The Father Figure

Edited by
LORNA McKEE &
MARGARET O'BRIEN

TAVISTOCK PUBLICATIONS
LONDON AND NEW YORK

First published in 1982 by
Tavistock Publications Ltd.
11 New Fetter Lane, London EC4P 4EE
Published in the USA by
Tavistock Publications
in association with Methuen, Inc.
733 Third Avenue, New York, NY 10017

Printed in Great Britain by
J. W. Arrowsmith Ltd., Bristol BS3 2NT

British Library Cataloguing in Publication Data

The Father figure.
1. Family   2. Fathers
I. McKee, Lorna   II. O'Brien, Margaret
306.8'7   H0518
ISBN 0-422-77720-X
ISBN 0-422-77730-7 Pbk

Library of Congress Cataloging in Publication Data
Main entry under title:

The Father figure.

Bibliography: p.
Includes index.
1. Fathers — Addresses, essays, lectures.
2. Father and child — Addresses, essays, lectures.
I. McKee, Lorna.   II. O'Brien, Margaret.
HQ756.F37   306.8'7   81-22298
ISBN 0-422-77720-X   AACR2
ISBN 0-422-77730-7 (pbk.)

Contents

vi   Contents

To our fathers, mothers, and families
for their inspiration

The Father Figure

and we feel that it has been a success. We would also like to thank all the fathers and would-be fathers who, through their accounts of family life, ultimately made this book possible. In addition, special thanks to Lyn Fox and Roger Buckland for collating and typing the references and to Moira Gomes for her typing assistance.

Lastly, our thanks are also due to some friends whose support has made the task of editing this book bearable and sometimes pleasurable: all at 457, Kate Corrigan, Judith Farrar, Patricia Palmer, Chris McKenna, Jenni Wilson, Peter Waldron, and most of all, Roger Buckland and Nick Tiratsoo.

M. O'B.   L. McK.
APRIL 1981

List of contributors

ANGELA BROWN
MRC Medical Sociology Unit, Institute of Medical Sociology, University of Aberdeen

JACQUELINE BURGOYNE
Department of Applied Social Studies, Sheffield City Polytechnic

DAVID CLARK
MRC Medical Sociology Unit, Institute of Medical Sociology, University of Aberdeen

TONY HIPGRAVE
Department of Social Work, University of Leicester

CHARLIE LEWIS
Department of Psychology, University of Nottingham

NIGEL V. LOWE
Department of Law, University of Bristol

TREVOR LUMMIS
Department of Sociology, University of Essex

LORNA McKEE
Department of Sociology and Social History, University of Aston in Birmingham

MARGARET O'BRIEN
Department of Applied Social Sciences, North East London Polytechnic

DAVID J. OWENS
Department of Sociology, University of Cardiff

MARTIN P. M. RICHARDS
Child Care and Development Group (formerly Medical Psychology Unit), University of Cambridge.

JOEL RICHMAN
Department of Applied Community Studies, Manchester Polytechnic

MADELEINE SIMMS
Institute for Social Studies and Medical Care, London

CHRISTOPHER SMITH
Institute for Social Studies and Medical Care, London

Preface

Our empirical interest in fathers emerged coincidentally back in the mid-seventies. At that time it seemed as if we were working in a minority area and without an identifiable research group from which to draw support and guidance. A number of writers in this volume found themselves in the same position, experiencing academic isolation and limited means of communication. Only through chance meetings, random contacts, and the passage of time did it become apparent, as this book will go on to show, that this solitude and peripherality was being challenged and that we were fast becoming part of a developing and popular research tradition.

The chapters in this volume stand as corrections to a research programme that has emphasized the mother-child bond and neglected the role of the male parent. Their common feature is that they place father centre stage and give him an exclusive 'hearing'. However, it is our belief that once a sufficient body of knowledge about fathers has been established, commonality will give way to diversity and the orientation to fathers alone will be amended and superseded. We feel that we share with our contributors a role in pioneering a new entrée into family life, but at the same time we feel that our 'father-centred' tendency is one that is ultimately in transition.

We would like to take this opportunity to thank all the contributors for their hard work in making this volume possible. They have worked conscientiously and co-operatively, meeting our deadlines, responding generously to our often harsh criticism, and making us feel that it has been worthwhile throughout. They gave up their time to meet together and to exchange in person their ideas and efforts so that the book would have a coherent and overarching salience. For this we are grateful,

PART ONE

History and ideologies of fatherhood

1

The father figure: Some current orientations and historical perspectives

LORNA McKEE AND MARGARET O'BRIEN

'The power of fathers has been difficult to grasp because it permeates everything, even the language in which we try to describe it.'

(Rich 1976 : 58)[1]

The conclusions that fathers are 'forgotten contributors to child development' (Lamb 1978 : 245) and that 'discussion of fathering is becoming fashionable' (Fein 1978 : 122) appear at first glance to be contradictory. However, what they in fact reflect is a temporal shift in the state of knowledge and research on the topic of fatherhood. From the mid-sixties through to the early eighties, the face of family research has witnessed a gentle revolution. Fatherhood has become a distinctive and prestigious substantive issue, and 'mother-focused' research programmes have become increasingly outmoded and criticized. Some commendable and comprehensive reviews of this literature now exist.[2] There has also been an acceleration of interest in sex roles more generally, with an emphasis on men's liberation and masculinity.[3] Much of the fatherhood research in Britain tends to fall into three major categories: the transition to fatherhood; fathers and infants; and men's experiences of fatherhood in single-parent and remarried families. To a certain extent, this book reflects the current 'empirical reality', and attempts to bring together for the first time a representative array of studies being conducted in this country. As such, it is both retrospective — capturing and communicating what has been quietly and imperceptibly going on in the sphere of family research — and prospective — perhaps providing some hints of the tenor of future family research where the 'mother-focused paradigm' may be said to be slipping or losing its appeal. The book also necessarily addresses some of the theoretical and ideological dimensions of fatherhood.

This being a first book, and perhaps indicative of a 'first phase', our selection of contributors was influenced by a variety of factors. Some contributors are included for being 'first' in the field and were among our early personal contacts. Others are there because we wanted accurately to reflect the diversity of disciplines approaching the topic of fatherhood and the plurality of methods available for such investigations. Still others are there because of their break with the study of conventional nuclear family structures, a developing trend in family research. By tying the book so closely to the quality and type of research being conducted in the empirical field, there are obvious gaps and deficiencies in the range of our material. There is an absence of research findings: for example on fathers of older children; on role reversal; on communal and cohabiting units; on the impact of work on men's family roles; on grandfathers; on fathers in ethnic minorities; and on fathers from a cross-cultural perspective — all issues that we consequently fail to include. As well as the obvious value in cataloguing and relating the early and existing British work on fathers, we feel a book such as this should also attempt to address some questions: why fathers have suddenly become a popular research topic; what sorts of insights have been afforded by inclusion of the father; what deficiencies exist in our current orientation to fathers, and what shape the research might take for the future. We will only be able to pay brief attention to each of these questions here, but feel that they are compelling and central, and should be repeatedly broached as data on fathers continues to be amassed. After a discussion of some of these current concerns and orientations, we will then go on to consider some aspects of the role of the father in former times.

Why have fathers become a popular research topic?

No single answer can be given to this question. However, it seems to us that the overriding impetus has come from a combination of certain structural occurrences and societal changes, all of which challenge traditional male and female roles and necessarily affect the character of modern family life. These changes include the impact of the Women's Movement of the 1960s and 1970s on women's perceptions of their maternal and domestic roles; the increase in the number of women in paid employment and their improved job opportunities (however limited); the increase in the number of single-parent families, especially male-headed families; the spread of unemployment, particularly male unemployment; the limitation of family size (family planning); the diminution of the first-time married, two parent, two children family structure; the shortening of the working week, particularly for manual workers, and the concomitant increase in leisure hours that potentially permits a more home-centred life-style; the emergence of a small Men's Liberation Movement (mainly in America); the continued privatization of the nuclear family; and the cultural support for an ideology of child-centredness (see Newson and Newson 1974) connected with the assumption of parental responsibility and duties towards children (Flandrin 1979; Backett 1980). As men's and women's external social roles become more parallel, diffuse, and volatile the possibility of variation, fluidity, and interchangeability within the home becomes more real. Many of the changes described raise the issue of sex-gender relationships in general and the position of women in particular, and as such demand that equivalent information be gathered about both sexes. Paradoxically, as information is gathered about women, men are forcibly brought into the dialectic and evidence about their family behaviours must also be accumulated. It is possible to speculate that the increased preoccupation with fathers might be an expression of the move toward women's equality, with men being expected to share childcare. Alternatively, it could represent a backlash against women, where men, facing competition from women at work, are attempting to compete with women in the home and to appropriate an area in which women were previously autonomous. Research has barely addressed and not yet answered the question of which of these social realities is evolving, but it is a question to be faced squarely.

The explanation that sees external pressures projecting fathers into the research limelight is mooted in the chapter by Richards. He takes the view that researchers have turned their attention to fathers for pragmatic reasons; to coincide with the growing involvement of men with their children; to counter feminist attacks that psychologists, through their exclusive concentration on mothers, have promoted a view of childcare as naturally and inevitably women's business; and to provide research insights and solutions for childcare experts and professionals who have found the 'mother-centred' monographs deficient. Richards is acutely concerned with the consequences of this research tendency, feeling that it has led to poorly formulated research, an uncritical and patchy body of knowledge on fathers, and a lack of theoretical sophistication in research design and interpretation. He makes constructive suggestions as to how this situation might be amended and we will turn to this later when we are contemplating the way forward for fatherhood research. Although it may be true that research on fathers has escalated largely in response to wider social changes, we suggest that some pressure may have come from within academic disciplines themselves. It may be that researchers are discovering and expressing dissatisfaction with existing theories of the family which have lost their coinage, accuracy, or relevance; the sustained attack on the thesis of maternal deprivation being a prime example (Rutter 1972). Or it may be, as Richman suggests in his chapter, a case of researchers transferring their expertise and skills from one area to another, associated one. Almost by chance, a new research problem is generated in an adjacent field so that studies of fathers derive naturally from studies of mothers. If this is true, it is not altogether surprising that researchers should, as Richards argues, initially translate their theories and methods of investigation from mothers to fathers (Kuhn 1970; Lakatos 1970).

Some interesting observations on why past studies have concentrated primarily on mothers have been offered by Dinnerstein (1978) and Chodorow (1978). They argue that this dominant preoccupation with mothers is in the main a reflection of the organization of contemporary gender arrangements. Although there are many 'intragender differences and intergender similarities' (Chodorow 1978:215) in degrees of nurturance, most men do not 'mother'. Chodorow's thesis claims that 'women come to mother because they have been mothered by women. By contrast, that men are mothered by women reduces their parenting capacities' (Chodorow 1978 :211). Women's central role in mothering is said to reproduce the existing social relations of subordination and domination between the sexes. The major message of her book is in fact that women and men should work together as nurturers to break this cycle of domination. Although Dinnerstein reaches a similar conclusion, her explanation of female subordination is somewhat different. She contends that the vital task of every 'mother-raised person' is to harness or contain the absolute power they were subjected to in the early mothering relationship.

> 'For the girl as well as the boy, a woman is the first human center of bodily comfort and pleasure, and the first being to provide the vital delight of social intercourse. The intial experience of dependence on a largely uncontrollable outside source of good is focused on a woman and so is the earliest experience of vulnerability to disappointment and pain.'   (Dinnerstein 1978 : 28)

This 'first' parent has control over the life and death of the infant and Dinnerstein (1978 : 161) believes that adults experience a 'terror' of 'sinking back wholly into the helplessness of infancy'. Because this absolute power is concentrated in one sex, the female, both sexes then go on to seek paternal authority as a sanctuary from early maternal domination.

The exhortations that flow from these theses for men to share more in early infant care have obviously influenced family researchers so that investigators have begun to explore fathers' perceptions of the 'personal' in the same way as feminist historians, for example, have begun to explore women's experience of the public sphere (see Rowbotham 1973).

Just as Dinnerstein and Chodorow have attempted to delineate what it means 'to be a mother', and 'to mother', questions are now being asked about what it means 'to be a father' and 'to father' and what might be the primary differences and similarities between mothers and fathers. Most of the chapters in this book are concerned with the experiences of 'being' a father, in the sense of nurturance and provision, while only the chapter by Owens looks more directly at 'fathering' as the siring and begetting of children. However, at this early stage it is not possible to detail how these alternative meanings of fatherhood relate to each other or to the meanings surrounding motherhood.

A further 'internal' explanation for why fathers are no longer neglected may be found within a given research tradition itself — namely within the interactionist and phenomenological perspective of sociology. This perspective places the emphasis on the actors' subjective meanings and perceptions of social reality. In family research it relies on uncovering how family members construct, negotiate, define, and sustain their family relationships and realities. As such, the mutuality of family life is underscored and fathers as well as mothers and children are drawn in. The chapter by McKee was inspired in this way, and in her work she shows how mothers' and fathers' beliefs about participation in infant care mesh together and are mutually influential in determining who does what and how they feel about it (for another example of work in this vein see Backett 1980).

What sorts of insights have been afforded by inclusion of the father in family research?

Just as it was impossible to find a precise or simple answer to 'Why fathers?', it is equally difficult to spell out conclusively what the research on fathers has achieved or uncovered. The chapters that follow, and the literature reviews cited earlier, should allow the readers to draw their own conclusions. However, here we can usefully sketch in broad outline some of the issues being explored and some of the assumptions being tested. Much of the research to date can be heuristically classified into 'adult-', or 'parent-', and 'child-centred'.[4] Studies that are 'parent-centred' can be said to be primarily concerned with how the mother or father views, experiences, and enacts parental roles. Mothers and fathers are reviewed largely *vis à vis* one another, and their differences and similarities are recorded. The problems that arise concern the biological predispositions of males and females; definitions and prescriptions of masculinity and femininity; the exposition of sex-gender stereotypes; patterns of marital decision making; marital power, authority, and deference; the division of household and childcare labour; the synchronization of family roles with wider social roles and institutions (such as medical institutions); the impact of life-events and transitions (such as pregnancy and childbirth) on individuals and couples; and attitudes toward and the meaning of being a parent (whether young or old, black or white, heterosexual or homosexual, middle-class or working-class, unmarried, married, or remarried, two-parents, multiple parents, or lone parents). Sometimes, the comparisons between mothers' and fathers' behaviours and beliefs are made explicit, in other cases they remain implicit. What unifies the 'parent-centred' studies is that the parent's perspective is paramount and the parent's testimony is valid for its own sake. All the empirical chapters in this book can be said to adhere essentially to a 'parent-centred' model, an orientation now notably well developed for mothers (for example see Oakley 1979, 1980; Graham and McKee 1980). Important progress in family research has also occurred through a 'child-centred' emphasis. Studies that are 'child-centred' may use adult or parental informants/subjects but the evidence gained has a primary relevance *vis à vis* the child's development, growth, and experience. Mothers' influences as compared to fathers' influences, while critical, are only significant in so far as they affect the total care environment of the child. The research problems embodied by this framework include the effects of parental absence (especially *paternal* absence) and separation; the development of gender-identity; the aquisition of language; cognitive development; the growth of personality and sociability — 'the integration of the child into the social world' (Richards 1974); and the emergence and expression of sexuality. The theoretical model that Richards explicates in his chapter can tentatively be placed here, seeming to identify ways in which sons learn to father. Apart from his contribution, this book does not contain any other direct examples of a 'child-centred' focus, although in Lewis's review of attachment theory and observational studies many such researchers are alluded to. A future volume could tackle or begin from this omission and make 'child-centred' studies its focus.

Regardless of whether studies have been 'parent-centred or 'child-centred', there has been a common tendency to view parental influences as moving in a downwards direction from parent to child. However, recent work has increasingly challenged this prevailing assumption and has shown that children, even small infants, initiate and affect parental responses (Lewis and Rosenblum 1974; Richards 1974a; Korner 1971). It is argued that an interactive approach is necessary, and meaningful results can only be obtained if mothers, fathers, and children are treated as mutually influential participants in social interaction (Clarke-Stewart 1978). Hipgrave raises this point in his chapter, and explains that the experiences of lone fathers cannot be bracketed off from the way they are affected by their children. It would seem that this 'triadic' and essentially 'neutral' orientation to family relationships will become increasingly accepted and expected; and studies that rely on naive assumptions about the direction of influence will be outdated. Similarly, this orientation to give equal credibility to mothers, fathers, and children will, from the outset, guard against the presumption that mothers and fathers influence their children differently (Clarke-Stewart 1978; and see Lewis, Chapter 10).

Some of the findings from the 'parent-centred' studies reported in this book provide fascinating insights about the status of fatherhood *vis à vis* motherhood, about the face of masculinity, about male attitudes to marriage and procreation, about how families divide up their childcare duties, about how men experience and view pregnancy and childbirth, and about how they cope and survive as primary caretakers and in reconstituted families. The papers by Owens, McKee, and Simms and Smith show that many men regard marriage and having babies as inextricable parts of the adult career pattern. It is something they adhere to without questioning and treat unselfconsciously − until things go wrong. As Owens shows, involuntary childlessness hits some men hard, first because it defies the 'natural' life-cycle plan, second because it challenges their virility (although this concern was not voiced equally by all his respondents), and third and most important, because it robs their wives of a 'career' and they feel a sense of regret and responsibility for this 'theft' of their wives' rights. Simms and Smith suggest that this favourable orientation of men to marriage and parenthood may lie in the particular biographies and circumstances of the young working-class men they interviewed. They noted that two-thirds of their sample themselves came from families where parents had married young and had many children, so that in becoming teenage fathers they were perpetuating a customary life-style. Furthermore, early marriage and parenthood provided for many of these men a release from overcrowded homes, and an independent base.

Both Simms and Smith and McKee also attend to the issue of how domestic work and childcare is shared out between couples. McKee pays special attention to fathers' participation in infant care, suggesting that measurement and interpretation of this is complex and multi-faceted. She argues that it is a contemporary issue, brought about by certain historical changes in the structure of the family. Her position is that men's values and behaviours may not always be consonant and that any appreciation of social change must take account of this possible mismatch. Simms and Smith present a picture of high engagement of fathers in domestic and childcare work, with only a small percentage not contributing to any household chores and 96 per cent feeding the baby at least occasionally. It would seem that this concern with 'who does what?' is going to be a recurrent theme as more studies expand to include fathers or couples in their brief. The issue of participation is important because of the evidence it supplies about men's and women's sex roles more generally, about the position of women in society, and about patterns of marital power, decision making, and negotiation. It also portrays information about the affective environment of child-rearing.

Images of men in affective or emotional settings are also contained in the chapters by Richman and Brown. Here, as we follow small groups of men through the experiences of pregnancy and childbirth, we see them reacting in ways that are unfamiliar and traditionally 'non-masculine'. We capture them in 'womanly' poses — crying, feeling help-less, being lost for words, talking romantically and mystically. Both authors show how expectant fathers have attained a marginal and ambiguous status, their vulnerability in pregnancy stemming from their physical remoteness from the pregnancy and, at the birth, from the medical definition of the physicality of birth. In both ethnographies, the cultural stereotypes of masculinity are implicitly challenged or shaken, and the stereotypes of male resilience, combativeness, and toughness seem curiously absent. Findings that reveal men in such unusual postures play an important part in larger debates about sex-gender typing and sex-gender differentiation.

Likewise, depictions of men acting as primary nurturant figures can add to our understanding about the contours and nature of masculinity. Through in-depth interviews with lone fathers, O'Brien and Hipgrave delineate exactly what this status entails for men. Hipgrave presents us with the statistical evidence that lone fatherhood is becoming steadily more common and through a comprehensive review of the research literature, backed up by his own empirical data, shows that they face recurrent and persistent problems of *time*, *money*, and *feelings*. He points out that these problems are scarcely acknowledged and poorly met by the wider society. O'Brien's work endorses Hipgrave's con-clusions and at the same time asks us not to review lone fatherhood as a homogeneous category. From her findings, what is significant is the route by which these men found themselves caring for their children. After marital separation, some fought to retain custody of the children; others had lone fatherhood thrust upon them by their wives' desertion; while still others negotiated the transition to lone fatherhood with their wives. This latter group perhaps represents an emergent trend among separating couples, some of whom may be attempting to contest conventional parenting norms. O'Brien's work implies that the means by which lone fatherhood is achieved has important consequences for both parents and children.

The need to avoid or decode global classifications is a theme also developed by Burgoyne and Clark in their discussion of stepfathers. They identify the complex 'pathways' by which families can be reconstituted depending on whether each or both parties has been married before, have been parents before, where the children live, and what has happened to the former spouse. Just as lone fatherhood is on the increase, the authors point out that remarriage and step-parenthood is a growing and familiar family structure today, and for this reason, stepfamilies and single parents deserve study. The chapters included here do much to draw our attention away from the conventional family form (first-time married, two children, two parents, mother homemaker, father breadwinner) which itself is becoming a relatively rare relic (Rapoport and Rapoport 1980; Coussins and Coote 1981). These contributions are valuable not least for widening our concept of 'the family'.

Are there any deficiencies in our current orientation to fathers?

While the issues raised by the inclusion of fathers in family research are expansive and manifold, our review cannot just rest with being descriptive but needs also to be critical. We have already seen that Richards has levelled some criticisms at the research on fathers for its neglect of theory. Lewis, McKee, Simms, and Smith also take researchers to task, but mainly because of the methods they employ, the simplistic assumptions they make, and the consequently suspect conclusions they draw. Lewis carefully reviews the work of developmental psychologists on fathers and suggests that three areas (the study of new-born babies, the 'strange' situation experiments, and observations of parent-child interaction in 'natural' settings) are all tied to assumptions derived from attachment theory. He sees this as inherently problematic, both because the applicability of attachment theory to fathers has bever been satisfactorily explored and because the observational methods generated by this model are in and by themselves limited. Lewis contends that direct observation should be complemented by other methods, especially those that allow parents to define and expound their own perceptions about being a parent, and should not be an end in itself.

McKee and Simms and Smith raise the qualitative versus quantitative debate in their chapters. McKee spells out some of the limitations of social surveys in approaching the question of fathers' participation in infant care and makes some constructive suggestions for how surveys might be improved, drawing on grounded data from a small group of fathers. She puts the case for a dialogue between methods. This dialogue is sustained in the paper by Simms and Smith where they demonstrate the strength and value of social survey methods, and quite rightly argue that national data on fathers, and especially working-class and young fathers, is lacking. The two chapters should be read in tandem, we feel, as they create an interesting polemic.

That such intense discussion should hinge around the appropriateness and adequacy of the methods used to investigate fathers is not all that surprising. As we have shown, the study of fathers is in a process of opening up and ripening and we can loosely draw on Kuhn's pre-paradigmatic metaphor here to reflect on how a body of knowledge emerges and develops. He says:

> 'The pre-paradigm period, in particular, is regularly marked by frequent and deep debate over legitimate methods, problems and standards of solution, though these serve rather to define schools than to produce agreement.'   (Kuhn 1970 : 48)

It is possible that what may well be happening is that the early alignment of researchers through their common interest in fathers is breaking down, and instead researchers are again diversifying into discrete research traditions, finding their bed-fellows hostile or unacceptable. We would find this retreat into a polarization of ideas and approaches saddening and firmly take the view that there is no one 'best' methodology. Instead what must be sought is the method best fitted to the research problem or goal in hand. Similarly, we feel that researchers should attempt to communicate across the divides to gain a more holistic appreciation of phenomena. This book is inspired by this commitment to a plurality of methods and further by a belief in interdisciplinary cooperation.

Indeed, one of our main assertions is that social scientists have been too insular and exclusive in their approach to fatherhood. They have particularly ignored the contributions to our understanding of the position of fathers that the disciplines of history and law afford. For this reason, we are pleased to have representations of this work in our book, in the chapters by Lummis and Lowe. Lowe has closely documented the shifts in the father's position from one of legal sovereignty to one where the 'welfare principle' predominates and the child's needs are given priority. This massive legal 'about face' is one of the largest structural changes to have been recorded with regard to parent-child relationships, yet it often goes unacknowledged by social scientists. By turning a blind eye to legal sources, sociologists, psychologists, and anthropologists often deny themselves a rich bedrock of data and brick up an important entrance to the interpretation of their contemporary findings. Similarly, lawyers themselves suffer from isolation and would benefit from exchanges that point to the sociological and ideological relevance and meaning of their statutes and judgements. Lowe's chapter sets social scientists a series of puzzles. Why did fathers maintain such power? What did this mean for family members in an emotional context? What relationship did fathers' rights bear to husbands' rights over wives? How and why did fathers' rights decline? And what pressures were exerted to bring about social change and by whom? This story has not yet been written, but Lowe's paper importantly and accurately sketches out the plot. Lummis too points out the myopia of the sociological work on fathers. He accuses sociologists of generalizing from very limited and specific data, of perpetuating erroneous cultural stereotypes, particularly of working-class fathers, and of simplifying and distorting their historical references, especially by the belief that modern fathers (in particular middle-class fathers) are more egalitarian than their forefathers. Using oral testimonies from East Anglian fishermen and their wives born at the turn of the century, he demonstrates the presence of compassionate and participant fathers in this community and successfully demolishes the myth of 'the drunken, brutal, working-class father'.

How might research on fathers advance?

Lummis's thesis on the historical role of fathers leads us on to one of our main observations about how research on fathers might advance, and that is, paradoxically, backwards. By this we mean that researchers should endeavour to glean further insights about fathers in former times. This has a value in itself as family history develops but it is also important if contemporary findings are to be contextualized and if conclusions are to be drawn about social change.

THE HISTORICAL CONTEXT OF FATHERHOOD

(i)   *The pre-modern period*

In our own preliminary foray into the annals of social and family history we are astonished and impressed by the volume of material that either reflects implicity or explicitly on the position of fathers, but we have found no text that *exclusively* looks at the position of men as fathers. The sources themselves are plentiful and diverse and some of those that we would advocate and that have often been successfully employed by family historians include the Bible, the writings of moral theologians (Flandrin 1979), catechisms (Flandrin 1979), religious and royal edicts, marriage contracts, inheritance settlements, portaits, photographs, and paintings of family scenes (Ariès 1962), census material (for example Laslett 1971; Laslett and Wall 1972), tax records, parish registers, 'medical geographies' (Berkner 1973),[5] memoirs and biographies (see Roberts 1978), diaries (see Macfarlane 1970, in which he analyses the diary of clergyman Ralph Josselin and provides a rich account of fatherhood in seventeenth-century England), legal statutes and cases, and literary evidence. Recourse to any of these sources will be bedevilled by all the usual and endemic problems of documentary and comparative method: problems of why the data was collected in the first place and how; problems of generalization; problems of social class, occupational and regional variation; and the more thorny problem of a greater preponderance of source materials on the upper classes the further back in history one goes (Berkner 1973; Laslett 1976). There are also the problems of forging satisfactory links theoretically and methodologically between disciplines, which cannot be overlooked or minimized (Stedman-Jones 1976; Rock 1976; Thompson 1976). However, we feel this should not deter sociologists or others from finding out about the historical dimension of fatherhood, but instead should make them cautious and alert in their endeavours.

As so little has been published by social scientists on fathers in history we feel it is apposite to introduce briefly some of the findings from our own search. We can do little more than whet the reader's appetite and assert the relevance of this exercise. We mostly rely on secondary sources for our preview and are aware of the hazards and limitations of this. What is striking is that some very general tenets emerge from the historical data against which any discrete observations about fathers have firstly to be placed. These can be summarized as follows: that the concept of 'the family' is not static throughout history but subject to definitional and structural modifications in terms of co-residence and kinship (for example, Flandrin 1979; Poster 1978; Barrett 1980) and consequently that the 'family' as equalling father-mother-child(ren) is a relatively recent configuration; that social change is not necessarily linear or continuous (Hareven 1977; Poster 1978); that change in social behaviour and values may not be coterminous (Scott and Tilly 1975); that regional, occupation, ecological, and social class factors influence family structures (see Anderson 1971; Thompson 1977; Meacham 1977; Poster 1978); that it is not enough simply to know about the size or composition of the 'domestic cell' (Flandrin 1979): we need to know about the nature of intra-familial as well as structural relations, and relations between the family unit and the wider society (see Morgan 1975; Poster 1978).

Expanding some of these points, Flandrin, for example, using an analysis of meanings of the 'family' drawn from French dictionaries, shows that in the pre-modern period 'families' could either comprise large numbers of co-residents not necessarily linked by birth or marriage *or* groups of blood relations who did not co-reside. In this context the father's sphere of influence was not necessarily restricted to his biological offspring, or even just to those living with him. Commenting on the father's position at that time, Flandrin says:

> 'The authority of a king over his subjects, and that of a father over his children, were of the same nature . . . neither authority was based on contract, and both were considered 'natural'. The king and the father were accountable for their governance to God alone.'
>
> (Flandrin 1979 : 1)

He describes how during the sixteenth and seventeenth centuries, the father's domain of authority extended to wives, children, servants, lodgers, and others, and over such matters as the making of wills, the transfer of property, the choice of a marriage partner, the selection of an occupation, and the issue of where to reside. He quotes one jurist of that period, Pierre Ayrault, who wrote 'the father is like a dictator . . . on his voice shall depend all that is subject to him' (Flandrin 1979 : 130). Another contemporary wrote 'we should consider fathers as gods on earth' (Flandrin 1979 : 130), while a third scholar advocated the extension of the father's power over the life and death of his family members, a right that had been abolished in late antiquity by Christian rulers.

This absolute or monarchical power of fathers is also described by Lawrence Stone, in reference to the period between 1500 and 1700. Stone's evidence is important, not least because of the argument advanced concerning social change. He suggests that the omnipotence of fathers was strengthened in this period, and whereas fathers lost some of their autonomy (for example, over marriage settlements) in the Middle Ages, it was regained and reasserted in the early 1500s. Speaking of the non-linearity or discontinuity of change in the father's position he says: 'In the sixteenth century, however, there are clear signs of a strengthening of paternal authority in the family. For a time, the power of fathers over children and of husbands over wives were both strengthened' (Stone 1975 : 34-5).

Some of the changes cited by Stone relate to the laws concerning the disposal of property, whereby the legislative rights of fathers to preside over inheritance matters was increased and children's subordination further reinforced. He also argues that certain prevailing psychological models about children resulted in parents attempting to civilize and 'break the will' of minors through physical repression. He documents the increase in child-beating and flogging during this period and suggests that during the seventeenth century: 'The early training of children was directly equated with the breaking in of young horses or hunting dogs' (Stone 1975 : 36). Several critics have berated Stone for his portrayal of the brutality and absolutism of pre-modern fathers, accusing him of generalizing from evidence drawn from a literate elite, thus misrepresenting working people's experience, and suggesting further that some occasions of parental affection, love, and mutuality must have existed (for example, Thompson 1977). What these comments underscore is the persistent need to differentiate between classes and between structural and emotional facets of family life.

One writer who achieves this is Mark Poster (1978) and in his account of sixteenth- and seventeenth-century family structures he makes vivid demarcations between aristocratic and peasant forms and experiences. In the aristocratic family he locates the father as potent and head of the 'House'. However, he shows this to be a seigneurial position and argues that direct care and control of children was delegated to servants, whose right it was to issue rewards or punishment. Like Stone, he argues that the prevailing ideology concerning children was that they needed taming.

'Fathers and mothers rarely bothered with their children, especially during the early, formative years. Childcare was considered beneath the dignity of an aristocratic woman. Children were thought of as little animals, not as objects of love and affection.'

(Poster 1978 : 180)

Poster's depiction of the peasant father is quite distinctive. While also maintaining power over wives and children, peasant fathers were liable to control and sanction from the community. He argues: 'Social authority was invested not in the father of the house but in the village itself' (Poster 1978 : 185). This is not to say that peasant fathers did not wield power but to suggest ways in which it was modified, contained, and supervised. One very general observation on which commentators of the pre-modern period, and for that matter the modern period, seem to agree, and one that seems essential for our understanding of the father's place today, is that parental *rights* (especially paternal rights) have given way to parental *duties*. This finding recurs across writers and although there is disagreement about when the change took place and what influenced it, there is a consensus about its occurrence (Flandrin 1979; Stone 1975; Roberts 1978; Newson and Newson 1974). Like other massive social changes, it is not represented as having occurred in a uniform or universal way, but the transformation from rights to duties was instead uneven, chequered, and gradual.

Flandrin traces the movement back to the earliest days of Christianity, seeing a tension between the absolute power of earthly fathers and God as 'the principal father'. However, he argues that the notion of parental duties only became properly established through the efforts of Protestant and Catholic reformers in the sixteenth, seventeenth, and eighteenth centuries. Flandrin bases his thesis on an analysis of the writings of moral confessors on the Fourth Commandment (the Fifth, in the Protestant faith), where he shows that little or no mention was made of parents' obligations toward children until the mid-1500s. Until this time, the emphasis was on filial duties to parents, but the situation changed and parental duties became increasingly important and numerous. From this time onwards Flandrin cites invocations to parents to provide moral and religious education for their children, and later for them to provide professional education, to settle their children, and to look to their future. Flandrin shows how this switch in ideology has a pertinence for today's child-rearing practices.

> 'The contradictory and repeatedly belied injunctions of modern psychologists and other educationalists, which cause such anguish, evident nowadays, are important only insofar as parents consider themselves responsible for the good or evil fortune of their offspring. It seems that it was the Protestant and Catholic reformers of the sixteenth and seventeenth and eighteenth centuries who first convinced parents of this responsibility.'   (Flandrin 1979 : 140)

What conclusions can be drawn about fathers in the pre-modern period? From these few sources, it would seem that many fathers in France and England on the one hand, enjoyed uncontested and unshakeable authority over all members of their household. Paternal authority resembled that of the absolute monarch and reflected the social reality that itself was characterized by hierarchical social relations and by the governance of the father, the husband, the master, and the lord. On the other hand, the way this authority was divested varies from class to class, aristocratic fathers being typified by remoteness and peasant fathers by their deference to village authority. Overlying all this was the increasing curtailment of fathers' rights over 'the family' brought about by Christianity and the encouragement of reciprocal duties between parents and children. However, as Chaytor points out, before coming to any definitive assessment of the father's position and the internal workings of family life during this period, we have to be aware that:

> 'We still know very little about sexual divisions within the households of the majority of the rural population, about the different activities and concerns of women and men, old and young, about how socialisation took place . . . '   (Chaytor 1980 : 48)

(ii) *The modern period*

A brief glance at the evidence on fathers in the modern period, especially Edwardian and Victorian fathers, reveals a similarly complex picture. Again social class, occupational, and regional differences abound and it is difficult to find any support for either a universal progressive democratization of family life or of the thesis of general cultural diffusion (implicitly supported by many family sociologists who argue that egalitarian trends amongst middle-class parents will spread downwards to working-class couples (Young and Willmott 1973)). The image of upper-class fathers as remote figures, noted in the pre-industrial period, also recurs in the later evidence on the Victorian 'paterfamilias' (Roberts 1978). In a study of the memoirs of 168 Victorians born between 1800 and 1850, Roberts argues that 'remoteness', however, was only one of a number of typical characteristics and fathers were also recollected in terms of sovereignty and benevolence. They were often absent on business, yet held a central and authoritative position in the family and often showered their children with indulgences. Beatrice Webb, describing her father, Richard Potter, industrialist and merchant, says:

'Notwithstanding frequent absence, my father was the central figure of the family life.'   (Webb 1971 : 35)

'He was the only man I ever knew who genuinely believed that women were superior to men.'   (Webb 1971 : 35)

'Yet in spite of this habitual self-subordination to those he loved ... he controlled the family destinies. My mother lived where it suited him to live and he came and went as he chose; his daughters married the sort of men he approved ... '   (Webb 1971 : 36)

Roberts uncovers two further themes about fathers in his analysis, which he claims seemed more characteristic of fathers in the later part of the Victorian era — he labels these 'self-conscious' and 'admonitory'. These traits seem to echo Flandrin's observations from the earlier period where fathers moved away from having rights over children to duties towards them. Like Flandrin, Roberts invokes the impact of religion as an explanation and attributes self-conscious and admonitory parenting to the rise of Puritanism or 'evangelism' in particular and urbanization in general. He cites examples of families such as the Cadburys, the Thorntons, and the MacCauleys. The clear message emerging from Roberts's insightful work is that even within the governing classes no single type of Victorian father existed. Our popular, yet contradictory images of the Victorian 'paterfamilias' can be corroborated, whether we imagine him to be hearty and backslapping, galloping across the fields with his son on the last day of the boarding-school vacation, or whether we envisage him dressed soberly in black, serenely presiding over family prayers. The benign and the austere co-existed.

Likewise, the Edwardian father cannot be neatly classified and while fathers at this time were universally heads of households and demanded respect, many variations are recorded as to how this authority was meted out. Paul Thompson (1977) using oral evidence from five hundred men and women drawn from the 1911 census shows how parent–child relationships varied enormously: between the upper, middle, and working classes and the poor; between occupational communities; across regions; and according to the nature and extent of male and female employment. He contends that rich children and poor children probably experienced least direct supervision from their parents, the rich being in the care of servants and the poor being on the streets. In the middle-class and working-class families he provides examples of stern and affectionate fathers, stern and affectionate mothers; rigid role segregation and absolute masculine domination; blurring of sex roles and marriage as a partnership; children as cowed and repressed and children as independent and equal. While the physical punishment of children was common in the industrial Midlands, it was rarer in the Shetlands, and while male participation in housework and childcare was frequently noted in areas of high female employment (textile districts) it was seldom observed in areas of heavy industry, where 'men's work was entirely segregated and physically exhausting (mining)' (Thompson 1977 : 85). Two quotes from Thompson's respondents help to reinforce the compexity of looking for uniform models of fatherhood from the past. A London sheet metal worker's wife speaks:

'tried to get them to bed before my husband came home — of course, he would be half past six to seven — if I could get them to bed beforehand. Or perhaps Alec might be up — but the two younger ones I'd always get to bed. 'Cause a man don't want yarney children when they come home to a meal.'   (Thompson 1977 : 58)

In contrast, a cowman's son comments on his relationship with his father:

'We was one: him and me was one. I'd always go to him with any troubles and he used to listen and if he could help me he did and when we sit on the couch like we did (we had a big old-fashioned sofa) he used to put his arm all round my shoulders. We used to sit there sometimes of an evening, cuddled up to him.'

(Thompson 1977 : 63)

Other interesting evidence on occupation and the place of work is emerging from the study of family economy in the transition from peasant society to industrial capitalism (Medick 1976). Medick shows that when some family units became centres of cottage industry (for example, weaving or lace-making) the 'traditional' separation of labour between the sexes broke down and became more diffuse. Women carried out 'male' duties and men, much to the chagrin of middle and upper strata observers, 'cook, sweep and milk the cows, in order never to disturb the good, diligent wife in her work' (Medick 1976 : 312).

If any lessons can be learnt from history we would suggest that this diversity of fatherhood in former times should warn contemporary social scientists against making naive general statements from their findings and instead guide them towards a delineation of the structural, economic, and cultural conditions that give rise to certain patterns of parent–child relationships and marital divisons of labour. This is why we feel that discrete ethnographies as well as national surveys have their part to play. In fact, we would argue that it is essential to investigate the specific *conjuncture* in which families are located in order to get a full understanding of men's relationship to family life.

A THEORETICAL APPRECIATION OF FATHERHOOD

We have earlier pointed to the fact that studies of fathers have been criticized for their poverty of theory, and we have indicated that Richards has tried to correct this in his chapter. Richards proposes the extension of object-relations theory and his thesis as to how this appertains to fathers is a fascinating one. We ourselves would like to postulate that the study of fathers might be approached through a re-evaluation of the concept of 'patriarchy'. However, we feel the word itself will have to be questioned because of some of its rigid associations and persistent limitations.

Weber used the concept of patriarchy to describe a specific form of household arrangement in which the father dominated other members of an extended kin network and controlled economic production (Shills and Rheinstein 1967). That is, in a patriarchical system the father governed by social authority and economic force. In later usages of patriarchy, particularly by radical feminists, there has been a tendency to generalize the concept to include all men, not just fathers (Millet 1972; Firestone 1972; Rich 1976).[6] This slippage from 'father' to 'men' is critical to our position, for we see patriarchy as embodying two types of domination, the domination of children and of women. This tendency to confound the power of fathers with the power of men has also been noted by Barrett. Commenting on the problems of patriarchy, she says: 'The concept of patriarchy as presently constituted reveals a fundamental confusion . . . between patriarchy as the rule of the father and patriarchy as the domination of women by men' (Barrett 1980 : 16).

It is of interest that psychoanalysts (for example, Mitchell 1974) have kept to the 'original', 'pure' meaning of patriarchy, but rather than locating their description at the concrete level of parenting they point to the importance of the law or authority of the father at an unconscious or symbolic level. Just as the theoretical development of the notion of patriarchy has come about most notably among psychoanalysts and feminists, its most recent and sustained critique has also come largely from these groups (see Rowbotham 1979; Barrett 1980). Some of the additional drawbacks to the concept of patriarchy as commonly assigned include its implication of a 'universal and historical form of oppression which returns us to biology' (Rowbotham 1979 : 970); its inability to capture occasions of women's resistance to male oppression; its lack of historical specificity and sensitivity to change; and its failure to capture moments when women and men have not been in conflict but, for example, have struggled together for social improvement.

We feel that the idea of a dual domination of children and women needs to be put back into 'patriarchy' and we feel that what is needed is some historical concept of parent–child relationships, especially father–child relationships, that can identify and explicate the varying subtleties, differences, and complexities of the father's role and the position of children over time, such as we have detailed earlier in this chapter. It is necessary to develop a concept that allows for an appreciation of the dialectical influence of parent on child and child on parent, that can embody the concept of inequality between parents (fathers) and children and that can be used to delineate age and generational hierarchies from ancient to modern times. As we see it, such a concept should make it possible to explore *'paternal-filial relationships'*, especially the way in which fathers have maintained authority over children under different economic and cultural conditions; how children have responded to and contested this subordination; what kinds of repressive instruments fathers (and mothers) have used; whether boys and girls have been governed and reared differently; and how maternal and paternal authority meshes together. Some of the themes that could be elucidated with this re-emphasis are notions of parental love – motherly and fatherly love; child-centredness and self-conscious parenthood (Newson and Newson 1974); shared parenting; favouritism versus 'equality' of offspring; use of domestic space; exploration of family rituals (meals, etc.); and the enactment of 'parental projects' (Morgan 1975). In this way it will be possible to reply to Poster's assertion that the history of women's and children's domination has not yet been written.

SOME IMMEDIATE RESEARCH RECOMMENDATIONS AND CONCLUDING REMARKS

As well as identifying two general directions — the historical and the theoretical — in which fatherhood research could move, more specific research priorities present themselves both from the areas covered and from those left uncovered by this book. We have already suggested how the experiences of certain groups of fathers have been neglected (such as fathers of older children and grandfathers), but investigators could also turn their attention to the wider social context in which men carry out their family practices. There needs to be more research on the impact of male unemployment, reduced hours of work, and increased leisure time on family life. In addition, the effects of government, employer, and trade union policies on men as fathers requires clarification. It could be beneficial to know about the operation of schemes such as maternity and paternity leave, flexible working hours, and the provision of childcare facilities on the well-being of all family members. Such information would allow the results of actual policies to be carefully monitored and inform new and perhaps better recommendations for the future. Another fruitful research exercise in this area could be a 're-reading' of certain social service and government documents with fathers in mind, so that changing ideologies surrounding the role of fathers could be highlighted.

It may well be that legislative changes alone will not bring about a massive upheaval in the current division of childcare. For it has been well established that attitudinal and behavioural shifts do not always occur at the same pace and even those fathers who have aimed to be more participant do so in conditions where strong stereotypes and social prejudices prevail. Perhaps research findings will ultimately conclude that utopian and complementary practices have to be encouraged, such as the positive rewarding of men who elect to care for their young children either full- or part-time, perhaps through economic benefits; the shortening of the working day for the parents of young children; the establishment of support groups for non-sexist parenthood and deliberate breaks in the process of sex-typing; the provision of facilities for expectant fathers in maternity hospitals; the guidance of fathers in the handling of small babies; an increase in the numbers of men working in settings with young children — day centres, infant schools, and crèches; and the exposure of discrimination against particular groups of fathers, such as lone fathers, or gay fathers (Lindberg and Fredriksson 1973; Millgàrdh and Rollén 1975; Palme 1975). To what extent these changes can be accommodated within existing social relations remains to be seen.

Lastly, in order to implement some of these research programmes it may be necessary to devise new and innovative research techniques. As well as the earlier suggestion for a plurality of methods, both in large-scale and small-scale studies, we would emphasize the value of longitudinal projects of families where *all* family members are studied throughout their lifetimes. For it is our conviction that it is not enough for research merely to turn from mothers to fathers, since this can only be a short-term and remedial strategy. Theoretical and empirical sophistication must be accomplished so that studies encompass all family interaction and dynamics, including mothers, fathers, and children, and extending to the wider kin and community.

Fatherhood research as contained in this book not only encapsulates a lively present, it is suggestive of a commanding academic future. Finding out about fathers, and campaigning for a change in their situation may have important consequences for women and men, for we share with Poster the hope that 'When men share housework and child care with women, important mechanisms of patriarchy are threatened' (Poster 1978 : 199).

Notes

1   For example, for this book no generic term could be agreed upon by contributors when the gender of the infant or parent was unclear — so individuals use their preferred conventions.

2   A SELECTIVE ACCOUNT OF REVIEWS ON FATHERHOOD
    Nash (1965)
    An early American article which examines and criticizes the pervasive influence of 'matricentrism' on psychological accounts of child development.
    Benson (1968)
    An early American book with a strong Parsonian orientation. Discusses the 'passing of the patriarch' and men's breadwinning and instrumental roles. Emphasizes the 'special' important qualities of fathers.
    Taconis (1969)
    An early British overview of the social science literature on fatherhood (draws from community studies as well as child-rearing research). Discusses own empirical study on fathers of five-year-olds.
    Biller (1974)
    An American book with social learning theory perspective. Reviews research on effects of father absence on children's social, cognitive, and personality

Lynn (1974)

An American book which attempts to draw together some biological, anthropological, historical, and current material on fatherhood. The examination of contemporary research is influenced by a social learning perspective.

Lamb (1976)

Lamb in his introduction to an American collection of readings about fatherhood, attempts to review the theoretical and research literature concerning the father's role in child development. His primary goal is to demonstrate that fathers do have an effect on the psychological development of their children.

Russell (1979)

An Australian article which critically examines sociological and psychological mother-centred research traditions. Presents some empirical data on male participation in dual- and single-worker Australian families.

Parke (1979)

A comprehensive overview of father–infant research (mainly American).

Berardo (1980)

Part of the *Journal of Marriage and the Family* decade review of family research. Looks ahead to family research and theory in 1980s. Suggests that the whole area of reconstituted families will be an important topic of this period.

Walters and Walters (1980)

A further article from the decade review on parent–child relationships between 1970 and 1979. Reviews some methodological issues of this research.

Parke (1981)

A short American book which introduces many aspects of fatherhood to the undergraduate reader. Includes sections on the expectant father; fathers and child development; divorce and custody.

In America it is interesting to note that four journals have devoted special issues to fatherhood:

The Family Coordinator **25** (4) October 1976
The Family Coordinator **29** (4) October 1979
Journal of Social Issues **34** (1) 1978
The Counselling Psychologist **7** (4) 1978

Meanwhile in Britain an inter-disciplinary Fatherhood Research Study Group now exists. It has met five times and averages an attendance of about fifteen or twenty members. For information, contact authors of present book. In addition, a research register, listing as many as thirty-two researchers actively interested in men as fathers and family members, has lately been compiled:

Fatherhood Research in Great Britain J. McGuire and N. Beail. September, 1980. Thomas Coram Research Unit, University of London.

3   A SELECTIVE ACCOUNT OF REVIEWS ON MEN AND MASCULINITY

Farrell (1974)

An American men's liberationist text, outlining the variety of restrictive aspects of current male roles.

Fasteau (1974)
A similar book to Farrell's, but more concentration on the relationship of militarism, sport, and the traditional male role.

Pleck and Sawyer (1974)
A useful collection of American articles covering many aspects of men's roles, in particular some useful contributions on men and young children; the problems of men working in child-care centres; male liberation and 'manliness and self disclosure'. Influenced by the men's liberation movement.

Tolson (1977)
One of the few British books on masculinity and men's role in society. Influenced by a 'feminist' perspective. Discusses sexuality, socialization, men's relationship to women; and has a useful chapter on the links between masculinity and work.

Harrison (1978)
A useful review of the literature on men and masculinity.

Dubbert (1979)
A historical approach to the shaping of American masculinity. Draws from a variety of sources including fiction and political life. Interesting section on the 'frontier' mentality of masculinity.

Scanzoni and Litton Fox (1980)
Another article from the decade review which explores the meaning of the term 'sex role' and the way it has been investigated in social research.

Morgan (1981)
An illuminating analysis of British academic machismo with particular reference to sociological theory and research practice.

4 These labels are used for convenience, and, like all labels, betray the complexity of much of the work done which straddles the two categories. Some research cannot neatly be placed in one or the other model and this must be borne in mind.

5 Berkner makes the point that these are especially useful for studying working-class living conditions, being compiled by concerned doctors and middle-class reformers from about 1800 onwards.

6 It is not possible here to do justice to the complex and varied ways in which patriarchy has been used. For a useful recent discussion of its usage, see for example Rowbotham (1979) and Barrett (1980).

2 The legal status of fathers: Past and present

NIGEL V. LOWE

The object of this chapter is to consider the legal position of fathers.[1]

The law has changed significantly from the days when a father's right to bring up 'his' legitimate children was regarded as sacred and virtually inviolable. Today, the rights that the law automatically vests in the parents of legitimate children are shared by the mother and father, while in court proceedings both parents' interests are secondary to those of the child. This chapter will first examine the volte-face of the law but the main thrust will be to consider the current legal position and judicial attitudes.

Generally, the chapter will concentrate on the position in court proceedings rather than on the inherent rights of fatherhood, because this particularly highlights the legal attitude towards fathers and reflects the tendency of the law in this area to provide remedies rather than rights. The main proceedings referred to are custody cases, by which is meant cases in which the court decides who should be legally entitled to bring up the child.

Historical perspective

FATHERS' RIGHTS AT LAW

Legitimate children

It is clear that legally fathers had long stood in a dominant position with regard both to their family in general and to legitimate children in particular. In the eighteenth century Blackstone wrote:

'The legal power of a father (for a mother, as such, is entitled to no power, but only to reverence and respect) the power of a father, I say, over the person of his child ceases at the age of twenty-one; for they are then enfranchised by arriving at years of discretion, or that point which the law has established . . . when the empire of the father or other guardian, gives place to the empire of reason. Yet, till that arrives this empire of the father continues even after his death for he may by his will appoint a guardian to his children.' (Commentaries on the Law of England Vol. 1 : 453)

The nineteenth century abounds with cases demonstrating the strength of the father's so-called 'empire'. In *R v De Manneville* 1804, a father who had separated from his wife forcibly removed an eight-month-old child while it was actually at the breast and carried it away almost naked in an open carriage in inclement weather. Despite this, the court said it could draw no inferences to the disadvantage of the father and upheld his right to custody.

In *R v Greenhill* 1836, a wife left her husband because of his adultery and sought an order giving her the right to bring up their three daughters (aged five, four, and two), who at the time of the hearing were living with her. She contended that she had not done anything that rendered her unworthy or unfit to have custody of the children. The father admitted his spouse's propriety both as a wife and mother but nevertheless sought to rely on his right to bring up 'his' children. The court upheld this right, even though he was cohabiting with another woman. The court was concerned about the children's possible contact with the adultress, but upon being satisfied that there had been no such contact nor would there be future contact, it was prepared to accede to the father's wishes that the children should be brought up by their paternal grandmother.

These cases poignantly illustrate the prevailing attitude of the last century, namely that a father's control over his children should be upheld save in rare cases where he had forfeited his parental rights. Though not easy to establish, forfeiture in theory comprised gross moral turpitude, abdication of parental authority, or seeking to remove the child from the country.

It is easy now to condemn this approach, since it apparently ignored both the mother's and, more importantly, the child's interests. However, the law did no more than reflect the general attitude of the time. Many judges genuinely felt that it was in children's interests to be under their father's control. As Bowen L. J. said in *Re Agar-Ellis* 1883: 'To neglect the natural jurisdiction of the father over the child until the age of twenty-one would be really to set aside the whole course and order of nature and it seems to me it would disturb the very foundation of family life.' Cotton L. J. commented in the same case:

> 'When by birth a child is subject to a father it is for the general interest of children and really for the interest of the particular infant that the Court should not, except in extreme cases interfere with the discretion of the father but leave to him the responsibility by exercising that power which nature has given by the birth of the child.'

It may be commented that the few child disputes that the courts were called upon to handle involved wealthy families where frequently neither parent would have personally brought up the children, and certainly would not have done so unaided. Given this background some of the decisions preserving the father's control may not have been quite as draconian as they appeared.

Illegitimate children

With regard to illegitimate children the law was brutally simple in that it was established that fathers had no rights (nor liabilities) and in particular could not claim custody (*R* v *Moses Soper* 1793). It became established that the right of control vested in the mother.

THE GROWTH OF MOTHERS' RIGHTS

The inevitable corollary of the strength of the father's position was the weakness of the mother's. This was especially so in the early 1800s, but the position changed through Parliamentary intervention. The Infants Custody Act 1839, passed as a direct result of *R* v *De Manneville*, mentioned above, gave the Lord Chancellor and Master of the Rolls a discretion to grant to the mother, provided she had not committed adultery, custody of her children under seven years old, and access to any of her children. The Custody of Infants Act 1873 further extended the Chancery Court's discretion to grant to the mother custody of her child up to the age of sixteen and the embargo relating to the mother's adultery was dropped. The Act also allowed a wife to enforce an agreement under which the husband gave up his rights and duties over his children in her favour, unless in the court's view the agreement was not for the child's benefit. Finally by the Guardianship of Infants Act 1886 the courts' discretion to grant the mother custody was extended to all her children under the age of twenty-one.

None of the above provisions gave mothers rights as such but were concerned to extend the *courts'* discretion to grant orders in the mother's favour. However, the 1886 Act did provide that upon the husband's death the mother became the sole guardian of the children (or joint guardian if the husband had appointed someone) and gave mothers the right to appoint a guardian with effect from their death.

This legislative concern for mothers was part of a general response to pressures for reform from the upper and monied classes to improve the legal position of wives. Perhaps the most significant Victorian reform was to treat each spouse as a separate entity each capable of separately owning property (Married Women's Property Act 1882). In the children context the move to establish maternal rights proved to be of only passing significance and indeed equalization of parental rights was not achieved until the implementation of the Guardianship Act 1973. In the event the more significant changes came about as a result of a growing awareness of children's interests.

THE EVOLUTION AND DEVELOPMENT OF THE CHILD WELFARE PRINCIPLE

A striking feature of the early law was its apparent lack of concern for the child. By the end of the last century, however, it was apparent that there was a growing awareness of the child's welfare. Precisely what triggered off this awareness is an interesting question but in the main, development was a judicial one. (There were occasional statutory references to the child's welfare: under the 1873 Act agreements transferring fathers' rights to mothers were not enforceable if the court thought that it would not be for the child's benefit while under the 1886 Act the courts were required, when hearing custody cases, to have 'regard to the welfare of the infant'.)

It is difficult to pinpoint the beginning of the change of attitude by the judiciary nor is it certain as to how quickly there developed a 'child welfare principle'. Some argue, and indeed it has been judicially stated (Lord Guest in *J v C*, 1969) that by 1925 the courts had come to regard the child's welfare as the dominant consideration, but others doubt this. What can be said, however, is that there was a marked shift away from the purely parent–orientated decisions that so dominated the nineteenth century, and that although this trend was not consistently followed, by 1925 as J. C. Hall (1972:248) has put it, 'the tide was flowing strongly in favour of the welfare of the child as the predominating consideration'. In any event the Guardianship of Infants Act 1925 provided *inter alia* that in deciding issues concerning the custody or upbringing of a child all courts were required to regard the welfare of the child as the *first and paramount* consideration. It was also stated that neither parent's claim was to be regarded as superior to the other.

The striking difference between this Act and the 1886 Act with regard to the weight to be placed on the child's welfare is evidence of the remarkable change in legal thought within a short period. Whether the 1925 Act was intended to do anything more than further the process of equalizing parental rights whilst at the same time extending the courts' discretionary power to override the absolute rights of the father in custody cases is perhaps debatable. However, the more enduring effect has proved to be the unequivocal establishment of the paramountcy of the child's welfare, which principle now forms the cornerstone of the current custody laws.

Applying the paramountcy test

The statutory entrenchment of the welfare principle by the 1925 Act (now consolidated in s.1 of the Guardianship of Minors Act 1971) by no means ended the development of the law. Indeed it took some time for the courts to accept that the welfare principle was the *paramount* consideration in all custody cases. In *Re Carroll* 1931, for example, the Court of Appeal ruled that despite s.1 of the 1925 Act it was still the law that the court 'should not sanction any proposal, excellent in itself, which does not give effect to the parents' views on education, religion and secular'. This decision was eventually overruled in *J* v *C* 1969. It is only since 1976 (see *Re K* and *S(B.D.)* v *S(D.J.)* 1976) that it can be unequivocally said that matrimonial conduct is not in itself a determining factor. Such conduct will only be relevant in as much as it reflects on a person as a parent. In other words the interest of justice as between mother and father does not outweigh the welfare principle.

There was a dispute too, as to whether the welfare principle applied to disputes as between parents and third parties. This was resolved in a crucial decision, *J* v *C* in 1969 where the House of Lords decided that the welfare principle did apply and that even so-called unimpeachable parents would loose custody of their child to a third party if the child's welfare so demanded. In other words the paramountcy of the child's welfare outweights the interests of even unimpeachable parents in custody disputes against third parties.

The sum total of these decisions, particularly *J* v *C* is that the child's welfare has virtually become the *sole* consideration, though in ascertaining this all the various factors of a case have to be weighed.

The meaning of 'welfare'

Judges rarely articulate the meaning of 'welfare' though Lindley L. J. said in *Re McGrath* 1892:

'the welfare of a child is not to be measured by money only nor by physical comfort only. The word welfare must be taken in its widest sense. The moral and religious welfare of the child must be considered as its well-being. Nor can the ties of affection be disregarded.'

One can go further and say that the court is concerned to promote as best it can the future well-being of the child (in the widest sense) the important basic considerations being to secure the child's future stability, security, and happiness.

The 'welfare' test vests in the court a considerable discretion. It is a flexible test in that notions of what are in a child's interests will change both in the light of fresh knowledge and understanding and with the prevailing attitudes of the day. What was thought to be in the child's interests in the past might not be so regarded today and conversely today's values and judgments may not be upheld in the future. One example of changing attitudes is *Re Thain* 1926. A father was seeking custody of his seven-year-old daugher, who had lived all her life with another couple. With respect to the possible effects of such a move the judge commented:

'I can quite understand [the immediate distress] but, at her tender age one knows from experience how mercifully transient are the effects of partings and other sorrows and how soon the novelty of fresh surroundings and new associations effaces the memory of former days and kind friends, and I cannot attach much weight to this aspect of the case.'

No court today would be so dismissive of this point for it is now realized just how harmful in the long term such disruption could be for the child.

The modern position

THE POSITION IN COURT PROCEEDINGS: DECIDING WITH WHOM THE CHILD SHALL LIVE

Function and powers of the Courts

The crucial decision upon the break-up of the family is deciding which, if either, of the separating parents should continue to look after the child. If the parents are divorcing this question must be referred to the court and solved to its satisfaction before the decree absolute can be granted (Matrimonial Causes Act 1973, s.41). Outside the divorce context, the parents may, if they choose, bring the issue before the court. However, the court's function in all proceedings is to resolve disputes, if there are any, or to confirm the parties' agreed arrangements according to what is thought to be in the child's best interests. The court is not *bound* by what the parties have already agreed though in practice such arrangements are rarely upset unless they are obviously not in the child's interests.

The precise orders that can be made depend upon which court is involved. The Divorce Court has *inter alia* the choice of making a simple custody order or a joint custody order. A sole custody order made in favour of one party confers on that person the right to bring up the child with sole power to make short–term decisions that inevitably arise in a child's day–to–day upbringing. It also confers on that party the right to take more long–term decisions, as, for example, determining the child's education. As will be seen the parent not granted custody (the 'non-custodial parent') is not totally deprived of a say in 'his' child's future but importantly under the new custody order 'he' loses the immediate right to bring up 'his' child.

A joint custody order vests in both parties the formal power to take long-term decisions relating to the child. However, since such an order is coupled with a 'care and control' order vesting in the successful party the day–to–day rights to bring up the child, the unsuccessful party still loses the immediate rights of upbringing and is legally in a position that is little different from having no custody at all. In psychological terms however, joint orders can be very important.

A court is not bound to grant custody or care and control to either party, and orders may be made instead in favour of third parties such as grandparents. If in the court's view there is no suitable person to bring up the child, then in exceptional cases it has the power to commit the child to the care of a local authority. Custody orders can also be subject to supervision by an independent person such as a court welfare officer.

Other courts have a broadly similar choice to that of the Divorce Courts, save that they make 'legal' custody orders which confer rights over the *person* of the child and not 'his' property. The joint orders take a different form in that legal custody must be vested in one party but the court can specify what other rights other than 'actual custody' (that is day–to–day control) should be vested in the non-custodial parent.

Reported decisions

Reported custody cases represent a tiny minority of court decisions, but nevertheless their importance goes beyond the particular instance because they collectively form the basis of a body of law upon which others are advised.

Apart from the paramountcy of the child's welfare it is constantly stated that there are no rules when deciding custody cases, nevertheless it is evident that certain factors are generally taken into account. Of these none seem more influential that the notion 'all things being equal young children are better off with their mother'. This phrase is repeated time and again and two examples will illustrate the apparent strength of the mother's position.

In *Greer* 1974 a mother was granted custody of two girls aged eight and five even though she had left the father and the children; had not brought up the children for two years prior to the hearing (though she did have regular access); had, prior to leaving the home been 'markedly inefficient and lazy about her domestic duties and more interested in her career than working in the house', and was in full-time employment. In reversing the previous decision the Court of Appeal thought that too much stress had been placed on the mother's previous shortcomings especially in view of her subsequent unblemished record when having access and not enough on the factor that young children were better off with their mother. Scarman L.J. said:

> 'it would be inconsistent with the true interests of the children to make an order disturbing the natural rhythm of childhood which in their earlier days was with their mother, who should be the secure and loving figure around which things should revolve, although . . . the father should be there as well.'

In *M* 1979, the mother left the matrimonial home taking her three-year-old daughter with her. The father was in the army, but planned to leave it in about eighteen months time. He had had difficulty having access. The judge granted custody to the father because he was greatly impressed with him and thought that access was more likely to be effective. It was recognized that as a serving soldier he would have difficulty looking after the child, but the judge felt that he would 'by hook or by crook' manage it. This decision was reversed on appeal, Stamp L.J. commenting that he 'could not regard that as in any way justifying removing the child from the care of the mother with whom she had been throughout her life and putting her in the care of the father'. Significantly, he added: 'However good a sort of man he may be he could not perform the functions which a mother performed by nature in relation to a little girl'.

It will be noted that the 'mother' factor applies, if at all, to young children. There is no rule as to what is regarded as 'young'. Though it is likely to have more force if the children are under five, the courts have applied the consideration in relation to eight-year-olds (see *P* v *McK* 1973). Lord Denning M.R. once said (in *W* v *W* & *C* 1968) that 'all things being equal it was better for a boy of eight to be with his father rather than his mother'. This sentiment is certainly not to be regarded as a rule and indeed there must now be a real doubt as to whether this could now be cited as a meaningful proposition (see *Re C(A)* 1970).

Where teenagers are concerned the position is different, at least in the sense that the courts do not admit to a preference for mothers; in any event the child's own views will be a relevant and possibly decisive factor (see *Marsh* 1979).

Another important general consideration is the *status quo*. It is now recognized that moving a child out of a familiar environment can produce lasting psychological damage. Hence, the longer a child has been in the actual care and control of one parent, the stronger that claim to custody becomes. The *status quo* argument is subject to the important proviso that it must be satisfactory in the first place. As Ormrod L.J. said: 'The *status quo* argument is not a very satisfactory one unless the *status quo* has been at some time established as an appropriate solution to the problem' (*Re P* 1979). As *Greer* shows on occasions, at least the 'mother' factor may be thought to outweigh the *status quo* consideration (see also *Ives* 1974, where a father lost custody after looking after the children for four years). Despite these limitations, however, it seems that the courts do think very carefully before disturbing the *status quo*.

The mother and *status quo* factors are but general considerations which must be judged against the particular facts of each case. It may be that the mother can be shown to be unsuitable. Examples of where this has been done range from showing that the mother was mentally unstable, excitable, a past alchoholic, and associating with an evil man, to showing that the mother simply could not cope (see *T* 1974, *Stovold* 1974, *Arensman* 1975, *Hutchinson* 1978, and *Re G* 1980 respectively). However, where such more obvious evidence cannot be brought then the general considerations tend to predominate.

Empirical evidence

In one sense the empirical evidence backs up the impression given by the reported decisions that the law favours mothers. Various studies (there are no national statistics) have shown that between 70 and 80 per cent of custody orders are made in favour of mothers.[2] However, it has also been found that in the vast majority of cases, sometimes as high as 99 per cent of the sample, the courts have confirmed the *status quo*. This has led Eekelaar to write (1978 : 227–28):

'Thus though occasional instances of judicial preference for a wife may be found the empirical evidence confirms the trend apparent in

more recent reported cases that courts are unwilling to disturb a
child's settled environment. The high proportion of awards to the
wife does not necessarily ... imply a presumption in favour of
mothers, but rather reflects an unwillingness to alter the parties' own
arrangements.'

To what extent this comment accurately reflects the current law is
debatable. *Status quo* is no doubt highly significant but it is submitted
that it would be premature to suggest that no significance is attached to
the applicant's sex. The empirical evidence shows that the courts are
more likely to disturb the *status quo* where the children are living with
the father. It has also been found that even in uncontested cases judges
are more likely to seek a welfare report when fathers have care of
children and they are more likely to declare themselves not satisfied
with a proposed arrangement that the father should have custody that
with a proposed arrangement with the mother (see Murch 1980:296–
97). These findings, it is submitted, are evidence of a continued anxiety
about entrusting custody to fathers. Furthermore, there continue to be
judicial statements to the effect that young children are better off with
their mother. In short it is submitted that the legal climate still favours
mothers and that solicitors would be justified in advising a father that
where the child is living with the mother something would have to be
shown against her if he is to gain custody and if a young child is living
with the father there is a distinct possibility of the mother gaining custody.

Justification for the current position

Few would quibble with the idea that in custody cases the child's
welfare is the first and paramount consideration. However, not un-
naturally there has been criticism of the apparent preference for mothers
in applying the welfare principle. To what extent can the court's suspicion of fathers be justified? It seems fair to say that the judicial
attitude does not stem from an assumption that fathers have no role to
play in child rearing. As Roskill L.J. said: 'This Court needs no persuasion
and no citation from the writing of psychiatrists on the benefit of a
father's care and a father's attention which I unreservedly accept is
exceedingly important' (*Grayling* 1979). However, the traditional attitude seems to be that mothers are normally 'the better bet' at least for
young children. There seem to be two bases for this position. First,
there is the practical problem of fathers being able to cope. If they are
in full-time employment they cannot give as much personal attention to
the child as the mother who is not working. No-one can gainsay this
problem (though many mothers face the same problem) but the courts

do seem to make it particularly difficult for fathers to overcome this disability. They seem suspicious of a man who is prepared to give up or has already given up work to look after his children. Fathers may also be in no better position if they find another partner. The courts seem more anxious about mother-substitutes than father-substitutes because it is assumed that the mother-substitute will take the more active role in the child's upbringing and it is believed that she will prefer her own children to her step-children (see *Willoughby* 1951, and *Re F* (1969)).

The second reason for preferring mothers seems to be the belief that young children most benefit from a maternal upbringing, coupled with the idea that it is a woman's natural role to bring up 'her' children. This attitude is certainly questionable. The former notion probably lacks scientific support (see King 1974) while it is understandable that both sexes would be critical of the 'role labelling'.

Despite the arguments, the court's attitude does reflect the current norm in society. As Ormrod L.J. said in defence of the *prima facie* proposition that mothers should have custody of their young children:

'It is a proposition of good sense as most people would agree. Normally children of this age are in fact looked after and brought up by their mothers. That is because, as things are in this society, that is the most convenient and generally speaking the most satisfactory way of dealing with children of that age. It is not anything more than that. It is an important factor — to be borne in mind — but it is not a factor which must take precedence over everything else. Of course not.' (*Re P* 1979)

Fathers bringing up their children at least by themselves remain in the minority and society does tend to make it more difficult for them to do so (see Chapter 11). Is it therefore so unreasonable of the courts to demand of a father in cases where there is an adequate mother, to show cogent evidence of his ability to bring up his children to their advantage?

The position of fathers deprived of custody and care and control

A custody order does not terminate the legal relationship between the non-custodial parent and the child. There will remain, for example, an enforceable duty to maintain the child and, as will be seen, the non-custodial parent will normally be granted access if that is desired. Fathers will also retain the right to apply to the court to prevent the child's surname being changed.

Recent cases (*Hicks* 1979; *Almond and Dipper* 1980) have empha- sized that non-custodial parents are not deprived of a say in the longer term decisions relating to the child. It has been said that it is a misunderstanding to believe either parent has a pre-emptive right over the other and that the parent having custody (or care and control) should discuss with the other matters affecting the child's welfare. If the parties disagree either may return to the court to have the dispute resolved.

How far this is a practical development is debatable though it does illustrate the court's concern for parents to realize that no matter what order is made both have a continuing role to play in their children's upbringing even if their own relationship has broken down.

THE POSITION IN COURT PROCEEDINGS: DETERMINING VISITATION RIGHTS

It has long been and remains the case that the court will be slow to deny access (that is, the right to see the child) to a parent. Under the modern philosophy this is because:

'the companionship of a parent is in any ordinary circumstances of such immense value to the child that there is a basic right in him to such companionship. ... [Hence] no court should deprive a child of access to either parent unless it is wholly satisfied that it is in the interests of that child that access should cease and that is a conclusion at which a court should be extremely slow to arrive.' (per Wrangham J. in *M* 1973)

The normal practice when granting access is to leave the parties to work out the arrangements for themselves. If they cannot agree the court will be prepared to make a more precise order, for example, that access should take place every Saturday afternoon.

The readiness to grant access against the custodial parent's wishes flies in the face of one school of thought (Goldstein, Freud, and Solnit 1973) which holds to the view that the court should have no power to order access and that such decisions should be left entirely to the custodial parent. This is because it is thought that nothing should be done which might impair the critical relationship between the child and the custodial parent. It seems right, however, that the matrimonial courts should encourage continued joint responsibility for the child, particularly in the difficult immediate separation period. The custodial parent's opposition may only be a temporary reaction and a formal access order may help to preserve contact, which would otherwise be lost, until things settle down. Granting access against the custodial parent's wishes seem justifiable at least in the first instance, provided the continued relationship is in the child's interest. It must be acknowledged, however, that the court's options are limited in the case of an intransigent custodial parent. In *Moore* 1980, for instance, custody of a girl (aged seven) had been granted to the mother with reasonable access to the father. The girl enjoyed and benefited from seeing the father, but the mother resented the access and pressurized the girl to stop seeing her father. Eventually access stopped and the father went back to the court. The mother's action was found not to be malicious but due to a 'wholly irrational' and emotional reaction against the father whom she blamed for the breakdown of the marriage. In all other respects she was a 'first-class parent'. The court considered that the likely result of making a fresh access order would be that it would be disobeyed. The sanctions for such disobedience, that is, fining or imprisoning the mother or even transferring custody, were all thought to be inappropriate. Accordingly, acting in the child's best interests, the court denied the father access.

THE POSITION OUTSIDE COURT PROCEEDINGS

Inherent rights vested in fathers of legitimate children

Fathers of legitimate children are automatically vested with certain rights (and duties) that can only be restricted or terminated by court proceedings or more usually by agreement between husband and wife. Space forbids a detailed account of these rights. Suffice it to say that some are statutory rights vested independently in each spouse, for example withholding agreement to adoption; objecting to a child's marriage; and appointing a guardian to act after the parent's death. Other rights have emerged via case-law or custom and are more immediately associated with the upbringing of children. These range from the day-to-day rights such as physically controlling and disciplining the child and probably consenting to the child's (at least if under sixteen) medical or dental treatment, to longer-term powers such as determining education and religion.

The non-statutory rights were once vested exclusively in fathers, but in the one significant development of the abstract rights of parenthood it is now provided that the mother enjoys the same rights as fathers. It is not clear, however, how these rights are to be shared. Under the Guardianship Act 1973, s. 1, either parent can it seems exercise their rights regardless of the other, whereas under the Children Act 1975, s. 85(3) the exercise of parental rights is limited by the other's disapproval. The difference between these co-existing provisions, however, is theoretical, because if the parties do disagree over their child's upbringing; one of them will probably take the matter to court.

Apart from these shared rights, children customarily take their father's surname and while this may not in itself be a father's 'right', once conferred it cannot be changed (at least by deed poll) without his or the court's consent. Children's nationality and domicile are determined by that of the father, though this is an incident rather than a right of fatherhood. Against this it has been decided (*Paton* v *BPAS* 1978) that fathers have no right to prevent their wives from having legal abortions. This decision was based on the father's 'no right' over foetuses as opposed to the mother's 'right' but the effect is to leave the mother in control.

It would be wrong not to mention the duties cast upon parents: for example, maintaining children to the appropriate standard (a burden commonly falling on fathers) and ensuring that the children receive full-time education. Even the so-called 'rights' become less important as the child becomes older. As Lord Denning M.R. poignantly said: 'custody is a dwindling right which the court will hesitate to enforce against the wishes of the child the older he is. It starts with the right of control and ends with little more than advice' (*Hewer* v *Bryant* 1969).

Putative fathers

Fathers of illegitimate children ('putative fathers') have no automatic rights over their offspring save the right to succeed on their intestacy. No distinction is drawn between those who have played an active part in their children's upbringing and those who have not. Indeed, though the legal disadvantages to the children have been reduced, scant attention has been paid to the putative father's position, the only development being to allow him to apply for custody, in which proceedings, the 'welfare principle' will be applied. In adoption proceedings he has a right to be heard if he is maintaining the child (in which case he must be notified of the proceedings) or if he expresses a wish to be heard.

The Law Commission (Working Paper No. 74 1979) advocates the abolition of the status of illegitimacy and as a corollary that all fathers should be treated equally. Many would agree that fathers living in 'stable union' with female cohabitants should be treated no differently from married men, though whether one should go further and treat *all* fathers alike is much more controversial. One problem the Law Commission pointed to was the difficulty of adequately defining a distinction between 'meritorious' and 'unmeritorious' fathers. Be that as it may the common reaction seems to be that the Commission has gone too far. Their full report is awaited with interest.

Step-fathers

Like putative fathers, step-parents have no automatic rights over their step-children. If they have married a divorcee they are entitled to seek joint custody with that spouse, otherwise they may have to apply to the High Court to have the child warded.

In the past, many couples applied for a joint adoption order but this is now discouraged for it is thought that the child would be normally little benefited by the application since he will continue to live with the applicants but have his legal relationship with his other parent terminated.

It may be thought that the current position is unsatisfactory, particularly in the event of the natural parent's death, since the step-parent cannot, without taking legal proceedings, prevent the non-custodial natural parent removing the child. There are, however, no proposals to reform this area of the law.

Conclusions

Over the last century fathers' rights over their legitimate children have substantially declined. Whereas formerly they stood supreme both in and outside court, today, they are in a more or less equal position with mothers outside the court, and when proceedings are brought their interests (as well as the mothers') take second place to the child's. However, as we have seen, the application of the 'welfare principle' in court proceedings seems to favour mothers more than fathers, at least where young children are concerned.

Putative fathers have fared no less well. They began by having no rights or duties over their illegitimate children and today they still have no rights automatically vested in them, though they are entitled to apply for custody and to acquire such rights.

How might the law develop in the future? There seems little prospect of fathers recovering their former supreme position, nor is there any reason why they should do so. It seems right to place fathers and mothers on an equal footing *vis à vis* automatic rights outside the court. Vesting automatic rights in some putative fathers seems the most likely development. This may become a more significant issue if cohabitation is increasingly seen as an alternative to marriage. Such a development might be accelerated if adequate definitions could be found to distinguish 'meritorious' and 'unmeritorious' fathers.

Whether the law will develop 'rights' any further is more problematic. It is a noticeable feature of the law in this area that it has developed in terms of remedies rather than rights. Hence, although the trend has been to promote children's interests at the expense of parents the law has stopped short of providing for 'children's rights'. Though there have been suggestions for a Bill of Rights for children or a Children's Charter, it is submitted that the law is right to stop short of this. The establishment of a charter, for example, seems to invite disputes where none existed before.

As far as custody proceedings are concerned it seems right that the child's welfare should be the first and paramount concern. Not everyone will agree with the application of the principle, but the welfare concept is a flexible and developing one. Already the courts seem more ready to grant joint orders and indeed it might not be unreasonable to suggest that such orders should be normally granted unless the court is persuaded otherwise. Whether fathers will overcome the basic prejudice of society against them being the sole parent, which is reflected by the court decisions, time will only tell. However, such changes are not out of the question. For example with more women going to work, and more men unemployed, it may not be so fanciful to contemplate a reversal of roles which in time would be reflected in court decisions.

Table of Cases

Re Agar–Ellis (1883) 24 Ch. D. 317
Almond v Almond, Court of Appeal Transcript No. 629 of 1980
Arensman v Pullman (1975) 5 Fam. Law 183
Re C(A) [1970] 1 All ER 309
Re Carroll [1931] 1 KB 317
Dipper v Dipper [1980] 2 All ER 722
Re F [1969] 2 All ER 766
Re G (1980) 10 Fam. Law 190
Grayling v Grayling, Court of Appeal Transcript No. 415 of 1979
Greer v Greer (1974) 4 Fam. Law 187
Hewer v Bryant [1969] 3 All ER 543
Hicks v Hicks, Court of Appeal Transcript No. 412 of 1980
Hutchinson v Hutchinson (1978) 8 Fam. Law 140
Ives v Ives (1974) 4 Fam. Law 16
J v C [1970] AC 668
Re K [1977] Fam. 179
M v M [1973] 2 All Er 81
M v M [1979] 9 Fam. Law 16
Re McGrath [1893] 1 Ch. 143
Marsh v Marsh (1978) 8 Fam. Law 103
Moore v Moore, Court of Appeal Transcript No. 028 of 1980
Re P, Court of Appeal Transcript No. 320 of 1979
P v McK (1973) Times, June 27
Paton v BPAS [1979] QB 276

R v De Manneville (1804) 102 ER 1054
R v Greenhill (1836) 111 ER 922
R v Moses Soper (1793) 101 ER 156
S(B.D.) v S(D.J.) [1977] Fam. 109
Stovold v Stovold (1974) 4 Fam. Law. 183
T v T (1974) Times, July I
Re Thain (1926) I Ch. 676
W v W & C (1968) 3 ALL ER 408
Willoughby v Willoughby (1951) :148

Notes

1 I would like to thank A. Borkowski, Lecturer in Law at the University of Bristol and R. A. H. White, Research Officer with the British Adoption and Fostering Agencies who kindly read over earlier drafts and Frances Lock who patiently typed various versions.

2 Summarized in Eekelaar's excellent book: *Family Law and Social Policy*: 227. The major English studies are S. Maidment: *A Study in Child Custody*; J. Eekelaar, E. Clive, K. Clarke and S. Raikes: *Custody After Divorce*; Northumbrian Probation and After Care Service (1976) and two Bristol studies conducted by M. Murch. All these studies are referred to and compared in Murch (1980).

3 The historical dimension of fatherhood: A case study 1890-1914

TREVOR LUMMIS

To comment on the role of the father in history briefly and yet relevantly will require a focus that is specific in time and place. This study uses data gathered on East Anglian fishermen and their families,[1] in order to question the common stereotype of the drunken, brutal, working-class father. This stereotype has prevailed in much sociological literature and has influenced our image of fathers in former times. The data and the discussion will be grouped into three areas. First, the degree to which the father's obligation as the main wage-earner enforced his absence from the family; second, the degree to which he contributed to childcare and domestic labour when free of the first task; finally, the degree to which time and income free from the previous two areas was shared with the family or spent as a 'male' with a peer group. But before turning to these I would briefly like to consider the historical image as it appears in sociological studies.

The dominant image conveyed by sociologists of the family is concisely expressed in one of the most widely known studies of a working-class community: 'The husband was not only mean with money. He was callous in sex, as often as not forcing a trial of unwanted pregnancies upon his unwilling mate. He was harsh to his children. He was violent when drunk, which was often' (Young and Willmott 1962 : 18). The authors of this study located a decisive shift in attitudes, towards lenience and family involvement, as occurring during or since the Second World War. A similar image of fathers and description of their behaviour appears in another study and once again the impression given is that fathers are becoming more benign: 'There is little doubt that the image of the stern, dominating father or the absent father who took no interest in the children, leaving them to mother, is fast disappearing' (Zweig 1962 : 23). In short, fatherhood in the past is presented as a Whiggish contrast to the present, with fathers becoming more domestic and humane as the present time is approached.

In the following pages it is argued that working-class marriage was in fact more generally an affectionate partnership of caring parents jointly concerned with preserving the family. That poverty, poor housing, and overwork resulted in deviations from this standard is indubitable. But in accepting the more dramatic deviant as the norm, such studies appear simply to repeat the class-biased image of the father that well informed observers of working-class life before 1914 knew to be a slander:

> 'Philanthropic people, as a rule, set so little value upon the family life of the poor, that they honestly believe that the one function performed by the father is to earn wages, and if these can be supplied from some other source they imagine that matters will go on very much as they did before — or even decidedly better. No allowance is made for the loss of companionship to the wife, of mental stimulus and moral restraint: none for the counterbalancing influence on the upbringing of the children, nor even the rough housework which commonly falls to *his share until he has a son old enough* to take his place.'
> (Loane 1910 : 222)

The emphasis has been added to underline Loane's view that fathers and sons shared domestic labour as a matter of course.

The fishermen's working pattern obviously restricted their opportunity to fulfil their paternal role more than most occupations. In East Anglia there were three distinct patterns of work-enforced absence and these are used as categories to analyse the degree to which the father's role as the family wage-earner affected his performance as a father. There were driftermen who were away from home for up to twenty weeks at a time, but also had four months at home without work; trawlermen, who were away for four or five nights a week regularly throughout the year; and inshoremen who worked almost normal hours in that they returned home most days. Also used in this analysis is the category of 'non-fishermen' which covers a variety of manual occupations.

The first area of discussion, that of the male's contribution to domestic work and childcare, involves some comment on their role as a spouse as well as a father. It is argued that this is relevant because it is in observing the total domestic activity of his father that the child forms expectations of appropriate behaviour. A sociological study of the fishing industry provides a stark image of the domestic attitude of such men: 'Some fishermen quickly come to regard their wives merely as providers of sexual and cooking services in return for a weekly wage'

(Tunstall 1962 : 162). This view is roughly congruent with an earlier study which found that miners had little time with, or for, their families and spent most of their surplus money and non-work time with peer groups outside the home. (Dennis, Henriques, and Slaughter 1956). Save in the first dimension of providing the wage necessary to raise a family, these men are little more than biological sires. This behaviour is explained by the 'exteme' nature of the waged work. Both are tough, male-only worlds, the values of which reject domestic life in favour of peer-group leisure activity and spending; wives getting a 'wage' regardless of the variable earnings of the spouse who keeps his earnings secret. On the evidence of the fishermen's wives such behaviour was not normal in East Anglia:

> '*Would your husband bring the money home all right even though he liked his drink?*
> Oh yes. Yes. He used to come home — and bring it and we'd share and share alike. Oh yes, we never had nothing no different then.'
> (3032 p. 7)[2]

> '*What happened when he was trawling, did he have the stockerbait money as his pocket money and you have the rest?*
> He would bring it all home to me and I'd give him — what I liked.
> *So you always managed the money did you?*
> Yes, yes. Yes! (3029 p. 42)

Among the trawlermen (and inshoremen) the 'share and share alike' was a typical response. This situation clearly reflected the short absence away from home of the man, but even so the woman usually had responsibility for allocating the family income.

This situation was greatly reinforced in the case of driftermen whose absences lasting several months necessitated the total surrender of all money to the wife:

> '*Did you ever discuss with your husband how the money should be spent?*
> Oh no. No. He used to come home at the end of a voyage, he'd come home and if there was anything to take, he'd come home and lay it all on the table.' (3042 p. 39)

> '*How did you manage money matters as you were away so much?*
> I never did see after the money until three years ago, I — the wife got so deaf and couldn't see — I always give her the money. I came home from the fishing one year, I think that was about 1921, any rate, I shuffled the pound notes out to the wife, I gave her fifty two,

enough to make a pack of cards. Now, I said, I don't see no more of it. She knew how to look after it better than I did.' (3077 pp. 73–4)

Giving all money to the wife to control was accompanied by a keen appreciation of the size of the family burden shouldered by the wife and the knowledge of just how essential a capable wife was to a fisherman. Nevertheless, within the context of enforced absence these men gave all possible finance to their families.

Informants were asked if their fathers did anything in the home. A very rigorous interpretation of the evidence proved that 38 per cent did, 28 per cent did not, and 33 per cent were unclassifiable. The distribution of 'don't knows' makes it impracticable to tabulate the difference between the various sections of fishermen. But it does appear that driftermen gave most help in the house and this might be expected considering their pattern of work — being home for long periods with no other work to do. The pattern of work, however, proved less crucial than might have been expected as a wife's right to some help seems to have been an accepted norm. Only two of the men appear to have refused to help in the home out of principle. The major reason for helping or not appears to have been a genuine sense of reciprocity and equal effort between parents:

'*Did your father help in the house at all?*
No. I mean, the old girl used to say to him if he wanted to help, no, you sit down father, you've been at work all day long and one thing and another — (he was working from) — five o'clock in the morning 'til here about six or seven o'clock at night'. (3020 p. 30)

The balance could change, however, and in the following extract the fact that his father did help in the house was being pursued:

'*Was it a bit unusual in those days for men to help in the house?*
No. No, the men always used to do some housework more or less.
A lot of people say that's a new thing, helping in the house.
No, not here. Because lots of them used to do things in the house, you know, to help the women out, because they most all had families, five or six was moderate — and eight and nine was — So they had to help more or less when they were home.' (3054 p. 49)

Apart from the obvious limits placed on the amount of help through the necessity of being absent from the home the division of labour in the family (waged and unwaged) seems to have been organized around an equal distribution of the amount of labour required to service the family. It is worth making the point that housework is a flexible procedure according to standards maintained and very few interviews reveal the obsessional scrubbing of steps, polishing of stoves and so forth that seem to feature in accounts from northern areas. In one account from East Anglia the standard was maintained by the male:

'Yes, he was a good father and a good husband. My children never knew what it was to get their own water in the morning to wash with. Before they went to school he'd clean their shoes.
Would he do any other jobs around the house?
On Friday night he used to say to me and my dear old mother — go in the other room I'm going to clean through. And he'd clean through my kitchen. I had a big cooking stove in there, with big white plates at the back, and he'd make that shine like a bit of glass.'
(Int. 3029 p. 29)

This informant married in 1904 so this is direct experience from pre-1914 and supports the evidence taken mainly from the informants' childhoods. All confirm that the level of housework was pragmatic and restricted to necessary tasks.

Certainly there was little chance of boys growing up with the idea that domestic labour was exclusively a female preserve. As many boys (68 per cent) as girls (70 per cent) report having to help in the home as children. There was some gender-typing regarding the type of task performed with boys more often cleaning yards and running errands while girls worked more in the home, but the most crucial aspect again seems to be the necessity of getting the work done. Thus, there are examples of boys who had little time for play because they had to mind infants and of girls who ran all the errands simply because there was not a sibling of the 'appropriate' age and sex to perform the tasks.[3]

Informants were asked how well they were disciplined in the home and which parent(s) administered corporal pubishment. It is evident from the responses that corporal punishment was rarely ever used and that childhood was on the whole comparitively unrestricted and free from fear, although in most homes the threat of chastisement was the ultimate deterrent. In an attempt to take the evidence beyond the anecdotal and to measure the role of the father the data has been tabulated.

Table 3(1) demonstrates a number of interesting features. One is that in the majority of known cases no physical method of socialization was used at all. Where it was used, it was the women rather than men who applied it, although unless placed in the category of 'No Role', the father concerned would take part in the general process of disciplining and socializing the children.

The effect of occupational absence is immediately obvious. A

Table 3 (1) *Parents who used chastisement as a form of discipline*

Parent	Using corporal punishment %	Not using corporal punishment %	No role %	Not known %	Cases
Inshore					
Mother	40	50		10	20
Father	20	60		20	20
Trawlers					
Mother	50	42		8	12
Father	25	42	33		12
Drifters					
Mother	44	31		25	16
Father	25	25	31	19	16
Non-Fishermen					
Mother	33	42		25	12
Father	17	42	8	33	12
Urban					
Mother	53	28		19	32
Father	22	34	22	22	32
Rural					
Mother	29	57		14	28
Father	21	54	11	14	28
Totals					
Mother	42(n=25)	42(n=25)		17(n=10)	60
Father	22(n=13)	43(n=26)	16(n=10)	18(n=11)	60

substantial proportion of the men who were obliged to be away from home withdrew from any active role. However, the interviews show that this was not through indifference, but as a result of the pragmatic recognition that the mother had to maintain order by herself for much of the time and that children therefore had to obey her alone. This dimension is also reflected in the lesser use of chastisement by mothers who had the daily support of the fathers — the non-fishermen and inshoremen. There are undoubtedly a number of factors affecting the level of corporal punishment that cannot be pursued at length: there is a difference, for example, between rural and urban areas that may well reflect the importance of environmental circumstances; but if attention is focused on the actual incidents that resulted in corporal punishment it is evident that such punishment was administered when a child's actions brought the family into conflict with the authorities or neighbours. It was, therefore, administered as a result of public pressures rather than private family rules or through the wilfulness, drunken or otherwise, of the father concerned. That working-class children play in public space may well involve their parents in public conflict more frequently that is the case with other social groups. This possibility is supported by the qualitative evidence which shows that it was in the fishing villages (most isolated from the power of other social groups) that the children had least fear of punishment in spite of their fathers being on hand: 'I was never punished — and not many other boys were either' (3059 p. 23) is from Essex. 'I don't know that any of our family ever got hit — I don't remember any children being hit about here at all' (3003 p. 24) is from Suffolk. From yet another Suffolk village it was related how if fishermen complained of children playing around their boats the children would retort 'Come near us and we will throw stones at you' (3014 p. 4). It is clear that they had little fear of their fathers or of any adults, an attitude identical to that noted by Stephen Reynolds who lived with a fishing family in Sidmouth around the turn of the century (Reynolds 1910).

The final focus of attention is on the leisure habits of the men, especially on their drinking habits, for it is these that have been held to be responsible both for their brutality in the home and for their selfish spending outside.

The East Anglian fishermen of pre-1914 were much more home-centred in their leisure time than either the fishermen of Hull in the 1960s or the miners of the 1950s. When they did go out it was during the day, not in the evenings. Although they were away from home for months at a time, even the driftermen spent little money on their own leisure activities. This was partly due to the fact that they would work seven days a week, except in Scotland where law prevented Sunday fishing, but then the day was usually spent quietly resting:

' — but very few people ever went ashore, in the latter years I went to Lerwick I never went ashore myself. I have been there fifteen weeks, never gone ashore, only on the quay, you know, just on the quay.
What about Aberdeen and those places?
If you went to Aberdeen, you might call there one night perhaps, go ashore and have a few drinks but — on the whole they weren't a very boozy lot. There was exceptions, they'd have a drink now and again, but there was none of that.'   (3017 p. 27)

The one exception to this for the driftermen and their one collective celebration was the day they were paid off. It was the custom for the men to get drunk on that day and then to disperse to their homes. For most men that would be the end of heavy drinking. An exception to this seems to have been fishing villages where whole crews came from the same village and where there was a lifeboat shed to provide a centre for card-playing and drinking during the afternoons. There the celebrations appear to have lasted several days:

> '*What about when your father was home, did he go out much in the evening?*
> No. No, he sometimes used to go, perhaps a dinnertime, to have a pint of beer and a game of cards in the Ship. Where all the fishermen, they all used to meet there. But that was all. They never went gallivanting on pub crawls and things like that. But the day when they finished their voyage, what they call paying-off day, well, all the wives knew what to expect. They'd all come home tiddly. But my father was so funny when he'd had a drink that he'd make you laugh. Mother used to get very annoyed with him. "Sit down there" she used to say to him. But we didn't care, I mean he never sort of frightened you. You know some men — I mean my uncle next door, he was violent. My poor cousins were terrified of their father because he'd had too much to drink.'   (3051 p. 38)

That extract illustrates both reactions to drink, but these cases were rare and the more typical response shows the woman in full control:

> 'Sunday dinnertime he'd go out and he wouldn't come home not 'til they turned out at half past two. He used to say to my mother — where's the dinner mother? She'd say — That's in the cupboard. She never kept anything hot for him. Then he'd say — I suppose what is good hot is good cold. He never made a fuss about it.'
> (3021 p. 49)

This informant's father was an habitual drinker but there is no sign in these interviews of the authoritarian father chronicled elsewhere.

With the driftermen the very limited amount of money spent on drink appears to come from their consciousness that money had to last over a long seasonal lay-off (and their habit of giving all the money to their wives) for as one man expressed it they just had to 'equalize' their money over that period. A lunchtime yarning over a small quantity of beer seems to have been the only outlet and that was often infrequent: 'Father didn't go out much. Perhaps he'd go and get a pint on Sunday dinnertime and then he didn't go anymore. The latter part of the time when we were getting off his hands he might, I mean, at that time of day he daresn't go and spend money on beer — what about food?'

(3003 p. 28). That working men could not spend money on their own pleasures because of the responsibility to their family is evident from an earlier study in London. Pember Reeves focused her study on women and infants in Lambeth but in spite of her concerns and her admitted prejudice that she expected to discover that their husbands would drink as a matter of course stated that they 'cannot and do not drink' (Pember Reeves 1913).

Many of the trawlermen came very close to being non-drinkers: this moderation contrasts very sharply with Tunstall's study of contemporary trawlermen. The next extract from a woman who married a trawlerman in 1907 is all the more convincing for being incidental to the question:

> 'So you could tell a fisherman by his dress could you?
> Oh, you could then, you can't now. And their roll. The trawlers — fishing smacks, they all used to have a (mimed roll) and there weren't no drunkenness and that like there is now. No. They'd go and have a pint before they came home but you never heard of a fisherman round here being drunk. Mm.'   (3016 p. 6)

This is typical of the accounts from wives and children who stated that most men would drink only on their way home after they had unloaded the fish.

The qualitative evidence on drinking was difficult to categorize with any precision. The least satisfactory category is 'Heavy', as it includes all those where actual habits were not specified. It includes a few cases

Table 3 (2) *Parents' Drinking Habits*

	Heavy %	Moderate %	Occasional %	Never %	Not known%	Total Cases
Father	18	32	23	13	13	60
Mother	3	10	7	22	58	60

where drinking obviously caused some hardship but usually they are simply cases where the respondent stated 'Dad liked a drink' without quantity or regularity being specified. 'Moderate' mainly indicates those who stated their fathers only drank at lunchtime or who specified a similar limitation. 'Occasional' includes some who were very occasional drinkers indeed: 'He never drank a glass of beer or anything like that, he never had the money to buy beer. He might have a drop of whisky if the owner took him in. He wouldn't go in of his own.' (3006 p. 5). 'Never' usually means one committed to non-drinking on principle. These were mostly inshore fishermen. Being mainly self-employed and usually working in close proximity to a pub there was always a risk that the comforts of a warm bar would prove more attractive than sitting for hours in a freezing open boat:

> 'Of course in them days you see the pubs used to open here about seven o'clock in the morning. And the chaps'd get in there and they wouldn't — you wouldn't see 'em before they chucked 'em out at night.
> *Was there very much of men going down intending to fish and then not bothering?*
> No. No. But if there was a breeze and they couldn't get off, they'd go in the pub and that was — they were finished.'   (3050 p. 26)

Self-discipline had to be strong, but once again the general impression is one of prudent self-restraint.

The data on women is not full enough to allow a great deal of comment, although it is noticeable that about half the known cases would drink on occasions. This more frequently took place at home although a number in the sample met their spouses in a pub. One female fish worker reports always going into the pub with her mother for rum and coffee before starting work at 6 a.m. as well as for an evening's entertainment while she was single. But it is evident that as one would expect, the pub was mainly the resort of men, or, less frequently, of men with their wives. It is equally clear, however, that the opening quotation that imputes regular drunkenness to the working-class father is not supported by a large body of evidence taken from the wives and children of an occupational group with a reputation for heavy drinking.

Apart from this light drinking there seems to have been little in the way of formal leisure. Informants from Lowestoft and Yarmouth recall their parents attending the variety theatres. A few wives report similar outings, but by far the greatest majority simply stated that neither they nor their husbands went out in the evening. This is supported by the informants' memories of their childhoods, and the evidence suggests that the fathers were deeply involved with their children. About a quarter of them stated that their father could play an instrument and that he would play for them in the evenings, or play ludo and similar games. One-third stated that they always had days out together as a family when father was home (that is, with mother as well) but an additional quarter report that they always had a day out with their father but their mother never accompanied them. There is a further quarter, all boys, who would spend various lengths of time at sea with their fathers during the school holidays. Yet only 4 per cent state that they had a day out alone with their mothers. This may indicate a rather unfair division of labour in this field as between spouses, but it does establish that these fathers were in no way distant from, or brutal to, their children. The return of father from a trip was anticipated with positive pleasure in the overwhelming majority of cases.

It is worth considering why this data so signally fails to support the stereotype. Three areas suggest themselves as possible explanations; location, occupation, and the quality of the evidence. In my own view the latter is the most important of these. Most evidence for the role of the father in history is little more than anecdotal. Such evidence is usually a surface response and conforms to what is believed to be the social norm.[4] Many informants, for example, when questioned about their fathers' domestic role would respond by stating that men never did anything in the house in those days. It is only through reconstructing the household routine that the part played by the father becomes apparent. In one interview the informant (3011) stated categorically that his father never did anything in the home. But his father was a horseman who rose at 4.40 a.m. every day to go to feed his horses at 5 a.m.; he would then return to the house to light the fire (there was no gas or electricity) in order to cook breakfast and make tea before waking his wife who would then rise and see to the children while he returned to work. Now it might be argued that rising first, preparing a fire and so on before anyone else is even up constitutes not only regular, but rather unpleasant, domestic duties. (Although as this father appears to have done nothing else in the home he is categorized as 'Never' helping in the home.) But establishing the role of the father resolved itself into a matter of detailed interviewing if the informants' own generalized images of the period were to be penetrated. It is perhaps significant that another study using long and detailed interviews has also found a much more positive image of domesticity in working-class families in the North of England (Roberts 1977).

There is simply not enough evidence available at the moment to assess whether the image of the brutal, uncaring, working-class father is due to poor-quality evidence or whether regional and occupation groups do vary very much in their domestic attitudes. Regional variations may well prove important, for as Tunstall showed, the fishermen of the Humber had very different values from those of East Anglia. According to one account of Cornish miners who moved to the Durham coalfield around 1865:

'The men set to work to whitewash the houses, that they might resemble the cottages they had left behind. They had none of that feeling, still strong in the north, that a man has amply performed his share in the marriage compact when he has handed over to his wife the bulk of his earnings. They did not shame to help their wives to wash, or even to cook.'   (Welbourne 1923)

Whether this was normal behaviour for miners in Cornwall I do not know, and as these families were strike breakers they may have been more home-centred than was customary for good reasons. Certainly one of the big differences between the East Anglian fishermen and the miners was the lack of male-only work-linked social centres (Trade Union, Welfare Club) outside the home. Differences in the role of fatherhood may well be modified by the organizational and social demands of the occupational situation.

One would not wish to conclude with an impression of over-emphasis on the domestic role of men. Clearly, domestic labour and child-rearing were female responsibilities and the involvement of father has grown since the period of this study. It would be obtuse to argue the importance of the historical dimension to contemporary studies if there has been no change. What is needed is a better understanding of the attitudes prevalent in the past and how the role of fatherhood has been shaped by material conditions in both the national and domestic economy.

At the turn of the century many men worked long hours which entailed their absence from the family for most of the day: that was not a rejection of fatherhood but a necessary element of it. No matter how strong the paternal instincts of the father, young children could only see him for a few hours a week. Yet so many studies concentrate on the male at the workplace; or research women, kinship, children, and community from which men are undergoing an enforced absence for most of the day.[5] Mothers, too, often used 'father' as the last disciplinary resort to control children. Where fathers accepted the authoritarian role cast for them by their spouse it can be no surprise that many children remember their fathers as more distant and intimidating figures than their mothers. One reason why so many of the informants in the present study remember their fathers much more affectionately may well be due to the different pattern of contact imposed through occupational factors. Driftermen were absent for long periods, but then they were also home for long spells and so became as familiar as the mothers. This work pattern also meant that as the men were absent for long periods they could not be used as a disciplinary threat: the mother had to control behaviour herself. This occupational pattern of the fishermen obliged women to exercise the ultimate sanction of corporal punishment, and perhaps as a result of this the image of the brutal father is less prevalent.

If fathers were absent as a sanction they were also absent as a family support. In this sample the importance of the positive functions of the father are undoubted. The number of child deaths in each family where the father was necessarily absent from home was double that of families where the father was not absent (driftermen 16 per cent, trawlermen 17 per cent, compared to inshoremen 7 per cent, non-fishermen 8 per cent), a division that is not explicable in terms of poverty or similar factors. This evidence suggests[6] that fathers were a very positive influence in domestic affairs. If they were the selfish figures of the stereotype, taking an abnormal share of family resources and brutalizing their children, then families with resident fathers might be expected to be least successful in child-rearing.

It is in the relation to the wider economy as well as the domestic one that changes in the performance of fatherhood must be traced. It is a complex situation, for much of the laboriousness of domestic work has been removed: 'productivity' has been reduced from six or so children to two. But standards and expectations have risen and the necessity of the work to be done at regular intervals over a seven-day week has not changed. On the other hand the working week in the wider economy has been considerably reduced and concentrated into five days. This obviously not only requires a change in the allocation of duties between parents but also makes such changes possible.

Finally, one must return to the importance of the historical record to contemporary issues. It is quite evident that models and concepts explaining social change and the development of particular roles are unlikely to be informative or accurate if they are based on a false starting point. I would argue that the role of the father in the recent past is largely unknown and probably misrepresented through poor-quality anecdotal evidence. It is accepted that there are a number of reasons that may have made the fishermen of this time and place atypical, but this needs to be shown by thorough research. Tunstall's work cautions against any assumption (or model) that sees the role of the father developing on a simple trend from 'distant/brutal' in the past to 'involved/loving' in the present. The attitudes to domestic life and fatherhood related by Tunstall may well be due to the fact that the contrast between the hours of hardship and danger endured by the males and the comfort of home enjoyed by their wives is probably the sharpest one left in modern industry. It can be argued, however, that the contribution of fatherhood is still mainly in terms of his absence from the domestic scene rather than his contribution to it:

'They suffer in order to get the money: to buy things. They talk of getting a nice house of their own, for the kids, and many of them have achieved this. Of taking the wife and kids away for trips in the car. Of a good life for their families. A good life that is based on their sacrifice. When you're packing bags, self-sacrifice and a determination to see things through become central to your world; just as they do for wives and *their* sacrifice in the home.'

(Nichols and Benyon 1977 : 193)

The performance of fatherhood roles cannot be divorced from socially imposed divisions of labour which have excluded the male from the home as effectively as they have tied women to it.

Notes

1   The interviews were conducted by the author while Senior Research Officer for the Social Science Research Council project HR 2656/1, The Family and Community Life of East Anglian Fishermen, directed by Paul Thompson. There are forty interviews with males and twenty with females. The mean average date of birth is 1893 but 30 per cent were born in the 1880s and the data is mainly drawn from their own childhoods although the married experience has also been used where this occurred before 1914.

2   This and similar references are to the interview number and transcript page. Both tapes and transcript are preserved in the University of Essex Oral History Archive, director Paul Thompson.

3   Cf. Kerr 1958, where under children's work she mentions only girls, and boys appear to exist only as infants to be cared for by girls.

4   Assumptions about what is the norm also seems to affect the perception of researchers. For example, Young and Willmott (1962 : 18) cite Pember Reeves '"He makes his wife the same allowance, and expects the same amount of food. She has more mouths to fill . . ."' as an example of the selfish father. It follows on from their typification of him as drunken and brutal. But they could have cited Pember Reeves to the effect that she found that the men did not drink; she also explained that 'The father of the family cannot eat less. He is already eating as little as will enable him to earn a family wage' (Pember Reeves 1913 : 68). She, at least, rightly attributes the poor role performance of both father and mother to low wages and poor conditions, rather than to male chauvinism.

5   Young and Willmott, 1962, may be an example of this in that much of their research is concerned with the daily routine of women and children while the male is necessarily absent. They do, however, acknowledge the importance in the reduction of the working week in enabling fathers to have more time with their families.

6   The data is taken from Table 3(1). It should be emphasized that this table has no statistical validity and the suggested implication is drawn by the customary process of historical reasoning from the available data.

4 How should we approach the study of fathers?

MARTIN P.M. RICHARDS

Though the study of fathers remains a minority interest among re-searchers concerned with parents and children, work has undergone a considerable, and welcome, increase during the last few years.[1] In this chapter I want to discuss some of the directions this research has taken. My argument is that much of the growing body of research is, in effect, an extension of the long-standing tradition of work with mothers to include fathers. It arises more from a well-meaning attempt to balance the earlier almost exclusive concentration on mothers than from an examination of what might be exclusive or special to father-hood rather than motherhood or parenthood. At worst, men as parents are presented as alternative mothers and much writing is concerned with demonstrating their adequacy, if not desirability, as parents. Little of this kind of research rises above comparisons of the behaviour of men and women with their children.

There has been very little interest in the social institution of father-hood. Many questions about the ways in which the distinct male and female reproductive physiology may (or may not) give rise to differing expectations and experiences of parenthood for men and women remain to be explored. Socially we view paternity and maternity in rather separate ways. While notions of paternity often embody an idea of the acquisition of property, maternity is more related to concepts of giving and fulfilment — how do these influence men and women as parents? There are many questions about the development of male and female gender identity and its relation to parenthood. Instead of exploring these, most work has concentrated on the traditional issues that have dominated the research on mothers. The absence of a more specific and adequate approach to the study of fathers has unnecessarily limited, and to some extent distorted, our understanding of fathers and father-hood.

The reason why the research has developed in this way and has not produced its own orientation is related to the manner in which the expansion in research on fathers has come about. In some cases, new areas of research suddenly blossom because of developments within the research work itself. Researchers may, for instance, develop a new method or technique that brings previously unreachable areas within their grasp or a new theoretical formulation sets new problems or questions for empirical work. In these sorts of situations the new research is generated from within the research community. An example here is the expansion of studies of childhood and parents that followed the adoption of observational methods which had been developed originally by animal ethologists (see Blurton Jones 1972a). Other expansions of research follow a rather different pattern where the main impetus comes from outside, rather than inside, the academic world. This would be exemplified by the research on the effects of separation at birth of mother and baby. The extent of newborn separation has steadily increased since the 1960s with the building of special care baby units and development of specialized neonatal paediatrics. Concern about the possible effects of the separation was originally expressed by parents who had suffered separation and by paediatricians responsible for the care of these babies. Most of the early studies in the field were carried out by paediatricians (Klaus and Kennell 1976a; de Chateau and Winberg 1977) and only more recently have psychologists become interested in the field. An additional reason for an absence of psychological interest in the problems has been the dominance of attachment theory. According to attachment theory (Ainsworth 1969) separation effects arise from the breaking of established relationships. As it was held that it took several months for a baby and parent to become attached, early separation did not appear as a problem.

My argument is that the expansion in research on fathers has followed external pressures and has not come about because of developments within the research world itself. The outside pressures have taken many forms and have complex origins. They include such things as the femin-ist attacks on psychology for its more or less exclusive concern with mothers and support for the idea that childcare is exclusively the business of women (for example, Wortis 1972) and the increasing involvement of men with their children. This latter pheonmenon has been apparent to many of the professional groups who work with parents and children who have turned to psychology for information or help with the issues that this new trend raises but initially found little of relevance. Even today, popular books for fathers still outnumber publications for the professional world.

The academic world has responded to these pressures for research on fathers not least because this work seemed to satisfy the growing calls for social relevance in research. But as in other areas of reasearch where little work is going on but expansion is considered desirable for social, political, or economic reasons, moves to enter the field tend to be accorded little critical appraisal. Research is then too easily justified by its object of concern rather than any theoretical or methodological arguments. This has meant not only that the various processes that may operate to weed out poorly thought out or conducted research have been blunted in their application, leaving a body of research of more than usually uneven quality, but also that old problems, approaches, and theories have been carried over into the new areas. There have been few pressures to create new orientations or new theory. The old gibe that psychology is all performance with little competence may apply more closely than usual in a situation like this.

In the next section of this chapter I will outline briefly the main directions that recent work on fathers has taken. In each case I suggest that a body of work on mothers has been extended to include fathers without any very significant adjustments. I will then go on to argue that better theoretical formulations are required and that these must be derived from a consideration of the social institution of fatherhood.

Themes in research on fathers

OBSERVATIONAL STUDIES OF PARENT-INFANT INTERACTION

In the early 1960s the combination of a growing interest in techniques of direct observation and Bowlby's formulation of his attachment theory (Bowlby 1969-1980) led to the establishment of an active tradition of observational studies of mothers and infants. Initially, this research was largely based in Britain, but now it is more strongly represented in the United States of America. The main aims of observational studies were to describe what mothers and infants did together, either at home or in some contrived situation in a laboratory, and to seek correlations across time between maternal behaviour and infant behaviour (for example, Bell, Weller, and Waldrop 1971; Ainsworth, Bell, and Stayton 1974; and Dunn 1977). To a greater or lesser extent, Bowlby's attachment theory has provided a theoretical orientation for these studies, though in recent years this has been largely superseded by an approach more concerned with the growth of communication between infant and parent than attachment (Richards 1974b; Lock 1978; Newson 1979). Originally, observation studies were exclusively concerned with mothers and infants. Many factors led to this constraint. Bowlby's theory assumed that the mother would be the object of early attachment and he relegated fathers to the role of providing financial and emotional support for their female partners. A very practical reason for ignoring fathers is that most childcare is provided by mothers, especially during the day, when researchers conduct their studies, so that samples that include fathers and their children are much harder to come by. However, the most important reason is the common assumption in society in general, as well as among many social scientists, that it is not only statistically usual for mothers to be the major caretakers of their children but that they are in some way better suited to the task.

As this latter assumption began to be questioned, a few people began to do observational studies of fathers (Lamb 1976b; Park, O'Leary, and West 1972; see Chapter 10 in this volume). Most of these studies seemed to be motivated by a concern to show that fathers' behaviour was the same as or very similar to that of mothers and that infants were equally likely to be attached to either. What was generally lacking, presumably because of the failure to replace attachment theory with anything more appropriate, was a concern with dynamics of interaction between father and mother and either of them with their male and/or female children. In fact, despite attachment theory's concentration on the female caretaker, it is surprising how its infant is always neuter and unsexed. The elements of Freudian theory used to build attachment theory excluded those concerned with Oedipus or infantile sexuality (Richards 1981).

Observational methods have been also widely employed in the study of early separation of mothers and newborn. Again in this field, one can trace a preoccupation with mothers and a later attempt to include fathers in the act but in exactly the same terms as mothers. Incidentally, the results of these studies show very similar effects with fathers and mothers (Rödholm 1981).

THE EXPERIENCE OF PREGNANCY AND DELIVERY

Interview studies of women's experience of pregnancy and delivery have formed a prominent part of a wider interest in female reproductive experience. Theoretical perspectives have varied from a generally feminist orientation (for example Oakley 1979) to a concern about the effects of changing obstetric practice (Chard and Richards 1977). Again, one can trace a shift in this literature over the last decade from a position where the concern was exclusively with women to the present where we have a growing body of studies that describe the experiences of men (see Chapters 6 and 7 in this volume). This shift parallels the growing frequency with which fathers are present at hospital deliveries and are included in antenatal classes. Given that a central theme in this research has been the participants' feelings, it is obvious that the same list of issues and problems will not do for both men and women and the research has, indeed, examined some topics specifically related to fatherhood (for example, the reconciliation of stereotypes of masculinity and the public expression of emotion or the handling of babies). However, the starting point of much of this research has been the growing dominance of medicine as the social institution that defines and controls the experience of pregnancy and birth for women. This has tended to become a point of reference for the studies of men too. Thus the research has concentrated on the men's experience of the medical system and the part it has allocated to them in the reproductive process, especially as helpers and companions for their partners. Less interest has been shown in the connections between men's feelings about their partner's pregnancy and delivery and other aspects of their own lives. Just as psychologists have concentrated on the study of women in their examination of childcare so have social scientists made the world of work the central area in the study of men. It is still rare to find studies that bridge this gap. Another topic that work on fathers has hardly touched is the possible connection between a man's feelings as a father and his experience of his relationships with his own father and mother.

MEN AS SOCIAL PROBLEMS

As has often been pointed out, much research in family sociology and associated areas of psychology has tended to regard any domestic arrangements apart from the intact nuclear family as deviant or as a social problem. The unmarried woman and her child, or more recently, the single-parent family, have been the staple fare of much of this sort of research. Again, the outside pressures on research seem to have led to this approach frequently being taken over into work on fathers. It is perhaps relevant that in 1973 when the National Council for the Unmarried Mother and Her Child changed its name to the National Council for One-Parent Famiies, it marked the occasion with a conference about fathers.

Though it has been the case in this research that 'single parent' in fact means mother, there are an increasing number of studies that examine the situation of fathers who are looking after children on their own. But, perhaps significantly, one of the earliest studies in this field was entitled *Motherless Families* (George and Wilding 1972). Once again, we find that when the attention has shifted from women to men there has been a tendency for the traditional conceptualizations to be

'd. So the basic orientation of many studies of lone fathers is
_ experience as a series of problems (as male mothers) and there
is a strong emphasis on the odd and unusual nature of their situation.
Much more unusual is a more neutral view of the variety of family
forms and a comparison of the reproductive alternatives open to
women and men (Rappoport, Rappoport, and Strelitz 1977). What is
also largely lacking is any male equivalent of the now extensive feminist
literature on the institution of motherhood (for example Rich 1976)
or the varieties of living arrangements with or without children. But
even here, the few examples that have appeared could be criticized for
taking their stance too closely from the women's movement (Pleck and
Sawyer 1974; Snodgrass 1977; Tolson 1977).

GENDER IDENTITY AND SEX ROLES

The final area I want to mention has a rather different history from
those I have discussed so far. In the study of the development of gender
identity and sex roles, at least one theoretical school had always taken
the position of fathers seriously thought it may be said to have studied
him by his absence. I refer to those who have held that boys' gender
identity is formed, at least in part, by a process of role modelling or
identification with the father. At least as far back as the Second World
War one can find plenty of studies that have compared boys in 'father
present' families and 'father absent' families (for example, Biller 1971).
The weakness here is that so little attempt has been made to study any
two-parent families, and so, although differences have been attributed
to father absence, there are no adequate models to suggest how those
differences may have come about. Further problems arise because the
male gender identity tends to be seen in such terms as aggressiveness or
the pursuit of stereotypically male activities and there is almost no
mention of the development of attitudes or feelings towards fatherhood.
Another difficulty is that the sterile debate between those who see
sexual differences as the product of social learning or other environmental factors and those who see them as inevitable products of biology
has clouded all other concerns in the field and this has tended to deflect
interest away from any concern with fathers and their influences on
their children.

Other perspectives

My summary in the last section of recent research on fathers has necessarily been very brief and therefore oversimplified. It does less than
justice to the diversity of approaches that is growing up and, in particular,

to those who have attempted to shift their work away from the traditional theoretical directions. Nevertheless, I think my main point stands, that research on fathers is constrained and distorted by the lack of an adequate orientation or theoretical framework. What has too often stood the the place of such an approach has been a substitution of men for women in the existing traditions of work on motherhood.

In an attempt to move on from the present, still unsatisfactory, position I want to discuss two areas that might form part of our conceptualization of fatherhood. The first concerns some biological ideas about fathers and mothers. I choose this area for discussion partly to point out the limited relevance of arguments derived from other species. However, one of the valid points that can be made from this perspective is the potential divergence in interests between fathers and mothers. This latter point is important because it challenges normative assumptions about a unity of interests within families and may help us to see the separate positions of men and women more clearly. It is my proposition that the currently fashionable assertion of an androgynous commonality for all parents, whatever their gender, serves only to gloss over important issues.

The second topic I choose for discussion is the development of men's attitudes and feelings toward children and toward their position as parents. Here I want to suggest that we need to take a developmental view in order to understand fatherhood.

SOME BIOLOGICAL ARGUMENTS

There are those who regard feelings toward children and the desire to care for them as behaviour that is inevitable and fixed by our genetic make-up. People taking this view also usually assume that there is a 'natural' division of labour whereby the major part of childcare falls to women (who, in these terms, are held to be especially fitted for this task). While it is obvious that breast feeding is not a task that can be shared between the sexes, there is no evidence that men are not only capable, but in many cases willing, to perform all other aspects of childcare. But rather than pursuing this fruitless debate between nature and nurture, it is perhaps more illuminating to consider some of the ways in which sociobiologists have considered the selection pressures that may influence the division of child-rearing labour between the sexes.

Looking around the animal kingdom it is clear that there is no universal answer to the question of which parent provides parental care. In many species neither does: for instance, in many pelagic fish such as the herring both sexes simply release their gametes into the water and take no further interest in their offspring. Among the birds there are species where the female builds the nest, incubates and feeds the young, others where all these tasks are shared with a male, and still others where these activities are only undertaken by the male. What determines which system is adopted? What some sociobiologists have done is to invent a kind of calculus of selective advantage that attempts to quantify the pros and cons of various systems in terms of selective advantage and disadvantage (Trivers 1972; West and Konner 1976). Though these models have no power to explain behaviour as they are simply concerned with the ways in which selective forces might have operated during evolution, they do help to make some important points about parents. However, in using them, it is important to realize that they grossly over-simplify selective pressures. They make the unlikely assumption that selective pressures will always remain equal except when exerted on the particular items of behaviour that the theory is concerned with.

Until the recent sociobiological work, parental behaviour and other behaviour which appears to involve costs (expenditure of energy, risks of mortality, etc.) to the individual doing it and a benefit to another individual, was generally explained on the basis of it being good for the species as a whole. However, despite many attempts, convincing ex-planations of how this process of group selection might arise in evolution have never been forthcoming. So sociobiologists have attempted explanations in terms of individual selection — natural selection being concerned with the genes an individual passes on, or fails to pass on, to the next generation. From the perspective of indi-vidual selection, parenthood, instead of being a cooperative venture, appears as a compromise between two sets of divergent individual interests. Offspring have half their genes in common with each parent so it is in the interests of a parent to ensure that as many offspring as possible survive to reproductive age. But neither parent is necessarily bound to have all their young fathered or mothered by the same indi-vidual. Let us make the reasonable assumption that the survival of young is enhanced by the investment of parental care. However, on the whole, the expenditure of energy in parental care reduces the number of young that can be produced. There are high number, low parental care strategies, as with the herring, or low number, high parental care stra-tegies, as with our own species. The same applies within a species between the sexes. A male could adopt a high number, low quality strategy. He could attempt to invest all his energies in impregnating as many females as possible and leave them to provide all the parental care. Or he could father fewer children but spend more time caring for them, which might in fact lead to a greater number surviving. Females would be playing exactly the same strategies. Trivers (1972) has further suggested that there are likely to be links between the mating system, courtship, sexual dimorphism, and the division of parental care (*Table 4 (1)*). While the evidence to support these relationships is rather mixed (presumably because all else is seldom equal — see above), these models do have the merit of drawing attention to aspects of reproduction and social organization.

In terms of the model in *Table 4 (1)*, our own species would seem to fall somewhere between the centre and the column on the left. Our

Table 4 (1)

Parental care	Male investment lower than female	Male and female investment about equal	Female investment lower than male
Mating system	Polygyny	Monogamy	Polyandry
Courtship	Male–male competition for females. Female choice.	Low intrasex competition	Female–female competition for males. Male choice.
Adult sex	Males larger, perhaps more brightly coloured etc.	Low sexual dimorphism	Female larger, perhaps more brightly coloured etc.

After Trivers (1972)

sexual dimorphism is relatively small (males slightly larger, differences in body hair distribution etc.), while a majority of societies practise occasional or regular polygyny. On this basis, one would predict that childcare would be to some extent shared but larger burdens would be carried by females.

However, in attempting to apply the model to our own species we should notice that one of its basic assumptions is unlikely to fit. The model assumes that parental investment can be provided by males or females and that all that matters is that the total investment is made by one or other or some combination of the two. This is a reasonable assumption for a bird species where the young are fed in the nest. Here, so long as sufficient food arrives it presumably does not matter if it comes via the male or female. Sometimes, of course, anatomical or physiological adaptions will more or less limit the provision of food to one sex — as with milk among mammals — so 'fixing' a particular division of labour. However, in a species like ours with its enormous emphasis on the culture and social skills that are passed from parent to young during the greatly extended period of childhood dependency, there is the question of providing knowledge and experience as part of the sum total of parental investment. It seems likely that in a cultural species with sexual divisions forming a prominent part of social life there may be an advantage in both parents involving themselves in childcare, as children may have the best chance of survival if they are exposed to both male and female culture. As a further complication, it might be that children of a particular sex have more or less to gain from parental care from one or other parent.

The most striking feature of the division of sexual labour among the various human societies is the great variety of arrangements that may be found — far more than among animal species. This, of course, is a reflection of the enormous importance of non-genetic information that is passed from generation to generation, largely from parent to child, and our ability to reflect on our social lives and to change them within the limits set by the social structures in which we live. This allows for wide variety between and within cultures and very rapid inter-generational change, far faster than in species where changes arise from modification to the genetic material. We moved from Stone Age culture to industrial society without significant genetic change. The overriding importance of our system of cultural transmission also means that models of behavioural development based on animal species are very unlikely to apply. As with the sociobiologist's model of mating systems and parental investment, these can only give us a viewpoint from which to observe our own behaviour, they can never explain it, and certainly can never tell us what might be desirable or natural. As I have already said, what is striking about parental care in our own species is the enormous variety of arrangements that can be found. While mothers tend to be the major caretakers of children, fathers' involvement ranges from almost complete absence (sometimes with other males taking a part in childcare, sometimes no males involved) to near equal partners. Knowledge of this variety can serve two important functions. First, it is a reminder that there are no simple answers to questions about desirable domestic arrangements. Those found in a particular society will reflect its history, social structure, mode of subsistence, and many other aspects of its culture. The other point is that by seeing the range of possibilites that exist we have a better base from which to reflect on our own situation. More formally, analyses of fatherhood within a number of societies can help us to build models that can be invaluable in analysing our society. As yet work on fatherhood has been very ethnocentric, seldom looking beyond the English–speaking industrialized countries. Some of this narrowness could be explained by the lack of appropriate anthropological research. There is an almost complete lack of cross–cultural surveys of the roles of fathers (but see Leiderman, Tulkin, and Rosenfeld 1977) let alone more sophisticated work which might begin to relate to the division of labour within and outside the home with other aspects of the social structure. Few of those interested in parent–child relations have undertaken cross–cultural comparisons, while the little that has been done has not had much to say about fathers. Yet, despite the obvious dangers in work which simply correlates crude indices of cultural divergence, work such as that of the Whitings (1975) provides a number of interesting ideas.

The other direction in which we may go to obtain some perspective from which to build a conceptual model of fatherhood is towards our own history. That is a theme that is explored elsewhere in this book (see Chapter 1).

GROWING UP TO BE A FATHER

As well as an adequate and historically specific view of fatherhood, we need to be able to answer questions about how an individual grows up to become a father. Or to put it in other terms, how are the expectations, needs, desires, and attitudes passed from generation to generation? Despite all the psychological work on sex differences (for example, Maccoby 1966) and gender role and identity (for example, Rosenberg and Sutton-Smith 1972; Mead 1949) relatively little attention has been paid to the reproduction of parental roles across generations and what there is has in large part been confined to mothers. However, some of this work comes from the psychoanalytic object–relations tradition, that lays particular emphasis on the different roles of mothers and fathers and the contrast between the developmental courses for boys and girls. So, though the primary concern of this work is women, it is possible to use it as a basis for elaborating the position for men without falling into the trap I described earlier of transposing theories about mothers to fathers.

In this final section I will elaborate a theoretical view of how patterns of parental relations are reproduced from generation to generation. My account leans heavily on the reworking of object relations theory provided by Chodorow (1978). At present these ideas remain at the level of an interesting and, perhaps, plausible theory. None of it has been systematically tested. However, given that these ideas go a long way to remedy the defects in attachment theory I described earlier, and that they could provide just the kind of focus that is required for studies of fathers, one hopes that they find a place in future psycho-logical work.

In the account that follows, for the purposes of simplifying the exposition I shall only discuss the present–day conventional nuclear family of Western industrialized societies in which the mother stays at home with the children (or, at least, is the major caretaker) and the father goes out to work. In doing this I do not want to suggest that such a pattern is universal or in any sense basic. But space does not permit the exploration of consequences of other arrangements. However, I hope the reader will at least be able to see the ways in which the framework could be used to analyse other situations.

At first, the mother's relationship with her newborn baby is one of total identification; in Winnicott's (1958) terms this is called 'primary maternal preoccupation'. The mother tends to withdraw from other relationships and to devote herself almost single–mindedly to the baby's care. Psychoanalysts often describe this response of a mother as regressive because it is partly a recreation of experiences she had in her own infancy. The mother is a cushion between the child and the outside world and she tries to interpret and satisfy his or her needs in ways that shelter the child from the harsher realities of daily life. For the child, the mother comes to represent dependence and passivity and a lack of adaptation to and isolation from reality.

From birth, the father will represent separateness and detachment. His contacts with the baby will be intermittent and more distant than the mother's. A father is a representative of the world outside the home, who first brings to the child knowledge about that world. He, and so that world, come to represent things like independence, activity, and progress. Because fathers are more distant they can be more subject to the child's fantasies than mothers and may be seen in much more stereotyped ways. So the link they provide with the outside world often distorts and brings the child a very conventional view of their culture.

As primary maternal preoccupation begins to recede, the baby's dependence becomes less complete and total. A first sense of autonomy and independence begins to emerge with a developing interest in other people and things. As this grows there is the first self-identification as a boy or a girl and the beginnings of awareness of the parents' gender. Children notice that not only are their parents of opposite sex, but that all of society appears to be organized in ways that reflect differences in position between men and women, fathers and mothers, and husbands and wives. This realization leads children to see their relationships with each parent in the form of a heterosexual couple, albeit in highly symbolic terms. At this point, in Freudian terms, the male child has entered the Oedipus complex and gender has now become the fundamental organizing principle of his own self-concept and that of his relations with others. This begins to replace the all-embracing dependency of the first tie with the mother.

In her detailed reworking of the Oedipal theory, Nancy Chodorow (1978) stresses that girls continue in a more or less exclusive relationship with their mothers for a much longer period than boys and when they enter their Oedipal phase their links with their mothers are not broken in the same way as for boys. Boys define their masculinity by what the mother is not and by moving away from her. Girls are led towards their fathers by the intensity and ambivalence of the mother–daughter relationship. The need to move away from the mother comes from the daughter's need to define herself in relation to someone who is unlike herself. Fathers may contribute to this process by responding to their daughters in a mildly erotic flirtatious way. Chodorow sums up the situation:

> 'Because mothers are the primary love object and object of identification for children of both genders and because fathers come into the relational picture later and differently, the Oedipus complex in girls is characterised by the continuation of pre-Oedipal attachments and preoccupations, sexual oscillation in an Oedipal triangle and the lack of either absolute change of love object or absolute Oedipal resolution.' (Chodorow 1978 : 133–34)

The girl's developing gender identity is more complex than that of a boy because it contains two contradictory elements: the nurturing, caring, and asexual maternal element, which derived from the mother, and the heterosexual element, which comes from the father. There is another difference in that girls' gender identity arises out of a personal identification while boys are more positional — more related to the abstract and non-personal aspects of the cultural norms and stereotypes. As boys develop their masculinity negatively — by what is not feminine — the development of their gender identity is, compared with girls, more separated from a close and powerful emotional relationship; it involves more the general characteristics of the male position and less the specific attitudes and values of the person identified with. This leads to a blunting and suppression of their nurturing and emotional side and an emphasis on the external attributes of power, economic position, and so on. They are growing into a world of work where their status will be defined by their occupation, and their emotional and family life will be seen as a secondary and an 'extra' part of their life. Their centre will be outside the home in the public world. Because a boy's masculinity becomes defined by negation, he learns to see women's economic and social position as less important than male ones. His relationship with his mother may contain elements of contempt as well as hostility. This can lead to ambivalent elements in adult heterosexual relations where women are seen not only as caring and supportive, but also as seductive, mysterious, and dangerous. In short, men's socialization prepares them for a world of male superiority in which they will strive in the world of work and remain withdrawn from the emotional world of family and children. Hetereosexual relations often become a search for a retreat and place of safety in a hostile and impersonal world. Close supportive relationships are difficult to find amongst other men in the competitive work world so men often become very dependent on wives. They may try to recreate an adult version of the primary relationship with their mothers that they so long ago abandoned. At the same time they may be seeking reassurances in their masculine stance which can reproduce the old hostilities and contempt for their mother. Such contradictory relationships sometimes cannot survive the arrival of a child which not only comes between the father and his would-be primary relationship but may also invoke old conflicts related to sibling rivalry and displacement. In addition, their long training in suppression of feelings can make men very unsatisfactory and demanding partners.

According to object relations theory of the kind I am outlining, a man's wish to father children arises from his positional identification with his own father. To have a child is to do as their father has done and it forms part of the stereotyped masculine identity they have accepted. It is important to note that the wish is one to create the position of father and not directly to form a father–son or father–daughter relationship. In this way the characteristic distance of the father from his children is reproduced for the next generation (supported, of course, by many elements in the social structure). The emphasis on biological paternity may provide the means for a father to assert and conceptualize in a very concrete way his link with his children, while, at the same time remaining physically and psychologically distant from them. Paternity is a kind of symbolic object − the coin of family relations, which like money in the work world comes to stand for and is the measure of a relation.

For girls the positional identification with the mother means close links between the affective relationship they have with their mother and their learning of a female identity. This provides for much more continuity for women between the families of each generation. Girls take attitudes and beliefs directly from their own mothers and these help to form their own attitudes as wives and mothers. Their femininity is taken directly from what they experience and see immediately around themselves. This stands in contrast to the much more idealized and fantasized masculine identity which men acquire and leaves girls in much closer and individual relationships with those inside and outside their families. A woman's position is more interpersonal and affective and is more defined from their place in the family (not the world of work) as daughter, wife, and mother. Their position in the public world is defined secondarily from their father and later their husband. He gives their name and their place in the economy.

Conclusion

In this chapter I have tried to argue that a satisfactory development of research on fathers must be based on an adequate conceptualization of the social institution of fatherhood. Research has too often simply substituted men for women in the longstanding traditions of work on mothers. Such work fails to elaborate what might be specific to make attitudes and feelings about parenthood and tends to leave unconnected male life inside and outside the home.

Much work remains to be done to elaborate our understanding of fatherhood. I have looked briefly at some concepts used by socio-biologists and a view on the development of gender identity produced by object relations theorists. Other chapters in this book explore other directions.

Notes

1 I am grateful to Shelley Day and the editors of this volume for their helpful comments on an earlier draft of this paper and to Phyllis Osbourn for her many secretarial and managerial skills. My work on ideologies of parenthood is supported by a contract with the SSRC.

5 The desire to father: Reproductive ideologies and involuntarily childless men

DAVID OWENS

Unlike the other chapters in this book, this one is not concerned with men who are fathers. Instead, it deals with men who are trying to become fathers and who have experienced difficulties in these attempts. I shall, therefore, be discussing not men *as* fathers, but men's reasons for wanting to father, and this discussion will include an examination of their reasons for trying to begin a family, the meanings they ascribe to parenthood, and the value they see in having children.[1]

Initial consideration of these issues leads us into the field of fertility intentions, an area in which a considerable amount of work has been done. Several large–scale surveys, for example, have concentrated on the usefulness or otherwise of 'ideal' and 'intended' family size to predict and explain achieved family size (Woolf 1971; Woolf and Pegden 1976; Cartwright 1976; Dunnell 1979). These studies have been instrumental in illustrating fertility intentions and behaviour amongst a cross–section of the British population, and, where the studies have involved a longitudinal element, have been significant in allowing us to examine the process of family formation over time (Woolf and Pegden 1976). However, informative though these studies are, they are not my concern here for two reasons. First, they do not deal directly with men, since in nearly all cases the data have been collected only from female respondents. Second, it can be argued that the studies deal with the details of reproduction, that is 'how many' and the 'when' of family building. Rather, I wish to address the more fundamental question of why men want children at all.

To some extent, this question is a product of modern times, since prior to the advent of effective contraception, couples' fertility was less obviously subject to regulation, and children more easily explained as 'by-products of copulation'. In fact, the situation is rather more com-plicated than this, given the considerable evidence that previous societies and present-day less developed countries have found means to control their populations with some degree of efficiency, at least at the aggregate level (Hawthorn 1970). Moreover, recent studies have indicated that in recent years in Britain, despite the availability of effective birth control methods, up to 48 per cent of births were 'either unintended, accidental, initially regretted or wrongly spaced' (Cartwright 1976 : 32). Neverthe-less, there is a good deal of evidence to indicate that couples are bringing their actual fertility into line with their desired fertility (Busfield 1972; Peel 1972; Peel and Carr 1975; Dunnell 1979). Consequently, we can say with some assurance that at least half the births in Britain today reflect parents' desires, and, therefore, that the study of people's motives in wanting children is legitimate and significant.

This chapter is not the first to discuss the issue of why people want children, although it is one of the first to explore it in relation to men. By and large, however, explanations of this question have been either psychologistic and tending to be based on unconscious needs or instincts, with heavy reliance on the 'maternal instinct', or highly rational with emphasis on economic theories incorporating utility models, cost-benefit analyses and, in the most extreme cases, likening babies to 'consumer durables' (Becker 1960; Easterlin 1969; Espenshade 1972). Recently, however, sociologists have directed their attention to these issues and have sought to explore normal reproductive behav-iour as a legitimate topic of concern. In particular, they have been concerned to demonstrate how culturally orientated theories can help explain reproductive behaviour. A clear statement of the thrust of this perspective is provided by Busfield (1974 : 11) who argues:

> 'A society or a social group's pattern of reproduction occurs in an ideological context where particular beliefs, both those about repro-duction *per se* and others that have reproductive consequences, affect, and are affected by, that pattern of reproduction. These beliefs provide a cognitive framework which structures individual action: they constitute the social reality in which reproduction takes place and they offer guidelines for, and justifications of, the actions of members of a society, which in aggregate result in a particular level of fertility.'

These cultural components are thus best conceived of as ideologies which form the basis for human behaviour, although as Busfield proceeds to note, they do not do so independently of economic and structural conditions. Indeed, in the long term these conditions may well shape the ideologies, but 'in the short term, ideologies probably provide a framework within which economic and social structural factors operate' (Busfield 1974 : 12).[2] From this point of view, therefore, in order to understand why people want children we must pay attention to the norms, values, and beliefs people hold about them, and about reproduction generally.

Macintyre adds to this perspective by pointing out the changes of assuming a monolithic ideology that people do want children, and argues that this aspect of their motivation has remained in large measure unquestioned, since it has been 'taken–for–granted' and 'part of the natural order'. In taking issue with the 'maternal instinct' theory she partly answered the call to explore those taken–for–granted beliefs about reproduction by showing how a range of such beliefs helped shape the pregnancy outcomes of a group of unmarried women (Macintyre 1977; 1976a; 1976b). In so doing she emphasized the need to explore the ways in which reproductive ideologies might vary, and the importance of enquiring as to 'whether, and what accounts for having babies are imputed or avowed in a society at any point in time' (Macintyre 1976 : 151).

'Thinking about children'

Despite the importance of understanding ideologies of reproduction, there has been little empirical work on them in Britain, although there have been some major studies of the value of children in other cultures (Arnold *et al.* 1975; Berelson 1973; Fawcett 1972; Hoffman and Hoffman 1973; Niphuis–Neill 1976). Of the few studies that do exist, a relatively full discussion of reproductive ideologies in Britain is provided in a study by Busfield and Paddon (1977) who explored them on the basis of interviews with women in East Anglia, although the ideologies concerned couples as opposed to women alone. In addition, the authors constructed five 'images of family life' which characterized the couples to a greater or lesser degree and which varied in terms of the extent to which they incorporated aspects of the dominant ideologies. I shall be concerned with describing only these dominant ideologies here, and shall restrict the discussion to those aspects of the ideologies that deal with marriage, parenthood, and beliefs concerning having children.

On the basis of their findings, Busfield and Paddon argued that the respondents become married because marriage conferred various rights and statuses which 'themselves were highly valued in society'. These rights included having children since 'only married people have a proper right to have children and if you want to have children then you should get married' (Busfield and Paddon 1977 : 117). Further, marriage carried with it the right to be treated as an adult and independent, and to be perceived as personally and sexually adequate. These factors were seen as more important to women than to men, since men could derive status more easily from their occupational roles.

Thus marriage was seen as providing the right to be a parent, and parenthood was valued for the status advantages that it implied, and the values that the children themselves would bestow. Thus, for example, women wished to be *mothers* and both marriage and children were instrumental to that end. However, marriage conferred not only rights, but duties, and one such duty was to have children. A variant of this idea was that children were viewed as essential to the survival and success of a marriage. Children were also seen to 'make a family' of a marriage. In these ways, marriage, parenthood, children, and families were seen as inextricably linked.

Children were also seen as having a value in and of themselves. In the short term they were seen as providing emotional and intrinsic satisfaction. It was seen as 'fulfilling' to provide for them and they could also be viewed as status objects. In the long term they were seen as an investment against future loneliness (though not necessarily as a means of future economic security). Finally, although there were costs perceived in having children, they were not systematically weighed against the advantages of having them in an utilitarian calculus and having children was assumed to be 'an experience not to be missed' (Busfield and Paddon 1977 : 140). Consequently, childlessness was negatively evaluated. Those who wished to be childless were stigmatized as selfish, while those who were unable to have children were pitied.

It is these ideologies that I wish to use as a basis for comparison with the findings of my own study outlined in the remainder of the chapter. These findings are based on interviews with some working-class men shortly after their or their wives' first attendance at an infertility clinic.[3] Using the crisis of involuntary childlessness as a focus, I shall attempt to document these ideologies, arguing that it is at a time of such crisis that many of the significant features are made apparent. However, given the difference in the fertility status and sex of Busfield's and Paddon's respondents and mine, such a comparison requires justification. The reasons for my making it are as follows. First, although some studies have been devoted to, or have included fertile men (Long 1979; Morton-Williams 1976; Simms and Smith Chapter 9), they do not provide a systematic coverage of the issues with which I am concerned. Second, the literature on involuntary childnessness is itself limited, and is either drawn from non–British societies (for example, Van Keep and Schmidt–Elmendorf 1975; Bierkens 1975) or, where it is drawn from British populations, has tended to be more concerned with the impact of childlessness than with the motives of the couples in wanting children (Burnage 1977; Smith 1978). Neither have these studies indicated clearly whether the data were collected from men or women, although a study by Humphrey (1969) is rather more explicit in this respect. Hence, I shall refer to these studies only in part. Finally, however, I shall draw on Busfield's and Paddon's findings because they do exemplify in some detail aspects of the ideologies of reproduction that have specific implications for childlessness, for as I hope to demonstrate from my study, these ideologies of reproduction orientated the respondents' behaviour in significant ways. Of course, I am not arguing that these ideologies are therefore universal. It is obviously not the case that everyone wants children, nor that those who do want children want them to the same extent. Nevertheless, there is evidence that these ideologies may be widespread (see also Macintyre 1976), and certainly most married couples do appear to want children (for example, Dunnell 1979). However, it is not the generality of the ideologies that I am trying to establish. What I wish to examine are the implications of these ideologies for conceptions of parenthood, the value of children, and the institution of marriage by specific reference to the beliefs and norms held by a group of childless men, and hopefully thereby to augment our understanding of these ideologies for those who do not hold them.

Men's reproductive ideologies before the suspicion of subfertility

The men in the study I undertook were asked about various features of their reproductive ideologies prior to the suspicion of subfertility, and the findings reported in this section are derived from their answers. In general, there was a broad similarity between the reasons for wanting children that were given by these men and those given by the couples with children interviewed by Busfield and Paddon. There were, of course, variations within these ideologies. Given their generality, however, and the fact that such variations were not numerous, I have chosen to present only the main themes. In this way comparison with Busfield's and Paddon's dominant ideologies is facilitated.

IT'S NATURAL

Particularly noticeable among the men interviewed was the extent to which the desire for children was taken for granted. Indeed, the most noticeable feature of the reasons that the men held for wanting children was the difficulty they found in articulating any at all. The question of why they wanted children usually met with blank embarrrassment and it was clear that the desire for them was assumed, or as many put it, that 'it was natural'. To want children was simply not questioned and in that sense provided a fundamental axiom of their behaviour. Thus the argument by Busfield (1974) that these ideologies are deeply internalized received strong support.

CHILDREN AS 'FUN'

Probing elicited some of the reasons the men had for wanting children. Particularly interesting was the fact that the main values of children were seen as expressive. The men looked forward to having children who were viewed as likely to provide enjoyment, pleasure, and companionship when older, and who as babies were essentially 'fun'. This emphasis on the companionship value of children had interesting implications for sex-preference, since the men expressed a desire to have boys to add to the enjoyment of life by participating in activities such as rugby or fishing. However, they also wished to have daughters so that these could be companions for their wives. Thus, as has been found elsewhere (see Williamson 1976), although there was an initial desire for a son, the ideal family was viewed as containing at least one child of each sex.

The emphasis on the expressive value of children is a move away from valuing them for other more obviously instrumental reasons. For example, reasons related to the continuation of the family, or the desire for a son as an heir were noticeably absent. Whilst this lack of interest in inheritance may be due to the class background of the men, it seems that there was a lack of a long-term perspective in general, since the men did not view children as providing a semblance of immortality, except in a few cases, nor did they seem concerned to have children as a means of achieving financial security or, contrary to Busfield's and Paddon's findings, as a source of companionship in their old age. The concepts of children as investments in the long-term held little salience, and the respondents had much more immediate wants for children.[4]

This lack of a perception of children as investments was reflected in the way the respondents viewed the cost of children. These were not seen as overriding, and were dismissed simply as factors that would be easily borne. Considerations such as 'they would tie us down', 'be a demand on our time', or 'place a financial burden on us' were not subjected to any form of scrutiny, and as such were not weighed against the advantages mentioned above to arrive at some form of careful decision. Thus, the results of the study provide a strong agreement that the question of whether to have children at all is *not* subject to any form of careful cost–benefit analysis.

MARRIAGE, THE FAMILY, PARENTHOOD, AND CHILDREN

Reasons related to wanting children were broader than those concerned with their intrinsic value, and confirmed a close connection between marriage, the family, parenthood, and children. Many of the men mentioned explicitly that they wanted children to make them 'a family'. Only a couple of the men had considered having children before becoming married, but all, as mentioned above, 'took-it-for-granted' that they would have them eventually. For these men, it was unthinkable that marriage should proceed without children. Children were the next natural stage in the marriage.[5]

Children were also seen as providing the husband and wife with the status of father and mother. Many of the men wished to be fathers so that they could enjoy the expressive values of children discussed above. Importantly, however, as I shall discuss at length later, they wished to ensure that their wives would become mothers and enjoy the associated status rewards. Nevertheless, the men had little idea of what fatherhood would entail and ideas of how it would affect them were extremely hazy. Most espoused some idea that they would participate with the wife in bringing up the child, but although the term 'joint' was sometimes used, it clearly meant something other than equal. These men did not foresee themselves as being nearly so heavily involved in the day-to-day tasks associated with children. Some felt that they would have to adopt a disciplinary role; others thought rather of 'educating' and 'elevating'. But these perspectives were not universal, and most men found it difficult to describe what they would do *as fathers*. Many candidly confessed that they had not thought about it much. Ideologies and expectations concerning fatherhood were, therefore, more characterized by their absence and lack of specificity than by anything else.

Views concerning motherhood were also vague, but less so than those described concerning fatherhood. Becoming a mother was seen as likely to engender major changes in the woman's way of life. Almost all the men expected and wished that their wives would give up work and look after the children full-time. It was believed that such full-time motherhood would provide 'fulfilment', and a reason given for wanting the wife to give up work was not only to bring the child up properly, which was certainly important, but also so that the wife would not 'miss out' on the rewards of child-rearing. Via children it was expected that the wife would become well integrated into the community, so that in addition to being fulfilled at a 'natural' level, children would provide both a career and identity and, in addition, consolidate social networks. This view of motherhood, however, carried poignant implications for the men and their perception of their marital duties, as I shall discuss later.

This idealized view of the benefits of children, the rewards of parenthood, but the relative lack of specific ideas about what parenthood involves, is not restricted to the men in my sample. Similar expectations in women who are becoming mothers together with the subsequent impact of the actuality of parenting, are discussed by Ann Oakley (1980, 1979) whose study indicates that becoming a parent also involves learning what parenthood is all about. Other chapters in this book note the same process with respect to men. In broad policy terms it is clear that preparation for parenthood is minimal and restricted largely to ante-natal classes more orientated to childbirth than child-rearing. Consequently, couples tend to fall back on their own childhood experiences or advice from parents to give them a guide as to how to parent, and whilst this is alleged to be more characteristic of the working classes (Humphrey 1969), is not restricted to them (see Oakley 1979). Further, women from all classes may use the ante-natal literature as a guide as to what to expect, but as Graham (1977) points out, this too may provide an inadequate picture of the reality of child-rearing. If the women's views of pregnancy and motherhood are unrealistic, then it is likely that men's are even more so. Consequently, we might have expected this sample to have put forward vague but traditional views of parenthood and headily idealistic views of the value of children. Nevertheless, it is not the veracity or otherwise of these perceptions that concern us here, rather it is their force in guiding and influencing the way individuals act. For these respondents, they were particularly significant in a way best summed up by Busfield (1977 : 140):

'Beliefs like this produce a situation where both men and women often think that having children is one of, if not the most important thing in life, and feel that having children is essential to a full and complete life.'

Expectations and anxieties surrounding the diagnosis

A possible consequence of holding these ideologies was that when family building was frustrated, the couples chose to seek medical help and eventually to attend a subfertility clinic.[6] Indeed, it can be argued that those who elect to have subfertility testing and treatment are the greatest upholders of the pro-natalist norms previously described. However, in so doing, the ability to comply with those norms is recognized as problematic and, as a result, certain features of these ideologies made more salient than for those whose compliance has not been denied.

Consequently, an examination of the reactions and perceptions of the men in an early part of their medical career concerned with subfertility is useful in illustrating the relative significance of obvious parts of their ideologies.

The decision to consult a doctor concerning suspected subfertility is difficult for many reasons. In particular, it involves the acceptance that there may be something wrong with either or both of the spouses. Further, awaiting the tests and their results arouses anxieties at the most profound level since a negative diagnosis may have implications for each of the spouses independently, but also for the structure of the marital relationship itself. Thus the impact of subfertility may be felt not only in psychological terms by each of the spouses, but equally fundamentally, subfertility may threaten the legitimate expectations and obligations of marriage proper as perceived by these men.

Of course, the nature of testing for subfertility is extremely intimate and sensitive since it involves the inspection of one's genitals and assessment of one's reproductive capacity. Thus, initiation of medical proceedings means having to undergo potentially distressing examinations with, of course, the possibility of surgery. This anxiety is documented elsewhere with respect to gynaecological examinations (Emerson 1970; Graham 1977a, 1978, 1981; Roberts 1981), but as I shall mention briefly, was characteristic of the men also. Important though understanding these anxieties is, however, especially in terms of making hospital practice more sensitive (see Smith 1978), I wish to focus on the deeper fears and uncertainties generated by the possibility of a negative diagnosis since they address themselves more directly to the reproductive ideologies already discussed.

THE SIGNIFICANCE OF THE SPERM TEST

To some extent the fear of a negative diagnosis for the men was muted, since there was a widespread assumption that any problem was likely to lie with the wife as 'there was more to go wrong'. Whilst this belief may have been bolstered by traditional views of the 'barren woman', it must be remembered that most of the men were producing what appeared to be a perfectly normal ejaculate.[7] Even so, many of the men were very apprehensive about taking the sperm test, and as more than one mentioned jokingly, delayed producing a sample for as long as they could reasonably do so.

The reasons for the men feeling anxious about the test are worthy of examination in detail, for there is considerable evidence that the diagnosis of infertility has a greater impact on the man than on the woman. Burnage (1977 : 47) notes of the childless couples she interviewed:

'Over half of the women felt that they were failures because they had been unable to conceive. They felt that they had let down their partners. This feeling was even more pronounced among men who were sterile or subfertile. The discovery that he is infertile can be an enormous blow to a man's ego and, combined with his wife's keen desire to have children, can leave him feeling extremely inadequate.'

A reason often given for this greater impact on the man is that the male is more likely to feel that his sexual capacity, equated with his virility, is threatened. Humphrey (1969 : 52) argues:

'awareness of sterility inflicts greater trauma on a man than on a woman in our culture . . . . Whilst a sense of failure may be common to both sexes, it is only the proud male who regards it as an affront to his sexual capacity. For him, procreation has always served as a means of demonstrating his virility, whereas it is well known that a woman's fertility gives no indication of her sexual responsiveness. And no matter how bravely he has accepted the discovery at a conscious level, unconsciously the equation with impotence is likely to remain.'

Humphrey proceeds to note that such a threat to virility is more likely to be associated with the lower classes (cf. Rainwater 1960) although some association is found in all. Hence we would have expected the threat to virility to be evident in my sample of working-class men.

Such threats to virility were not, however, easily discerned. Indeed, the vast majority of the respondents denied them. Most instead rationalized the situation by pointing out that 'you think you are not the first and not the last' or, as another put it, 'you can't help if if you are firing blanks'. Nevertheless, given the strength of Humphrey's arguments above, it would be naive to accept these statements simply at face value. Of course, it is possible that these men did not feel their virility was threatened because the concept held no salience for them, or because they measured it according to other unspecified criteria. But evidence that the men may well have felt insecure came from their wives, and many pointed out what they felt to be their husband's sensitivity on this matter. For example one commented, after I had interviewed her husband who had denied feeling a threat to his masculinity, that he had taken to heart remarks such as 'oh you haven't proved yourself yet like we have' from his brothers. Others pointed to the teasing that their husbands received that 'they didn't know how to do it'.

Thus, the problem of the threat to virility was not easily established, and perhaps this was to be expected given the sensitive nature of the situation in which the men found themselves. However, this inability to explore the concept of masculinity fully was not entirely detrimental to the exploration of the men's possible feelings of inadequacy. For whilst the respondents were not forthcoming about any potential blow to their self-concepts as *men*, they did speak of the threat that infertility would raise to the fulfilment of their role as *husband*. That they did so is significant for it allows us to examine the implications of fertility in a different light. From this point of view we can consider at the very least a complementary hypothesis to that of the loss of virility. I will suggest that it was also the significance of male infertility for the wife and the marriage that aroused the anxieties surrounding the sperm test.

MOTHERS, FATHERS, AND CHILDREN

To examine this contention, we need to remind ourselves of the men's reproductive ideologies concerning motherhood, fatherhood, and the value of children. Motherhood, in particular, was perceived as a highly valued status to which the wives should aspire, a fulfilling and all-embracing career, and children were seen as central to their lives. Given the adherence to the ideologies described, ideologies that emphasized the importance of children within marriage, it was the husband who had the prime responsibility of providing the wife with that career:[8] Hence, since it was important for the woman to *be* a mother, it was vital for the husband to *become* a father. In this sense, fatherhood could be viewed as a status instrumental to the creation of the status of motherhood.

It is in this context that the comments of the men concerning the threat of infertility should be put. Typical responses to the question of how the men would react if they were found to have a medical problem were that they would feel 'guilty', or 'to blame', or that they would be 'letting their wives down'. The latter description is particularly telling since it emphasizes not so much personal or psychological adequacy, as the failure to meet marital expectations. One pinpointed the distinction between virility and fulfilling these obligations in saying that he hoped the problem wouldn't be his since 'she'd be hampered with me then' and 'it would upset me more knowing I could never give her a child' and that 'I wouldn't feel less of a man, but would feel I'm not fulfilling a role'. One respondent voiced the logical conclusion that this view of marriage implies when he said that 'if a man can't have children he is depriving her (the wife) of something and he should say "If I can't have a family, then I should have a divorce" ', and added:

'if the test was negative, most probably I would have said I would have divorced her, because if you deprive a woman of a child, then you are depriving her of something which is very, very important to her, and no matter what my wife would have said to have eased my feelings on the subject whether she actually really meant that, it didn't matter or not. I would have felt uneasy especially when we were with other people's children, and I might have divorced her, but for her own sake.'

Not all shared this extreme view, most indicating that they felt some-how that they and their wives would cope. Nevertheless, the threat to the marriage and to the fulfilment of the marital role was real. Con-sequently, a positive test result came as a considerable relief and while not all were as euphoric as the respondent who said 'I could have jumped through the window with joy', some indicated that they could have cried, one saying that 'it was the happiest day of my life'.

On the other hand, a positive result was a double-edged sword. For this result for the man could mean that the wife had questionable fertility, and consequently would place strains on her. Nevertheless, the view of marriage we have discussed implies that she would not feel such a sense of failing her husband, since he could find some refuge in the occupational role. Hence, while the wife might regret the inability to have children for her own sake, she would not need to be so concerned for her husband. He, for his part, could afford to be more accom-modating and supportive, and in fact my respondents spoke less of divorce and more of the need to rally to their wives' aid. Humphrey (1969 : 53) sums up these sentiments:

'This is why the reverse situation, where the incapacity lies in the wife, usually offers more room for manœuvre. A fertile man can more readily 'forgive' his barren wife if he is happy in his career or other outside interests.'[9]

Summary and conclusions

This view of marital duties may seem surprising. Certainly it has been seen as a traditional obligation of the wife to provide her husband with children. As Flandrin (1979) and Poster (1978) point out, this was particularly important for the aristocracy, where the promotion of lineage and the ensuring of inheritance were crucial considerations. But in other less exalted classes, the provision of children by wives was important because of the labour value held by the offspring, especially if male. Where children are seen as producers either of goods or of income, these obligations are especially strong.

The reproductive ideologies I have been concerned with, however, emphasize different values of children. Although we would not wish to accept the extreme arguments of Becker (1960) that they may be likened to consumer durables, children were not seen as economic producers. In fact, there is little doubt that children today are consumers, and expensive consumers at that. But, as I have discussed, these economic factors were not considered in any detail, since other values of children were seen as more salient. Those other values were largely expressive, and also linked to concepts of what constituted proper marriage. Particularly important was seen to be the status of motherhood; children are of course essential to the attainment of that status and are thereby instrumental in allowing the wives to enjoy its associated status rewards. This paradoxically emphasizes the role of the man as a 'husband provider' in a much more than material sense.[10]

Nevertheless, to claim universal currency for these beliefs on the basis of the findings presented here would be seriously misleading. The very existence of, for example, voluntary childlessness and the increase in the number of unmarried mothers who are bringing up their children indicates that they are not. Macintyre's caution (1976b : 151) that: 'we run the danger of erecting what may be an unwarrantably monolithic and universal model of normal reproduction, and of assuming a homogeneity and consensus of motives and beliefs not found empirically' cannot be taken too seriously. Rather, what I have tried to do is to outline certain views of marriage, parenthood, and the value of children that are contained in these specific ideologies. Very different types of studies from the ones dealt with in this chapter would have to be undertaken to establish the extent to which such ideologies are general, and the sections of the population who adhere to them, and those who do not.

A final caveat concerns the role of reproductive ideologies and actual behaviour. The relationship between them is complex, and the general way in which I have treated ideologies here, distracts from the accommodations and adjustments that individuals make to them. An example may illustrate. Despite the strong association between the survival of marriage and children implied by the ideologies described by these childless men, it is not the case that involuntary childless marriages necessarily end in divorce. Indeed, the relationship between childlessness and divorce or even marital instability is far from clear-cut (Chester 1972; Gibson 1980; Thornes and Collard 1979), although it is the case that involuntary childlessness probably does cause marital tension in the short term. While it has not been the purpose of this paper to examine this process, such an analysis would provide remarkable insight into the management of marital crises generally. What we can say of course, is that much would depend on the ideologies of the wife, and I have not dealt with these here. As a result, the view has been one-sided and has not indicated how two people come to terms with a situation that provides them with serious problems and potential conflicts of interest. Consequently, reproductive ideologies can only be the background against which individual couples will make decisions. Indeed, we must remember that important though understanding these ideologies may be, they are but crude determinants of actual behaviour. The translation of cultural ideologies into individual action is always mediated by the subjective interpretations of these ideologies, situational exigencies, negotiation, and consequently, change.

Notes

1   I would like to thank the senior staff of the Professorial Unit of the Infertility Clinic in the University of Wales Teaching Hospital, where the research was carried out, for their permission to mount the study and their encouragement while it was being undertaken. Thanks are due also to the nursing staff who helped. A particular debt is owed to the patients who volunteered both time and sensitive information. The research was partially funded by a grant made available from the Birmingham Settlement.

2   An excellent study which examines the relationships between culture, social structure, and fertility was undertaken by Askham (1975).

3   Both husbands and wives were interviewed separately in depth and together. The data on which this chapter is based are drawn from the in–depth interviews with the husband. The couples interviewed were either skilled or semi-skilled manual workers, imposing considerable restrictions on the extent to which the data could be generalized.

4   The immediacy of these wants is not necessarily attributable to the respondents' childlessness which might be expected to emphasize a short-term perspective. These accounts were based on responses to questions on the men's ideologies *prior to* the suspicion of infertility. In any case, it is not certain that suspected infertility would necessarily reduce the salience of viewing children as, for example, sources of financial or other security in old age.

5   I have not had the space to develop the theme of the perceived stages in marriage and the life cycle. In particular, respondents saw having children as appropriate to a certain age and a certain stage of marriage, and these factors appeared to be influential in determining when the couple decided to seek treatment (Owens 1979). A discussion on the significance of the stages in the life cycle and their relation to other theories of the family is to be found in Rapoport, Rapoport, and Strelitz with Kew (1977).

6   The decision to seek treatment is complex and obviously involved the wives as well as the husbands. In fact it was usually the wife who first visited the GP concerning subfertility, although this was often after discussion with the spouse. Nevertheless, there is much more involved in the decision to consult

than simple adherence to the ideologies described. I have discussed this process in detail elsewhere (Owens 1979).

7　The men's belief that the woman is more likely to be at fault is incorrect. Medical evidence indicates that men and women have approximately equal incidences of subfertility problems (Stangel 1979).

8　There are alternatives to the husband fathering the child (excluding extra-marital liaisons), for example, fostering, adoption or artificial insemination by donor. However, these are not usually considered until it is established that the husband is unable, or unlikely to be able, to father.

9　This argument requires two major qualifications. First, it assumes that the man finds a refuge in the occupational role, and of course, he may not. Current unemployment figures indicate that many men can no longer do so, and this may result in greater pressure on their wives to produce children to offset the husband's lack of occupational satisfaction and status. Secondly, it assumes that the woman finds her work less rewarding than her husband. This was generally true of my respondents, most of whom had unskilled work which they looked forward to giving up. But it would not be the case where the wife had a career to which she was committed and which provided her with satisfaction. In this case, the pressure on the husband to 'provide' a child would be correspondingly less.

10　It could be argued that the inability to provide the wife with children would seriously affect the dynamics of the marital relationship, and undermine the status and legitimate authority of the husband in marriage. Bell and Newby (1976) develop the theme of the 'husband–provider' with interesting implications for the role of reproductive 'provision'.

PART TWO

Becoming a father

6 Men's experiences of pregnancy and childbirth

JOEL RICHMAN

As C. Wright Mills has emphasized, all studies are the result of the 'natural histories', which have steered the course of their production. I shall begin this selective account of some fathers' beliefs and responses to pregnancy and birth by describing how a research impetus emerged only as an unintended consequence of another enterprise. While investigating the social organization of a gynaecological department in a large general hospital, with the initial emphasis orientated towards the woman as client, I found matters of a much wider social direction soon appeared: not least, fathers 'forced' themselves into the social reckoning. It is of practical and symbolic significance to note that this occurrence is by no means unique. Other similar research had duplicated this preliminary stage. Although fatherhood, like motherhood, is one of the major cultural universals and an everyday event, it has few associated and distinctive characteristics, being typically subsumed under other categories and activites.

Unintended domiciliary birth and the discovery of fathers

It was during the hospital crises of 1973 that the significance of fathers at birth first became apparent to me, albeit in a dramatic fashion. The ancillaries' industrial action culminated in a strike and radically disturbed medical routines. Although the maternity unit was not as badly affected as other departments — most of the expectant mothers normally being short-stay cases and only exceptionally needing special treatment — a considerable number of women had their clientship severed. Overnight the established medical base-lines were discarded; primigravidae, those over thirty years of age, and even some Rhesus-negative mothers now had home deliveries.

These mothers were not ideologically prepared for home delivery, which was contrary to both the national trend and 'official' policy. A project was hurriedly devised to investigate this deviant occurrence of unexpected home delivery, looking at the medical and sociological factors.[1] Although the mothers were surveyed in the 'baby honeymoon' period, their very favourable responses were not dependent on the difficulty/ease of the birth. When all the factors surrounding the exceptional births were examined (for example, the supreme effort made by the domiciliary midwives, who used the occasion to demonstrate their community worth to the authorities in an attempt to resist their being incorporated into the hospital regime, where they feared they would become deskilled), the fathers' presence and aid at birth also surfaced as being highly relevant. (It had not occurred to the researchers, in the hasty design of the study, to ascertain the fathers' own responses, where possible.) On hearing that the hospital booking had been cancelled, 42 per cent of the expectant fathers (by mothers' accounts) first raised the subject with their wives of wanting to be present at the birth. More than twice as many were present for the domiciliary than had originally indicated for the hospital birth. They helped to normalize the home setting, where labour times were greater than they would have been in hospital: 15 per cent lasted over nineteen hours.

Towards the end of 1976 the mothers, who were mainly 'forced' converts to domiciliary delivery, were followed up to see where they had their next baby. In 1973, 80 per cent had indicated that they would want their next baby at home. However, in the follow-up sample, of the nineteen mothers who had second children only 15 per cent had home deliveries. Not only had the medical hegemony reasserted itself (with the falling birth-rate there was a political necessity to maintain the maximum rate of bed occupancy in maternity units) and the mothers reassessed their 1973 experiences by seeing some virtue in the hospital as a place for 'rest', but the fathers were also a crucial factor. The fathers were even less prepared ideologically for home delivery, considering pregnancy as an 'illness'. Hospitals were deemed to be 'safe places' and they helped to steer their wives towards them.

The abbreviated account of the atypical birth events of 1973 is not offered for extrapolation, one way or the other, in the intense debate between the merits of hospital versus home delivery, but is intended to illustrate how, when the social net surrounding birth is cast 'widely', fathers are trawled. This kind of event served to focus attention on fathers and such circumstances make the experiences of fathers of immediate relevance. A review of the literature on birth showed that others had shared my research experience.

Other discoveries of fathers at birth

During the early 1960s much obstetric research into the variations of pregnancy and labour sought explanations by focusing predominantly on the woman and her biological characteristics. Only when the inadequacy of the medical model became apparent and underwent modifications to encompass some of the social landscape, did the place of fathers begin to gain more recognition. In this context Rosengren (1962) was instrumental in demonstrating how women who adopted the sick-role during pregnancy could have husbands who were socially mobile in the class hierarchy or whose education was inferior to their own, among other factors. Pregnancy came to be understood as straddling a range of problematic social values. It is interesting to note that it was a common characteristic for fathers to be initially included in research schemes concerned with the difficulties of pregnancy not in their roles as fathers, but as husbands. Furthermore they were accorded a 'negative' valency, being a complicating and disturbing element.

In the early 1970s, observational studies of pregnancy became more prevalent and fathers were 'discovered' anew, but this time they were considered to bring 'positive' and unexpected benefits. I shall elaborate two instances of this. Tanzer (1976), one of the pioneers in introducing the Lamaze technique of labour coaching into the USA, set up a study for gathering empirical evidence about the efficaciousness of 'natural childbirth'. She wrote (Tanzer 1976 : 199): 'Although my research project concentrated on women and did not formally study *husbands*, much revealing information about *husbands* kept emerging' (my emphasis).

With hindsight, the initial formulation of the research issue appears incongruous, especially as the Lamaze technique introduced fathers-to-be participation into the pregnancy training. From the accounts offered by the mothers about their deliveries Tanzer (1976 : 205) was forced to swing to the conclusion: '*Men* may have a greater need to play a role in birth than had been realised. Childbirth may not be exclusively the domain of the female psyche' (my emphasis). In contrast we are told that the control group of conventional childbirth husbands and wives displayed no emotional transaction. The second example of the discovery of the 'new' father concerns Greenberg's and Morris's (1974) study on 'engrossment' — the impact of the newborn upon the father. Significantly, they introduce their paper thus (1974:520): 'The senior author (MG) first became interested in the father–child relationship as a *by-product* of his study of the early mother-infant relationship and the various influences upon this relationship' (my emphasis). Expressing astonishment at the scarcity of studies of the father–newborn relationship, particularly in the first week, they postulate that the potential for engrossment (a sense of intense absorption) with the newborn is an innate potential. Without providing evidence, the authors make the lavish claim that a father's 'early' engrossment is likely to continue as the child develops (to what age, we are not told).

Pregnant fathers

It is indicative that the terms 'pregnant fathers', or 'fathers in labour', are not in common usage. However, the expression, 'expectant fathers', used for example by Schaefer (1965) and Liebenberg (1969), does have slightly more currency. Only recently have extensive endeavours been made to study 'normal' fathers and birth.

Most of our knowledge has been distilled from deviance, pathology, and the quasi-history of tribal society (usually of the nineteenth-century exotica variety). The one consistent thread of continuity in the theme of pregnant fathers has been the Freudian investment. Drawing upon the reports of the couvade (birth rites of fathers) from pre-industrial societies, this data was used to provide further elaborations of the dynamics of the male psyche. Childbirth was interpreted as the mechanism for precipitating mental crises, whose manifestations could take many cultural forms. Pregnancy could reactivate the latent Oedipus complex: this line of reasoning tainted the child as the product of 'primordial sin', who would later become a phallic competitor. Additionally, the woman's pregnancy could cause 'womb envy', or 'Zeus Jealousy'. Lomas (1966), who drew his inspiration from Reik's (1914) compendium on the couvade, developed the scenario that modern obstetric practice could be best understood as the working through of man's envy of women's creative success. Lomas (1966 : 212) writes:

> 'In couvade the husband is significant: in our society one sometimes has the impression that it is the doctor; and the degree by which he takes control of her function — even the details of procedures such as ritual shaving and periotomy — put one in mind of female circumcision and Bettelheim's interpretation of this, as an attempt on the part of the male to master his envy.'

This is not the occasion to navigate fully the Freudian logic, only to comment that it has produced a version of pregnant fathers that is both one-dimensional and over-determined. Small clinical samples, sometimes derived from closed communities (USA military camps), have often been its mainstay. At random, Bucove's (1964) study of psychosis was based on three cases, concentrating also upon other medical complaints of pregnant fathers such as sickness, headaches, and eye complaints. Midwifery lore has long fostered a link between tooth-ache and expectant fathers. Another tack on pregnant fathers has followed the direction of their potentiality for sexual deviance. What Hartman and Nicolay (1966 : 234) classify as 'regressive, immature sexual behaviour', exhibitionism and paedophilia, form the bulk of the offences and are more likely during the first pregnancy.

Idiosyncratic though the above approaches may be, their value has been threefold. First, a research momentum in a neglected area was maintained. Second, the Freudian-linked approaches have demonstrated, usually implicitly, how modern society has provided no cultural apparatus for conveying the complex assortment of sentiments fathers hold about pregnancy. However, it is erroneous to assert that the private, ritualized form of psychiatric symptoms are the essential, functional equivalent of the past couvade, which was never universally observed. Reik conceded that point, but compounded the issue by his reference to the 'genuine couvade'. Anthropologists are now renewing their interest in the couvade. Douglas (1976) interprets it at the level of social relations and their manipulation. The couvade now becomes one version of how the symmetry of the social world can be made by creating the symmetry of the sexes within it. The third value of the Freudian approach derives from its focus on 'stress' as a triggering mechanism in psychiatric disorders: attention is thereby drawn to how intra-family relationships can be modified during pregnancy.

Researching pregnant fathers

It is against the backcloth of the above debates that I go on next to offer some sociological findings derived from my research conducted in a maternity unit.[2] The project was devised originally within tight perimeters for a practical end — to explore why some fathers attend birth and others do not — but a host of other interests were soon absorbed. Expectant fathers are becoming more prevalent in labour and delivery rooms, but there are still no national birth statistics recorded on this topic. (There are also no statistical frequencies of male 'illness', attributed to pregnancy.)

Most of the medical objections to the father's presence, that is on grounds of 'hygiene', or that it was a 'sadistic perversion' to watch birth, or that it would inhibit future sexual relations, or that fathers would create a nuisance (interfere/faint) are no longer sustained. Some fathers, however, gave me parallel explanations of why they did not wish to attend birth. One said: 'I don't want to attend birth, it is an intimate thing when it happens to your *own wife*. I will watch it on TV'. Fathers' legal rights to attend are uncertain. Much depends on what is decided at the time to be a 'medical interlude' in the proceedings.

Hospital literature is suitably vague about fathers' rights. While Californian fathers have taken legal action to clarify their rights, the English courts have received no such pleas. Fathers are now often welcomed, but mainly as 'aids', or in service roles. Mothers left alone in labour (one National Childbirth Trust survey put the figure as high as 13 per cent) may suffer from sensory deprivation and confusion; complicating birth. Although the data is sketchy, generally, fewer fathers attend induced births (Macfarlane 1977).

From an intake based on a single hospital no 'sampling' sophistication is claimed; opportunity and chance played its part in sifting fathers. Many were 'anxious' and when they left the birth were 'high', often in tears. Much of their talk with me resembled a stream of consciousness. If they wanted to talk about the hospital routine or other things that worried them then the interviews flowed in those directions. Edgell (1980 : 114) has aptly commented on the difficulties of family research: 'The private nature of family life represents one of the major obstacles to empirical research in this area . . . therefore fieldwork in family sociology can involve a double intrusion, into private relationships and private space'. In this situation the fathers oscillated between the private and semi-public space of the hospital. Both medically and sociologically the father's relationship with the foetus has been considered a 'secondary' one, mainly on the common-sense grounds that fathers do not carry the child, undergo no hormonal or physical change, do not abandon their work patterns, and do not enter directly into clientship with medical agencies. This notion can become, however, a self-fulfilling prophecy. The image of the father who is gainfully employed in the labour market and has little concern for domestic matters has held sway for a long time. Also, the image of the father instilling dominance and fear has helped to cloud the emotional potentiality of fathers.

These are some of the essential features about fathers that have emerged from my research:

(a) It is erroneous to consider pregnant fathers in over-generalized terms, and as possessing birth sentiments discrete from those of mothers. When discussing their feelings, especially about seeing the birth, fathers would use language usually associated with women. Like mothers, they cluster a constellation of meaning around the birth. In many ways the baby is intended to be 'problem-solving'. *Table 6(1)* very crudely taps some of these sentiments. When asked, 'Why have a baby?', the 'superficial' response was that it was the 'normal' thing to do. A sales manager replied:

'Something I have never even thought about. We married, we got

Table 6 (1) *The differences the new baby will make (figures in percentages)**

	More expense	Minimal	Creation of family	Restrictive	Increased responsibility	Completion of family	New challenge	More complexities	Uncert-ainties	Did not answer
Fathers attending birth (total 100)	5	9	32	19	8	8	8	13	10	9
Fathers attending labour only (total 50)	8	10	22	22	12	12	2	10	9	20

*Some fathers made more than one response, the totals do not add up to a hundred.

established. We got our home and the rest of it. We thought it would be nice; we could now be prepared to share our lives, you know, with someone else. So we decided to go ahead, we both love children. My brothers are married, with three and two children. I always enjoy being with them, and they seem to enjoy my company as well. When you set up your own natural environment, then you want to add to it. I think a child is a natural off-shoot to this. You get to a point when you feel your home is not complete without them. I don't mean it in the mercenary sense as an adornment to your house, like a car.'

On probing, more specific reasons appear. He went on: 'This time I want a son. I know its selfish. I love sport. I would like to enjoy it through my son'.

(b) Pregnancy was capable of generating not only practical and emotional interests, but also an intellectual one. Fathers were eager to learn about the biological processes. For example, 63 per cent of the birth-attenders and 78 per cent of the labour-only fathers had read book/articles on pregnancy, but more birth-attenders had read the hospital handouts; 8 per cent had read medical texts, none of the labour-only fathers had read any. No father had attended relaxation classes. A number of generalizations appear. First, an increased interest in the female reproductive system did not produce necessarily a corresponding interest in their own bodies. But some did become more 'health conscious', giving up/cutting down on smoking and 'exercising' more. Other studies on USA servicemen, report the same — some also drink more milk. The unconscious motive imputed is that these expectant fathers are fortifying themselves against the impending threat from the new 'challenger'. My fathers argued that the 'thrill' of pregnancy had invigorated them, or that they had to look after themselves more because they were taking on new responsibilites. Second, it was not inevitable that 'pregnancy-aware' fathers would want to attend the birth.

(c) Expectant fathers had distinct views about the necessity for observing the correct etiquette in spreading/controlling news about the onset of pregnancy. All could recall the occasion when they were first told. An engineer described it: 'I remember clearly when the wife told me she was pregnant. I met her one dinner time, we are both working, to find the results of the test. We then met her best friend. She is now a friend of both of us, but she is the wife's friend from a long time ago'. 'Normally', both sets of parents are told 'first'; the wife often tells the mother-in-law. When this was not feasible and a trusted friend or close relative were the first recipients, they were initially 'sworn' to secrecy. Pregnancy causes a critical evaulation to be made of the couple's social network. Fathers regard it as their duty to transmit the immediate news of the birth. Some had lists of people to contact, the sequence pre-agreed with their wives. One of the difficulties of researching fathers in hospital is their 'rush' to spread the news. Sudnow (1967) has shown how with the other life crisis, of death, great care is also taken to ensure that the knowledge of the event is transmitted appropriately. One father even partly attributed the miscarriage of the first pregnancy to the fact that the correct procedure for spreading the news had not been observed. He considered that 'providence' had been tempted by spreading the news 'too soon' and 'too widely'; non-relevant individuals had come to own this personal knowledge.

(d) The expectant fathers deployed an armoury of strategies of incorporation in their attempts to forge a special relationship with the foetus. There was an increase in joint shopping expeditions, especially for goods for the first baby and an acceleration in jobs around the house — the baby's room being the father's priority. At the extreme, there were two fathers who attempted 'to take over' the pregnancy. One concerned a man who was more than thirty years older than the mother; he had left his wife and had set up home with an employee of the firm where he was manager. He insisted on running the whole domestic set-up, attempting to 'sterilize' socially the mother-to-be. The foetus was endowed with transcendental qualities, removing the differences of class, age, and religious affiliation that divided the parents. Childbirth is still an occasion fraught with dangers and uncertainties and fathers expressed their fears about potential birth abnormalities. The reduced birth rate and media discussion has possibly intensified this anxiety. The fathers' accounts were sometimes punctuated with magico-religious sentiments. While denying that they were religious, fathers would nevertheless explain their feelings about birth in imagary and ideas with cosmic overtones — there being a 'power' and 'unity' existing in the world that held sway over their birth outcomes, which had to be reconciled. Oakley (1979:200) has recalled how Mrs Brady commented on her husband's behaviour: 'He goes down on his knees every night praying. Now you might think he is some kind of fanatic, he's not. He's worried that something might happen to the baby'.

Although explanations of the couvade offered by Frazer (Reik:1914) — that the rite was a magic act designed to protect the unborn — have been discarded, some of the explanations presented by fathers for their behaviour emulate that purpose. One executive froze his work career, refusing promotion and a move until after the birth, lest the changed circumstances circumscribing the birth increased the 'hidden' danger to it. One component of the tribal couvade (besides dietetic prohibitions) necessitates that the father restricts his work activity, and becomes more 'home-centred', geographically. Accounts of pregnancy, especially the first, report a diminution in sexual activity. Masters and Johnson (1966) reported that thirty-one men out of seventy-nine gradually ceased sexual activity, although they discovered that the majority of pregnant women experienced an increase of the sex drive around the four to five month mark. Those women who have an increased need to make love and experience intense orgasms into the last month are more likely to have an easier birth (Tolor and di Grazia 1976).

The 'unattractiveness' of the wife, or her discomfort during intercourse are the usual explanations offered. Some, like this self-employed tradesman talking about the second pregnancy, concurred: 'We stopped sex at about three months. It must be uncomfortable for her and to be frank it has never been the be-all of our relationship'. Some regarded it as unclean/improper for the male to persist towards the final stage of pregnancy. An unskilled worker added: 'One friend of mine had it (intercourse) a couple of nights before she had it. It's not right you know. He must be really low. I couldn't do it myself'. However, there was another set of meanings ascribed to this relinquishment: abstention was the 'sacrifice' the father was deliberately making as his special contribution for ensuring a successful birth, thereby reinforcing the medico–technical 'efficiency' also supporting the pregnancy. One skilled worker explained:

> 'We didn't actually discuss this. We never said, "Look we must stop this now, it's going to be injurious", for we had read it in books it wasn't. It was almost *built in* which said "look, don't". I went off it. She went off it. Possibly because of the first miscarriage, we wanted to *do everything right* this time. We weren't taking any risks at all.'

It could be argued, of course, that no 'great sacrifice' existed: this father's sexual needs were still catered for. His wife masturbated him, but neither regarded this as satisfactory, or typical of their normal sexual relationship.

(e) Fathers' pregnancy careers not only differ from mothers' by being more diffuse and opaque, but they also have a greater resonance with their occupational careers. The date by which mothers leave paid employment is not only legally mandatory, but the actual day is usually ceremonially observed. (In the sample, 64 per cent of those mothers whose husbands were present for birth worked during pregnancy.) It is paradoxical that the multifarious studies of organizational behaviour made by sociologists have not only neglected to depict women workers, but have failed, too, to recognize that pregnancy could be an explanatory variable in understanding the behaviour of male employees. Manual workers, particularly those having a first child, would describe how pregnancy made them more 'responsible' and 'mature'. Some would talk of having 'grown up in the past four months'. This is what one father considered to be 'responsible':

> 'I've always been one if the gaffer is funny with me, I've always told him what to do and walk out. There have been a few firms I've just finished from normally. I don't like to be dictated to. Since the wife has been pregnant, I've had to knuckle down a bit. I still speak my mind, but don't say "get stuffed".'

One shop steward was looking forward to the birth; the baby now legitimated an escape from his militant role, without his being accused of 'selling out". One teacher of twenty-five explained that the new baby had made him 'old enough' to apply for high-graded posts, formerly regarded as out of reach.

Although some fathers felt invigorated at work, especially during the early months, there were those who reported an increased tiredness and agitation as pregnancy progressed. Liebenberg (1969), whose fathers were well educated (72 per cent had degrees) makes the related point that several had car accidents in the early pre-natal period. White-collar workers with responsibilities would admit to having made errors at work. One extreme example was that of the partner in a small building firm who told me:

> 'In the last two months I have been really tense and tired, not really caring. Normally I work late (8.00 p.m.), but when 5.00 p.m. comes I'm just for packing in and going home. In the mornings I can't really get going. I've made stupid mistakes in marking out. My partners accepted it really well. They really pulled me through.'

The class ranking of organizations differentially affected pregnant fathers. Manual workers with no direct access home via the company telephone also had difficulties in getting time off to take their wives to the ante-natal clinic. Twenty-three per cent of fathers attending a week-day birth claimed to have lost money. Manual workers tend to receive a less sympathetic reception from their colleagues on announcing the pregnancy news. One described the progression of responses thus:

> 'At first they ribbed you about joining the club or losing your freedom and told horrific stories. But the older blokes ask if she is alright.

But nearer the time most seem to show some concern. Some of the young ones at work who have got a wife who's pregnant seem to be asking all the time, so they know what to expect.'

Men who work in offices with women can obtain a greater 'comforting', which some seek out.

(f) A father's pregnancy career is transactional with other values and relationships. Biller and Meredith (1975 : 39) distinguish three

'prevalent categories of fathers' attitudes towards marriage and pregnancy. (1) The father who eagerly accepts the responsibility of being a family man and considers pregnancy a gift and becomes very close to the wife. (2) The totally career-orientated husband who often regards prospective fatherhood as a burden . . . tries hard to reaffirm all his old habits and denies the need for change in his way of. living; he may want to take his wife on long camping trips. (3) The emotionally immature who is frightened at the prospect of having to support a wife and child; he faces the problem of transition from carefree adolescence.'

However, Biller assumes without warranty that the attitudes towards marriage and pregnancy will always be synonymous. Further, there is the implication that fathers' attitudes remain fixed. Pregnancy 'trajectories' can take dramatic shifts — fathers at first being absorbed with the foetus, then neglecting mother and foetus. The third category — 'emotional immaturity' — presupposes the existence of a precise developmental scale, against which corresponding social activities can accurately be read off.

From my evidence, it is possible to arrange, heuristically, the dominant pregnancy careers of fathers along four axes (Richman and Goldthorp 1978), remembering that each is a dynamic process with swings possible between the poles:

The father denies the existence of pregnancy and adopts strategies of disavowal: the psychiatric literature on USA servicemen describing how new postings are constantly sought, being typical.
The father adopts the stance that pregnancy is 'nothing unusual' and is the wife's responsibility.
The father wishes to share the pregnancy experience and develops special bonds with the foetus; increased emotional and instrumental help is given.
The father claims total identification with the foetus and attempts to sterilize socially the mother.

Fathers at birth

A number of indicators were gleaned unsuccessfully in a preliminary attempt to distinguish a propensity for attending birth. Even at the hospital some fathers are still weighing up the decision. The birth-attenders and labour-only fathers could not be distinguished on the frequency of accompanying their wives to the clinic; one-third of the birth-attenders had never been. Other signs of 'togetherness' — whether the pregnancy was 'planned', or whether the wife 'knew' how much the husband earned — were not revealing. Birth-attenders could not be distinguished on the grounds of ideological rapport with 'feminism'. Also, when the fathers' attitudes towards vasectomy were ranked, 48 per cent of labour-only fathers 'would consider' having one at some time as opposed to 34 per cent of the birth-attenders. (There is a national increase in both vasectomies and fathers at birth.) However, 8 per cent of the fathers at birth (2 per cent of labour only) were to be vasectomized subsequently and birth for them was the crucial temporal marker commemorating the termination of their own fertility. There was a hint that birth-attenders had canvassed widely the opinions of others in making their decision.

A kaleidoscopic pattern of motives are involved in the decision to be a birth-attender. There were the instrumental reasons offered by a policeman and an ambulanceman: they were keen to learn how the experts handled birth, should they be called upon to make an emergency delivery. There were also the reluctant conscripts who were attending for the 'sake of the wife'. Others described how the desire to be present evolved as part of a developmental framework of ideas: 'Originally I saw birth as being *sickly*. But I thought about it. The child is *mine* . . . I'm going to be there. Then I thought, I'm missing *life* itself. I know its there, but the critical moment is when it comes into the world'. Others describe the presence as a thing both had 'always wanted'.

One might see fathers as an anomaly that confronts a hospital's ideologies and organizational routines. Hospitals are highly structured ecologically: types of behaviour are only considered appropriate in given settings. Pregnant women are not expected to express pain in ante-natal clinics, or refuse to see their babies when delivered. Women entering hospitals are subjected to a series of events controlled by medical specialists that deny them any control or individual status: the powerful impose their dominant timetables, even dictating the time for the baby to be born.

The father may be said to present a potential threat because of the 'unknown' qualities latent in his being a stranger and marginal. He has not undergone any of the rites of incorporation experienced by his wife. Consequently, none of the institutional rhetoric of the hospital signposts his status. The room where he waits is not called 'the fathers' room'. Unlike his wife, he has not brought into the hospital any private property (except for reading material) with which he could colonize space and sustain an identity. As a stranger he is switched between remoteness and intimacy in relation to the birth. He occupies a 'status gap', interstitial between the well-defined medical hierarchy (usually high-status males), the midwives (female), and the mother/foetus, who are now the hospital's responsibility. Strangers in the 'gap', with their high visibility, are vulnerable — sharing neither the value systems nor the patronage of any of the dominant groups. Although maternity units have ceased to neutralize the lay threats of fathers by their complete exclusion, other techniques operate in that direction. On arrival with his wife, the father is treated as if he were 'invisible'. Being accorded no formal public acknowledgement, his difficulties are intensified should he wish to assert his 'rights' as a father. In my research fathers recall their 'entrance trauma' (especially acute for the first birth) with anger. They describe their wives as being 'taken away', or 'disappearing'. The format is the same. The midwife approaches the couple, confirms the mother's identity and the two go off. The father is left standing, often with no explanation, and remains so for some time. Fathers recognize their peripherality. Some see their wives as being reincorporated into a 'society of women'. One felt that his treatment was a deliberate punishment by the female staff for the burden of pregnancy he had imposed on the wife. Some referred to themselves as 'second-class citizens', or the 'third party'. During labour/birth the father can be 'activated', but as a background prop, supportive of the main action. The father is tagged on to the team involved in the delivery, but his status as the father is erased by the medical garb. His 'incorporation' into the birth drama is at the lowest level possible — as an 'extra' — with no predetermined part in the script. His mask (usually incorrectly worn) has no sterile function, but the emphasis on pollution and infection symbolizes that this is a hospital rite and not a familial occasion.

Despite the anomic ways the hospital meshes fathers in, most of those interviewed suggest that the excitement and joy experienced on first seeing their child makes it a supreme moment, which negates their own treatment. Ninety-three per cent said they would be present for their 'next' baby in hospital. The birth-attenders tended to consider that their wives had the 'easier' birth, whereas the labour-only fathers tended to see themselves as playing the more 'supportive' role. When the fathers were asked what improvements were needed in their conditions, the birth-attenders expressed more satisfaction with the present regime. (American insurance companies have also noted that fathers at birth raise fewer complaints and are less likely to sue the hospital.) The need for improved refreshment and sleeping facilities came higher than the need for more 'progress reports' from the staff. Ten per cent of the labour–only fathers and 7 per cent of the fathers who were at the birth complained about the lack of information. But it is a characteristic of studies made on users' evaluation of hospital services that the nearer in time the study is made to the completion of the treatment regime, the greater will be the satisfaction expressed by the users.

Conclusion

Studies of pregnant fathers are significant in a number of ways. Not least is their importance in presenting ethnographic evidence about the 'hidden side' of masculinity. Many fathers can be seen to break the 'first commandment' of masculinity (Farrell 1974 : 32): 'Thou shall not cry or expose feelings of emotion, fear, weakness, sympathy, empathy, or involvement before thy neighbour'. The social tide is running in the direction of fathers becoming more home-involved. This is not simply as a refuge from alienation, or, as C. Wright Mills observed, because bureaucracy is no testing field for heroes. Marriage now involves more emotional interplay between partners: the cause and effect is by no means explicit. Pregnancy provides males with one opportunity for emotional involvement. The medical services (not just obstetrics, but paediatrics) could do much to acknowledge and promote 'fathering', and Reik's (1914 : 89) words are still appropriate ones on which to end: 'It is not difficult to be a father, it is not easy to become one'.

Notes

1 In the 1973 study of unintended home delivery the sample consisted of sixty-five mothers. In the 1976 re-evaluation of these mothers' experiences, the sample was forty-nine. The fathers in these two studies are not those in the hospital study that I discuss later.

2 The data on fathers' experiences was collected by a variety of techniques in 1975. A sample of 100 birth-attenders and fifty labour-only fathers were surveyed. Nineteen were interviewed in depth. Other data was collected by indirect interviews and participant observation on walk-arounds. The study was one of a number made in collaboration with W. O. Goldthorp, Consultant Gynaecologist. Approximately 50 per cent of the sample had white-collar status. Seventy-three per cent of the birth-attenders were doing so for the first time. Forty-two per cent of the birth-attenders had previous children, compared with 34 per cent of the labour-only fathers.

7

Fathers in the labour ward: Medical and lay accounts

ANGELA BROWN

The ascendance of the medical model of pregnancy and birth over recent decades has led to a situation in which the great majority of couples having a child will encounter in the course of their experience not only their GP, midwife, and health visitor but also ante-natal clinics, and hospital labour and post-natal wards. The nature of these encounters between medical agencies and parent is relevant to the experience of the great majority of people having children and it is thus important to enquire into such contact as is made and the effect it may have upon the experience of birth.

The author has referred extensively elsewhere (Brown 1977) to the range of research relating to the father and the pattern that this research has hitherto taken. Three main inadequacies in the approach of investigators were outlined: namely a conceptual emphasis on the mother as parent to the extent that the father was diminished in or excluded from the research design; the use of the mother as a source of information on the father; and a concern with the effect of a lack of fathering, through paternal absence or deprivation on the development of the child. The latter, while a legitimate research interest in itself, was considered a somewhat negative focus of interest in an assessment of the body of work on fathering taken as a whole.

In recent years, a growing number of researchers have attempted to remedy this situation (Fein 1974, 1976; Lamb and Lamb 1976; McKee 1980; O'Leary 1972; Rebelsky and Hanks 1971; Richman, Goldthorp, and Simmons 1975; Richman and Goldthorp 1978; Wente and Crockenberg 1976) and a direct approach to the father has become the usual one in research in this area. Even in these studies, however, one aspect of this subject has been consistently neglected and an evident imbalance remains. This is the failure, where concern has been with the transition to fatherhood, to seek the medical viewpoint. In any investigation into a transition that is rarely effected without some contact with medical agencies, this constitutes a significant omission. The research on which this chapter draws was an attempt to redress this balance. A small group of men and their partners were separately interviewed before and after the birth of their first child and subsequently interviews were conducted with medical and nursing staff in the maternity hospital concerned.[1]

With the medicalization of birth has grown the legitimizing belief that the degree of monitoring and medicalization offered is essential or at least beneficial to the process of birth. This belief, held by many of the consumers as well as providers of this service, is important in relation to the effect that medical agencies may have upon those encountering them. If it is assumed that the definitions offered of any status or condition by medical agencies are both crucial and fundamental, then credence will necessarily be accorded to them. Most women, in the course of having a child, through pregnancy and birth, and subsequently in the first months of the child's life, will encounter most, if not all, of the agencies mentioned above. How many her partner, the prospective father, will encounter will vary more widely (with policy, facilities, and inclination on the part of providers and fathers) and it is reasonable to postulate that the nature and extent of his experience of these agencies, the omissions as well as inclusions of the father in the contact made may affect his perception of his role and function as a father to the extent that such credence is given.

The dominance of the medical model of procreation influences the behaviour of individuals in two ways. Not only does belief in its legitimacy affect the status and function of those involved, but this belief in itself argues for the hospitalization of birth. The hospital setting, as will be seen, further determines the roles adopted by the various actors.

Perceptions of fathers in labour: peripheral to the process?

The author's interviews with fathers both before and after the birth of their first child in hospital and with medical and nursing staff in the hospital concerned reveal an apparent lack of function on the part of the father to be a prominent perception in both sets of accounts.

The fathers' accounts pointed to three factors in particular as engendering this feeling: (a) helplessness in the fact of their wife's experience of labour; (b) being an encumbrance — a feeling of being in the way stemming from periodic removal and unfamiliarity with the hospital setting and procedures; and (c) length and type of labour — there being a direct correlation between the extent of medication employed and the extent of the father's feelings of redundancy.

The following are representative of the type of comment frequently made:

> 'I felt detached from the proceedings. You know, you feel . . . that there's not very much you can do. Well, I felt that, that there wasn't a lot that I was doing.'

> 'And ye get the feeling you're just in the way, and the doctors keep talking to you and just . . . instead of getting on with the job they've got to tell you what's happening.'

> '(Wife) was doped up to the eyeballs, you know, and that in itself made it a sort of distressing experience for me. Because, eh (wife) was in a very unreal condition, and there was nothing very much that I could do.'

From these and similar comments emerges a perception of birth in which there is considered to be but one legitimate function, the physical. Within this function two roles thus derive their validity. The first is obvious, that of the woman in labour; indisputably and essentially physically involved and the individual from whom other actors, at least in this context, derive their meaning. Second, there are the hospital staff, who derive their validity as actors in the setting from two sources. First, they are seen as essential to a safe labour and delivery. Their knowledge of the physical process places them in control of the situation and in the position of power that the ability to impart or withold information brings. This element of control is extended and heightened by a further aspect of this knowledge particularly evident in hospital deliveries, namely medical intervention in labour and delivery routinely or otherwise employed, such as the administration of drugs, monitoring of labour, induction, use of forceps, use of caesarian section. The fact of hospital delivery brings us to the second source from which medical personnel derive legitimacy in the birth context, that is the hospital setting itself. Not only is medical knowledge, and thus the personnel who hold such knowledge, it is suggested, deemed essential to the process of labour and delivery, but such personnel are intrinsic to the setting itself with its routines and equipment, in a sense in which mother, father, and child are external. The power dynamics of the situation conspire to enhance the authority of the medical personnel over the patient — the mother — and her partner, the father.

This was a situation of which the doctors interviewed were themselves keenly aware. One indeed expressed the opinion that 'most of medicine is a power situation, imposing your will on someone else', while both senior and junior staff referred to a 'system which doctors have created to make the woman dependent' and to an atmosphere that was conducive to placing the woman 'more firmly below you (the doctor) in the pecking order' with all the back-up of 'nurses and high-technology medicine'.

The introduction of the father into this system concerned certain of the doctors who felt that he, being less directly in need of the doctor than his partner, less busy, and certainly not sedated, might be more pressing in his questions and more likely to pick up contradictions or to ask questions that the doctor could not answer. This relative detachment of the father hinges upon his aforementioned and apparent lack of function. While others of the medical staff might not have expressed the feeling, as did one doctor, that the father was 'an intrusion, a strange foreign element', all were acutely aware of his apparent peripherality and alienation from the setting. As one senior member of staff admitted, 'they *are* out of their depth'.

That many of the fathers did experience, in varying degrees, feelings of peripherality or redundancy their accounts bear eloquent witness.

'With such a long labour, with her being, you know, doped up on all these drugs, she was totally unaware of me. She still does not even know that I was at the birth.'

'because they all had jobs to do and a job to get on with and, you know, I felt I wasn't in the way but, you know, I felt as though . . . I really wasn't making their job any easier. And I certainly wasn't making (wife's) job any easier because she wasn't aware of the fact I was there.'

'In hospital they tell you they want you in but . . . I don't know whose idea it is to take the fathers down. The hospital don't want that.'

'Experience is only something you think about once you come out and it's something that you *make up*. You do, you *make it up*. Because there's no such thing as sharing that experience, I don't think. The husband is an "interested spectator". Very interested. Interested in the, you know, the safety and health of his wife and interested in the safety and health of the child. If he's an interested spectator, well there's no way in which he shares in that experience.'

These fathers evidently felt that they were able to participate on neither of the two levels discussed. They were not themselves in labour, nor were they in possession of medical knowledge or in a position to employ such knowledge. If the above contention has validity, that only physical and medical functions are felt to have legitimacy in the birth context, then these fathers, unable to participate either physically or medically, would necessarily define themselves as peripheral to the process. In this perception of events a third dimension, the emotional, and a perception of the father as a legitimate actor in the birth context *as* a father would appear to be either not countenanced or subsumed under the need to be physically involved.

Hacker (1957) has made a useful distinction between conflicts engendered by feelings of inadequacy in fulfilling role expectations and those resulting from feelings of uncertainty, ambiguity, or confusion regarding role expectations. A further study (Fein 1974, 1976), examining the ease of post-partum adjustment in relation to fathers' expected and actual participation in infant care has used a similar framework in stressing the importance of the development by the father of a coherent role rather than any one particular role. If Hacker's distinction is applied to the above accounts it may be seen that both types of conflict were operant for different fathers in the context of the delivery room. An analysis of the extent to which each was influential in engendering the feelings expressed would help in a more precise understanding of their perceptions of themselves in that context. The successful resolution of such conflicts may depend, to the extent that men's participation in labour is minimally physical, upon the elevation of the emotional aspect, in the perceptions of all actors, to the status accorded the physical.

Both medical and nursing staff considered that they made conscious and deliberate efforts to alleviate these feelings of peripherality. One senior obstetrician considered that the midwives 'regard it as a formal part of their duty to relate to the husbands' and another felt that most staff tried to invent jobs for him, 'to make him feel less of a sore thumb', It was felt, too, by several of the doctors, that the nursing staff were more successful in their attempts to relate to the fathers than were the medical staff. Reference was made here to the 'haphazard' discussion of fathers' possible feelings in the course of a doctor's obstetric training. While doctors, it was felt, knew something of the woman in respect of her role in the situation in which their contact occurred, that is as a woman having a baby, the man was not always felt to come into the doctor's remit and remained something of an unknown quantity to him. Such interviews as were conducted with nursing staff revealed a similar awareness of the possibility of feelings of redundancy on the father's part and a confirmation that they encouraged him in those activities that he could perform — rubbing his partner's back, wiping her face, giving her ice, and supporting her in second stage — expressly for the purpose of alleviating these feelings.

Indeed, the impression gained from interviews with both medical and nursing staff was of an involvement with their patients that was affected by more than purely clinical considerations. Responsibility for the clinical quality of the birth was certainly paramount but this concern did not preclude involvement with patients as individuals and interest in their particular experiences of birth. This is not to suggest that all hospital staff necessarily achieved a complete understanding of their patients' experiences but is meant to indicate the degree of involvement they themselves felt with their patients. The midwives, in particular, whose contact with couples was more protracted than that of the doctors, and involved proportionately more straightforward deliveries in which no intervention was required, were thus provided with greater opportunity to share the more positive experiences of birth with their patients. It is perhaps this difference in the nature and extent of contact made by midwives and doctors with the expectant couple that accounts for the doctors' suggestion that a more successful relationship was formed between fathers and midwives, despite the fact that the majority of doctors share not only gender, but the status of fatherhood with them.

If one turns to the fathers' accounts, however, one sees that the efforts of hospital staff to accommodate fathers met with variable success. Some of the men were both aware and appreciative of the staff's attempts to include them in the proceedings, as in the following instances.

'Well, they always say, in fact, that they prefer the fathers to be there if they want to be so there were no problems at all. Right from the start to the finish.'

'But even just asking a question about the instrument sort of things, she (the midwife) knew all the answers. But, I just kept saying, "What would happen", you know, "what if that doesn't work?" and all this. And she'd give me the answers and that, you know, she was on the ball.'

For others, however, the feelings of being an intruder predominated, despite apparent attempts at communication and inclusion.

'You just had to sit and wait, so I mean . . . they just sort of kept telling you about every five minutes or so, "It'll be a while yet". Ye ken they were forcing theirsel's to . . . instead of just walking in and walking out and talking to (wife), you know . . . well, once I was there, well, I couldn't exactly say, "I'm away".'

'Welcome though I was made until such time as they, you know, they came to deliver by forceps — I was made very welcome by the midwife and made very welcome by all the staff there — I did to a certain extent feel as though I was an intruder.'

'An ye get the feeling you're just in the way and the doctors keep talking to you and just . . . instead of getting on with the job they've got to tell you what's happening.'

While these feelings were the experience of the majority of fathers in this sample, a minority expressed no such feelings of peripherality and one notable exception actively involved himself throughout his wife's labour. In his wife's words: 'He just, you know, got his jacket off and got the gown on and I don't think his bottom touched a chair until she was born'.

These men felt both that they had been able to contribute to the labour and that they had shared the experience with their partners. Moreover, their reactions at delivery were described in extremely positive terms. One was 'in a dream' with excitement, another referred to the feeling of 'all joy in the delivery room'. This was in sharp contrast to a predominant feeling of 'relief' after delivery reported by other respondents.

While it is not possible here to discuss at length the reasons for the contrast between these men's experiences and the majority described above, it may be noted that they were all, in the words of one doctor describing the fathers who usually sought access to him, articulate people, 'well able to manage the mechanisms of our society'. The efforts of nursing and medical staff to overcome fathers' feelings of strangeness would need, perhaps to be directed particularly to those men who are less articulate and more likely to feel intimidated by and unwelcome within the hospital setting.

A further reason why such efforts should have failed where they did may be found, it is suggested, in the pervasiveness of the model of birth described earlier in this chapter and in the perceived pattern of legitimacy consequent upon it. It is interesting, in view of this hypothesis, that the most highly involved father likened his own function to the medical. He did not describe himself as having been involved 'as a father' but, having felt involved, described himself as 'like a doctor'. Even in this case, therefore, in which a high degree of participation was evident and which demonstrated that passivity need not necessarily characterize the father's role at the birth of his child, the extent of this involvement found explanation in terms of the medical role and function, thereby illustrating the lack of a coherent conceptual framework in which fathers' experiences of birth may be perceived and verbalized.

The medical viewpoint: objections to the father's presence – and some benefits

In discussing objections of the hospital staff to the father's presence a distinction must first be made between spontaneous and instrumental deliveries. It was generally and informally accepted among all the staff that fathers were permitted and indeed encouraged to be present during the former. The question of his presence arose over other than these straightforward cases. This acceptance of what is a relatively recent phenomenon was to be found among all hospital staff interviewed with no discernible difference related to age or the relative conservatism or liberalism of individuals on other factors. An exception to this general rule, however, lay in the question of the minor procedures, such as vaginal examinations, insertion of catheters, setting up of drips, that may be employed in the course of even relatively straightforward labours. Here, doctors varied in their opinions regarding the father's continued presence and in the actions taken in accordance with them. These will be discussed subsequently.

The father's observer status, his position as an 'interested spectator', lay behind the most widely voiced objection to his presence among the doctors, namely, that of pressure felt by the doctor from an added presence, intimately involved but not participating actively in the events taking place. As one remarked, even senior medical staff may feel under pressure from the father's presence. It was felt that the doctor could not be unaware of the fact that the father was there and that, in the words of one, 'he was a nuisance, disturbing the process of my decision-making'. Another vividly described how, in the course of a difficult forceps delivery, if he looked up, the husband was 'looking straight at you'.

Indeed, the fathers themselves were not unaware of these feelings and while sympathetic towards them, this awareness only aggravated their sense of intrusion. In the words of one father:

'I'm the same, if I'm doing a job and it's getting a bit tricky, I don't want anybody breathing . . . well, they're right, they're doing a job, you know, and the last thing they want is for somebody — who's got nothing to do with it — sort of being . . . well, if there's complications . . . even if things are straightforward.'

While the extent of this man's sense of alienation, as having, in fact, 'nothing to do' with the baby, was exceptional in the sample, his reluctance to be an encumbrance to medical staff was shared by other fathers.

'Oh, well, every time one of them [a doctor] came along I had to go.

I was mad, because I had to ring to come back which is more inconvenience for . . . somebody had to come and . . . Well, I suppose I could have just walked in, but ye didn't like, ye didn't know what the rules and regulations are.'

This factor, then, of pressure upon the medical staff was voiced as a serious objection to the father's presence in certain circumstances, by all the doctors interviewed. It should be said, however, that on balance quite definite obstetric advantages were felt to result from his presence in other, more optimum circumstances. Where the father was willing and enthusiastic to be present a majority of hospital staff felt that his support would enhance the quality of the labour, the woman controlling her labour better when a supportive partner was present than when he was absent. The same advantage was seen to extend to procedures such as suturing episiotomies where the woman with a supportive partner would be more relaxed, thus making the task easier. One junior doctor spoke representatively of this body of opinion in his insistence that fathers '*do* actively do something, just by being there'. Another considered that they could be 'superb' in fulfilling the functions of communicator, assisting in maintaining control and in providing external stimulation for the labouring women and spoke of their delight and sense of achievement when a labour and delivery had gone well.

Regarding the question of the father's continued presence during minor procedures, particularly vaginal examinations, opinion was, as indicated, more variable and the objection here was different from the ones already discussed. This objection, mentioned by just under half of the doctors interviewed and related to their sex though not to their relative seniority and experience, was the factor of increased self-consciousness on the doctor's part and uncertainty as to how the husband himself would feel. These doctors felt very aware of the father's personal relation to the labouring woman and naturally of their own masculinity, and a resulting discomfort in carrying out the procedure in his presence. As one of them put it, 'I don't want to impose on the husband my sex'.

While differences existed among medical staff in the extent of pressure or discomfort felt from the father's presence, it is fair to say that the decision to ask him to leave was subject uniformly to one main priority — namely the clinical quality of the birth. As one obstetrician succinctly phrased it, 'The first minute is a clinical minute'. This man nonetheless suggested the possibility, though not an actual occurrence, of a baby being insufficiently resuscitated owing to pressure that may be felt by the staff from the father's presence.

Further considerations on which decisions regarding the father's presence were taken were not wholly clinical, nor were they related solely to the doctor's own unease and resulting level of efficiency. The father's possible distress in staying in certain circumstances was mentioned by both doctors and midwives as contributing to the decision to ask him to leave. One clinician, for example, possibly more aware than others of the effect of removal upon the father, felt that if 'in trouble' he would 'make the decision regarding his presence that is least worrying for him' (the father).

Relevant in this context is a further point that was made by a minority of the doctors of the possibility of pressure upon the father, from his partner or peers, to be present during the labour and/or delivery. The fear of being thought a coward was felt to be sufficient, in some cases, to persuade a reluctant father to attend a labour and delivery where he would not have otherwise wished to do so. This view was not shared by all doctors, however, others feeling rather that some women felt quite protective towards their partners and would not push them to a decision.

Effect of removal upon the father

The doctors were in general sympathetic to the men's desire to be with their wives during labour, even where they personally preferred them to leave and implemented this if it could be achieved 'tactfully'. Most considered that providing an explanation was offered, husbands would accept the reason for removal and co-operate with the doctor's wishes. It remains questionable, however, how far the doctors did in fact appreciate the effect of removal upon the fathers and the extent to which this might serve to underline their feelings of being an outsider, and increase the level of worry and stress experienced. The following comments may illustrate these points.

One father who had been present through most of his wife's twenty-one-hour labour and who was asked to leave, much against his will, when the decision to deliver by forceps was taken, compared the experiences of being present in the delivery room and of waiting outside:

'You know, it's nice if you're right up to date, you're aware of everything that's going on, you're not sitting wondering, you know, "What in the name of heaven's going on now . . . I hope there's nothing wrong that they're not coming through" . . . You know, you get all these sort of things running through your head. So you don't suffer from that sort of thing, you're in there, you know, so your information is hot off the press. But . . . that was the benefit to me. Being such a long labour if I hadn't been in, if I hadn't been involved in it, then it would have been a lot more worrying, possibly, to me than it was.'

Another who had known for some time before the birth that he would not be permitted to be present owing to a breech delivery found the one and a half hours between leaving his wife in labour and hearing that his son was born:

'. . . terrible, yes, I . . . "How long is it going to take, how long is it going to take?" I was asking the receptionist chap . . . and I was asking him how long these things usually take and when it got to be a bit longer than that I was getting worried, you know.'

A third man was asked to leave when his wife was put on a drip to bring down blood pressure.

'She says, "Oh could you go for just a couple of minutes?" So I gae'd into the waiting room, and eh . . . actually I was feeling that something, ken, something's surely happened here. Well, she only says tae me, "Oh, could you ging oot for a couple of minutes?" But the next minute she came through again and I says, "What was wrong?"'

And another:

'You see, if there's any complications you're just thrown out and that's it, ye dinna even know what's gan on . . . You're just whipped right out, and that's it. Ye'll be sitting, she'll [a nurse] sit ye oot there and naebody tells ye nothing.'

In two cases removal had unexpected consequences for the fathers concerned. In each of these cases the request was understood by the man to be for his temporary absence while some procedure was carried out. The next communication each received from hospital staff, however, was to tell them that their child had been born. Their own accounts best illustrate their understanding of events.

'I was there but the sister or somebody said I'd to go 'cos the doctor wanted to check her. This was at twenty to one. So I was sitting there at ten to one, ken, one o'clock . . . still there . . . eight minutes past she comes out and she says, "Congratulations".'

'Well, I was in there but they had to do something and the nurse says, "Would you mind going out a bit?" She says, "Oh you're nae looking too well anyway". But I would have stayed . . . if nobody had said anything I would have been there . . . but, you know, I was put away and I wasn't called.'

Here it may be seen how the fathers' inadequate understanding of events and procedures led to an outcome quite other than that which they had intended and how, if desired (for example, if perceiving the father to be feeling unwell) the hospital staff, with their greater knowledge and anticipation of events, may effect the father's absence with the minimum of delay or protest.

Accommodation of the father within the hospital setting

Relevant to any discussion of fathers' experiences of hospital must be the question of facilities, or the lack of them, for the expectant couple. This was an area discussed at some length with hospital staff and one in which there would appear to be considerable room for change and development.

Words such as 'archaic' and 'dreadful' were typical of descriptions offered by staff to describe existing facilities within the hospital to which this study relates.[2] While this situation is not necessarily typical of hospitals elsewhere in the country, the suggestions put forward to remedy it have wider application. Underlying these was an appreciation of the alien atmosphere of the setting for many parents and of the discomfort many felt within it. The father's discomfort, in particular, was felt to be increased by the simple lack of accommodation for him. There was nowhere, for example, for him to hang a jacket, nowhere he could sit 'without being hemmed in by machines'. Further, for someone who was purportedly welcomed for the duration of labour there was nowhere, in this particular hospital, for him to get any sort of refreshment, and only relatively recently had a room in the labour ward been converted for use as a fathers' sitting room. All these factors, it was felt, could be improved upon.

Little reference was made in the fathers' accounts to the inadequacy or otherwise of facilities but, as has been seen, ample reference was made by some to the discomfort they felt within the hospital. Certain of the doctors, while aware of these feelings, considered that changes in the design of delivery rooms to accommodate fathers would not be appropriate. It would be 'bending over too far', one remarked, 'to go out of our way to alleviate this uncomfortableness' if, he added, clinical considerations were thereby compromised. Nonetheless, it was the feeling of all that much could, and should be changed to encourage an atmosphere within the maternity hospital that was less institutional and more homely than that found at present.

Here, then, would appear to be an area in which much could be done to achieve a meeting of the needs of both hospital staff and parents. By lessening the institutional aspect of a hospital as far as possible and by paying proper attention to physical accommodation of the father, it might be possible to ameliorate in some measure, while remaining within the sphere of hospital facilities, the fundamental feelings of peripherality and redundancy experienced by many fathers. This in turn might begin to erode the perception of fathers as extraneous to the process of birth on any level that is considered significant. If fathers were to become more fully a part of the setting, both fathers and hospital staff might perhaps increasingly come to see the father as an intrinsic member of the event of birth.

Fathers in theatre

The question of fathers' possible distress came into particularly sharp focus regarding the issue of fathers in theatre, especially for caesarian sections. Here, the doctors were almost wholly and the nursing staff completely uniform in their feeling that this was an inappropriate place for the prospective father. Several reasons were put forward to support this view. Regarding the father's own feelings, it was felt that he would be unable to detach himself sufficiently from the proceedings not to be distressed. 'It would be difficult', one doctor remarked, 'to see how he could'.

Another widely voiced objection to fathers in theatre expressed by most, though not all, doctors concerned the question of asepsis. The father's ignorance of procedures, of what he may or may not touch and where he may or may not stand, was felt to be insuperable and severely to warrant his exclusion.

A third objection, less widely voiced, referred once again to restrictions placed on the medical team by the father's presence and to his perceived status as non-functional intruder. Were he there, it was felt, free discussion relating to his partner's case, or to other cases, would be impossible. One doctor referred to the psychology of the operating theatre, whereby the freedom to make remarks, often disrespectful, about the patient was necessary to the process of detachment on the part of the surgical team. Similarly, it was felt that teaching would be severely restricted by the presence of the father, with his personal relationship to the patient. One could not, one doctor commented, remark, for example, that 'there would be a stillbirth in a few minutes' if a section was not performed, if the father was also there to hear it.

A final objection in this context, again brought into focus by the particular circumstances of a section but which may nonetheless be addressed to the range of experiences of labour, concerns the basic question of why the father may wish to be present at the birth of his child. As far as caesarian sections were concerned, a distinction was drawn by all the doctors between elective sections performed under an epidural, where the woman was therefore conscious throughout, and those performed under a general anaesthetic. In the former, all felt that there might be instances in which it would be appropriate and even advantageous for the father to be present. Sections performed under an epidural would be those in which the woman had already expressed the desire to see her child born and, where her partner was willing to be present, he could 'experience the experience with his wife'. This was indeed held by all the doctors interviewed to be the sole reason for his presence. In those operations performed under a general anaesthetic, therefore, there was felt to be little point in his being there. Indeed, in one of the rare cases related in which a father had been present in theatre during a section for which a general anaesthetic was used the doctor performing the operation was somewhat critical of his motives. He felt extremely uncomfortable in the presence of the father and suspected that he 'wanted to see every drop of blood and . . . go back to work and tell his colleagues he'd seen it all'. The general view regarding fathers in theatre, in general anaesthetic cases, was expressed in the comment of one doctor that 'All he's going to see is the baby delivered'. This factor in itself was held to be of little importance to him.

Perceptions of the father-child relationship, in contradistinction to that between mother and child, emerged here in relation to the question of bonding. Some importance was attached to this question but it was widely held to be more important for the mother to see and hold her child as soon as possible than for the father to do so. Indeed, one even feared a negative effect on the father of seeing his newborn child 'emerging covered in meconium, or blood, its face perhaps distorted by forceps' though no such effect was mentioned for the mother. Another felt it best for the father to see his baby first with its mother.

This emphasis is to be found also in some of the literature relating to this subject. Earlier advocates of a maternal instinct (Deutsch 1947; Mead 1949; Ackermann 1958) attached a certain exclusivity to this notion, denying the possibility of a corresponding instinct in men. Later writers, retaining the idea of parental behaviour as instinctual, broadened their application of this behaviour to claim a corresponding 'father instinct' in men (Biller and Meredith 1974).

The acknowledgement of a capacity for nurturance in men did not, however, preclude the belief in a more fundamental capacity in women (Nash 1965). Nash considered, with others (Parke and Sawin 1976), that the process of 'imprinting' may play an important part in the formation of an affective link between parent and child and thus argued for greater contact and involvement between father and infant from the very earliest stage. He qualified this opinion, however, with the suggestion that such a process may be less important for women than for men, thus implying a belief in innate nurturant qualities in the female not matched in the male.

Such a position is reminiscent of that adopted by some of the medical staff in the present study in the shared supposition of a more dominant urge to nurturance in the mother than in the father, although with the latter the emphasis was on the seemingly greater importance of the affective link between mother and neonate than that between father and neonate. Where a father had not been present at the delivery of his child, then, for whatever reason, a delay of some fifteen minutes before he saw his child was felt by the medical staff interviewed to be 'sufficient for bonding'. Then, with the delivery and any attendant difficulties or pressures over, as one doctor phrased it, 'It's nice to see the clover leaf'. Here again, a perception of the situation emerges in which the father's emotional commitment to the delivery of his child is subsumed under wider considerations, be they medical or otherwise.

Perhaps significant in this context is the comment of one doctor that he had often heard a father say to his baby, as he first held it, 'I'm your dad', yet he had never heard a mother say, 'I'm your mum'. In this expression may be found, perhaps, an indication of the distance hitherto felt by many fathers between themselves and their unborn child and an attempt to express a physical and emotional relationship that had until the moment of birth been for him at one remove. If this is so, it surely argues for the importance of early and close contact between father and child.

Concluding remarks

Interviews with both fathers and hospital staff have shown that, despite efforts at accommodation on both sides, a certain disharmony exists between the needs of the two parties.

One area in which much could be done to achieve a meeting of these needs has already been discussed at some length, namely the question of facilities within the hospital and the hospital setting. It will suffice to reiterate briefly here that efforts towards lessening the institutional atmosphere of maternity hospitals and thoughtful physical accommodation of the father may do much, without compromising clinical considerations, to make him feel less conspicuous on introduction into a room designed for a function in which he was once held to have had no part.

Other points emerging from interviews with medical staff — for example, the almost uniform objection to fathers in theatre and the widely felt concern with pressure on the doctor from the father's presence in certain circumstances — would appear to be more intractable.

while presenting a marked degree of unity in their opinion on these subjects, however, the doctors placed some emphasis upon the importance of making individual judgements. As one senior clinician remarked, 'One of the marks of a good doctor is how far he is able to particularize a situation and escape from generalities'. It is perhaps here, in the recognition of the importance of individual judgement, that further steps towards a satisfactory experience of birth for both medical staff and fathers may be taken. There is no procedure, one doctor commented, from which fathers are categorically excluded, and nor can there be, one may argue, in a situation that is at once deeply personal and individual yet bound inextricably to some measure of specialism and expertise.

Notes

1   The material in this chapter is taken from a wider study on men's experiences of the transition to fatherhood which the author carried out while in receipt of a grant from the Medical Research Council. In 1977 fifteen men and their partners were separately interviewed approximately six weeks before and three months after the birth of their first child. The sample was obtained through the records at the Maternity Hospital and included six men of Social Class I, five of Social Class III (manual) and four of Social Class IV. Interviews with hospital staff were carried out subsequently in 1980. Five consultant obstetricians and three registrars were interviewed from the medical staff and from the nursing staff one nursing officer, four sisters, and five staff midwives.
2   Renovations to the labour ward in this hospital are planned at the time of writing.

8 Fathers' participation in infant care: A critique

LORNA McKEE

Studies of the family have become increasingly concerned with the father's contribution to childcare and his involvement in the life of the child. The focus on fathers' participation has allowed researchers to comment on a number of central sociological issues: on the nature and character of contemporary sex roles and definitions of masculinity and femininity; on the jointness/segregation of couple relationships; on the social or working conditions of full-time mothers; on the total care and developmental environment of the child; on the parent-child relationship; and on the generic and cultural meaning of parenthood. At the same time, attempts to measure and evaluate men's involvement with their children have been coupled with an interest in other aspects of men's household and domestic work and can be collectively referred to as the 'domestic politics' of the family (Oakley 1979:198). Researchers agree that the way couples divide up their home and family work is an important contemporary political issue, reflecting much about the power relations between men and women, between husbands and wives, and between parents and children (Oakley 1974; Moss 1980) and identifying a particular form of relationship between the family and the economy (Rushton 1979:32). However, our preoccupation with 'who does what?' within the family must be set in an historical context that recognizes both changes in the family form itself and changes in economic modes of production. The importance of how much labour men contribute to the rearing of their children and to the maintenance of their homes arises precisely because modern families, unlike peasant and early industrial working-class families, are no longer discrete economic units where all members are expected to contribute to the survival of the unit.

Instead, as family history has shown, the 'co-operative productive' interdependence of families has splintered: children have become almost entirely dependent family members; parental power over children has lessened; adults, especially men, usually generate their income away from the home and receive 'private' remuneration for their labour; the nature of domestic labour has changed and fewer tasks are tied to survival; total household numbers have fallen due to smaller family size and a reduction in the presence of servants, lodgers, and other relatives, leading to an increased privatization of family life; the inevitable connection between marriage and procreation has been broken; and child-bearing and child-rearing occupy a smaller proportion of the family life-cycle (Ariès 1962; Laslett and Wall 1972; Flandrin 1976; Anderson 1979).

More fundamentally, modern families are characterized by a type of economic organization that sharply ranks and separates domestic and productive activity, divides homes from workplaces, and provides few opportunities for women to participate equally with men in the sphere of work. In this family structure, which it is argued first emerged amongst the bourgeoisie of nineteenth-century Europe, men are commonly assigned the breadwinning roles, while women are assigned the tasks of homemaking and child-rearing (Scott and Tilly 1975; Poster 1978).

Each confers a different status and ideology: the one economic independence and superordination, the other economic dependency and subordination. This contrasts with the peasant family type where all members were economically active and individuals were not divisible from the family unit. Sex-role differentiation clearly did exist in peasant families and husbands maintained authority over wives; however, the sex-gender relations of modern families have a *different* and *peculiar* tenor attributable to the shift in the location and definition of productive work and in women's access to it. Feminists have largely been responsible for highlighting these structural inequalities of the modern family and for drawing critical attention to the differential participation of men and women in waged work. Their campaign through the Women's Movement of the 1960s and 1970s for more and more equal opportunities for women to express themselves *outside* the home has paradoxically compelled us to review seriously what happens *inside* the home. In short, the relationship between domestic and waged labour has been thrown into sharp relief and the home has become politicized. This is why the organization of infant care and domestic work and more specifically, fathers' participation in infant care and housework is important. It stands as a symbol of the sex-gender relations within a particular family structure, shaped by particular economic forces and embodying the forms of oppression women experience elsewhere in

society. But it is a contemporary concern and in former times the strug-
gles between the sexes must have cast up other issues and been sited in
other terrains (Anderson 1979:65; Oakley 1979; Rowbotham 1979).

Having briefly outlined the historical background to *why* fathers'
participation in infant care is a crucial area of study, it is now necessary
to ask *how* researchers have gone about their investigations. This is the
main concern of my chapter and I will focus chiefly on the social survey
approach for three reasons. First, social surveys have become the dominant mode of sociological inquiry. Second, social surveys have been
influential in shaping the categories and questions applied by other
researchers outside the survey tradition, especially ethnographers. Third,
there continue to be too few opportunities for users of different styles
of inquiry to pursue a constructive dialogue with one another. The aim
of this chapter is not to invalidate the social survey method but rather
to pick up on some persistent limitations in the way that it has been
applied to the father's role and to feed back insights gained about
fathers through an alternative technique. Primarily, my interest here
lies in uncovering whether social surveys have asked the right questions
about fathers, if more or different questions should be asked, if there
are any different ways of asking and seeing which lie outside the scope
of surveys, and if any different sense can be or should be made of the
answers given.

For my critique I rely on case-study material from thirteen couples
who were interviewed in depth about their perceptions of becoming
and being a parent. Each partner was interviewed three times (and
separately where possible) over a period of fifteen months. Informal
visits were also made to each of the families soon after the birth and the
research emphasis was on 'getting to know well' a small group of parents
and on exposing the meanings that they attached to their family roles.
This case-study approach is distinguished from a social survey by the
number of people selected for study, their representativeness, and the
number of questions focused on the father's role. Social surveys,
especially those employing questionnaires and structured interviews,
tend to extend their inquiries over a large number of cases, to aim for a
sample that is representative, and to have to restrict the number of
questions on a given phenomenon. Consequently, social surveys are
valuable for identifying patterns and variations for large populations
and for aggregates of individuals. The case-study approach is directed
less at the full variation of phenomena, being better equipped to explore
social processes and social relationships between individuals, including
the meanings that people attribute to the actions of others. Despite
these fundamental differences in what each method can achieve, and the
fact that the philosophical assumptions of the two approaches are often

at variance, this chapter will show that grounded data gathered through one route can have relevance and validity for the other. In commenting on the flaws discovered in the survey approach to fathers' participation I will use a heuristic division between empirical and interpretive flaws; however, this distinction is in no way an absolute or exclusive one.

Empirical flaws in the survey approach

In the measurement of fathers' participation in infant care the survey approach can be criticized first on two general points: on its narrow definition of 'participation' and on its narrow definition of 'infant care'. Participation is usually taken as 'direct' participation in the life of the infant, while infant care is chiefly taken as 'physical' caretaking. Typically, a small range of fatherhood practices is identified and these practices cluster around the father's involvement in caretaking activities (feeding, bathing, nappy-changing, soothing the crying baby, and attending the baby at night); his participation in domestic baby care duties (washing nappies, preparing bottles); his performance of social activities (walking out with the baby) and play; and, more recently, his attendance at childbirth (Newson and Newson 1965; Gavron 1966; Richards, Dunn, Antonis 1977; Gallagher 1978). The father's performance of these tasks, the regularity and frequency with which he carries them out is taken to be the summation of the father's role and the prime expression of being a father. However, the nonsense of this quantitative approach, when taken as a single index of the father role, can be seen if attempts were made to measure motherhood in this way. For example, in assessing mothers' involvement with their babies it is not enough to add up how many feeds they give daily or how many nappies they change. Clearly, we have developed more sensitive indices for assessing the degree and extent of maternal involvement and include in our assessment other variables, not least the baby's individual needs, the mother's other responsibilities, and what these duties mean in the total context of the infant's care. Similarly, while it is important to know what fathers *do* for their babies, this information needs to be reviewed alongside what the mother does, including other non-physical dimensions of infant care and the demands of the baby itself. The survey approach tends to assume a homogeneity of both mothers and babies and the data on fathers' engagement in infant care tasks is often presented in isolation and without qualification. When represented in this way it is difficult to know what the resultant figures mean, especially if they claim to embody something about the totality of fatherhood. If measures of direct participation in caretaking were set against other approaches to the father's role then they could be revealing and permissible as I will go on to demonstrate.

The case-study material suggests that it is possible to gain a fuller appreciation of the father's role by focusing additionally on how men feel about their economic/provider roles, by reviewing the way men's home and work roles interconnect, by tracing the part men play in decision-making concerning their children, by exploring the level of interest and knowledge men hold about their babies and their sensitivity to the baby's cues, and by examining how men engage in the educational, moral, and disciplinarian aspects of child-rearing. These areas expand our vision beyond direct and physical caretaking and provide a context in which it can be understood. I shall briefly outline the case-study findings along each of these dimensions to illustrate how the scope of inquiries about the father's role can be broadened. All the fathers interviewed in the present study felt they had the prime responsibility for providing financial security for their families and this was identified as one of the big changes wrought by parenthood. In many ways they felt more bound to their homes, their wives, and their jobs. They also cited ways in which they felt their jobs interfered with their opportunities for contact with the baby: home and work commitments were sometimes felt to be in competition with one another (see also Moss and Fonda 1980). Nonetheless, most of the fathers could foresee no alternative to adopting the chief bread-winning role when their babies were infants (one couple attempted role-sharing, dovetailing their working hours, but this later broke down) and only one father, a librarian, had given any serious thought to swapping roles with his wife.

Decision-making was investigated, particularly through questions about the baby's health: who would observe that the baby was ill, who would contact help, and who would decide which help was to be sought? Parents were asked to describe what happened with regard to the decision about whether or not to vaccinate their babies. In the main, parents were described as acting consultatively over 'major' health care decisions, but mothers carried most health care responsibility and arbitrated over 'minor' decisions (Kerr and McKee 1981). When fathers were systematically asked about the baby's sleeping/crying patterns their responses suggest that they felt themselves to be fully informed about the baby's daily behavioural pattern. They claimed a high level of knowledge about the number of feeds given, the timing of feeds, the type of food given (for example, why and when solids were introduced), the number of hours the baby was awake, and the types of occasions when the baby was likely to cry and why. Only one father reported ignorance about both the number of feeds given and the baby's sleeping/waking pattern and explained this in terms of his daily absence at work. All the other fathers answered these questions with confidence, going into minute details of the daily repertoire of behaviour. The accounts suggest that this knowledge was gained partly through direct observation and experience (all the fathers had at least a few days off in the immediate post-natal period) and by mothers reporting back daily happenings/routines to fathers. Mothers were described as playing a key role as correspondent of the baby's affairs. The majority of fathers also felt that they could distinguish different cries and knew why or when the baby was going to cry, and claimed that they could devise different strategies for soothing the crying baby. In some cases, this ability to recognize the differential infant cues was described as a learned attribute, in others it was perceived as instinctual. Fathers felt that they had a responsibility to provide comfort for their babies and also held well developed beliefs about how parental reactions to distress could influence the baby's later behaviour and personality. Likewise, the fathers took their responsibilities for educating the child, both morally and intellectually, seriously. Being a parent carried with it from the outset the expectation that the father should be interested in the child's welfare and self-conscious about the business of child-rearing. Most read in their brief as parents the need to provide comfort, succour, stimulation, and control.

Although this cursory overview of the fathers' perceptions of their role conflates and simplifies many complex findings (McKee 1979), it does raise some new and important issues for consideration and uncovers some previously hidden pathways to the study of fatherhood. Furthermore, it provides a context in which to place findings about physical caretaking. By developing the concept of participation in this way, it is possible to detect subtle differences between fathers, their values, ideals, and overall contributions to child-rearing, which are at first obscured if only the traditional measures are employed. By balancing the two sorts of data it may be possible to generate some 'true' or 'better' evaluation of high and low participation and to decide what this participation means for individual families. For example, two case-study fathers, Simon Shaw, postgraduate student and Evan Crowley, British Rail guard, came out on the physical caretaking scales as participating very little in the routine handling of their babies. They have never bathed the baby, rarely fed the baby, seldom attend to the baby in the night. Yet when this is seen in the context of other aspects of involvement, their experiences were very different and their knowledge about the baby very diffuse. On the one hand, Simon Shaw has carved out a very distinctive educational and intellectual role for himself (reading to the baby, talking to him, offering him unusual toys, food) and has taken this aspect of fatherhood very seriously. He has read extensively about babies both for personal and academic reasons and is highly engaged in assessing the minutiae of the baby's life. At eleven weeks post-partum he is keeping a detailed journal of the baby's progress. On the other hand, Evan Crowley sees his role in early infancy as minimal, is rarely at home — working long hours and relaxing after work with his friends — has not read anything about babies or infant care and does not know what the baby's daily routines are because of his absence from the home. These differences must affect not just their roles as fathers but the experiences both of their wives and their babies. Listening to their comments it is possible to detect the diversity of what fatherhood means to these two men and the way they enact being fathers:

> 'We've got some books with very colourful illustrations in them so I sit him on my knee just to get him used to the idea of being near me and listening to me speak about an object, not necessarily to *him* but about an object to him, about something. And it's easier if we have a book because then we can cater for the length of time he can concentrate. Or I wander round the flat getting him to look at things in the flat and using the same route each time and using the same words.'
>
> (Simon Shaw, postgraduate student)

> 'Well I mean you do your bit when you're 'ere. But I mean a bloke's never 'ere most of the time. Either he goes out for a drink on a night time or he's at work all day like. I mean, like I am, since he's been born I've been out at work seven days a week. I'm not in a great deal. But I mean you do your bit when you're in like, you hold, you get hold of him and things like that.'
>
> (Evan Crowley, British Rail guard)

As well as the narrow range of tasks identified by social surveys in the investigation of the father's role, another survey technique of *aggregating* tasks can be misleading and further betray the complexity of what is being studied. Typically, investigators try to create some composite or additive measure of participation which represents a sum of tasks performed regularly or often by the father. The selection of how many tasks and which tasks seems arbitrary and is rarely justified. In one study the 'high participation group' comprises fathers 'performing at least two categories besides playing "often" ' (Richards, Dunn, and Antonis 1977:28). While in another, the researchers divide the categories into: fathers who perform 'many', 'few', or 'no' tasks. 'Many' is taken to mean four or more tasks performed on a regular basis (Graham and McKee 1978:4). This aggregating of tasks, as well as making comparison across studies difficult, again is restricted to the *quantity* of fatherhood practices and does not reveal what the performance of those tasks means for the couple or how it affects the overall quality of child-rearing. One mother may find the burden of childbearing relieved by a regular, willing performance of one task by the father, perhaps one that she dislikes or finds distasteful, while another mother may still feel exploited even though the father might regularly do four tasks, but might not do them very well or might only do them under duress. The case-study findings suggest that weighting of tasks should be tied to the couples' evaluations of what is done and how essential it is to the overall context of child care. Couples' assessments of the extent of the father's involvement need to be matched against one another, and against 'real' rates of involvement before any general or holistic categories can be generated. Mothers' satisfaction with levels of participation also needs to be measured over time, as it has been shown that this can diminish as the baby grows older (Oakley 1979; Graham and McKee 1978).

Another persistent shortcoming of the way surveys have investigated fathers' participation is the lack of standardization in the period of infanthood under review. More importantly, researchers also tend to take this issue as unproblematical and to make comparisons across studies where the infants' ages vary from four weeks to twelve months (Richards, Dunn, and Antonis 1977; Graham and McKee 1978). In one study comparisons are made between fathers of one-year-old infants and fathers of children of an unspecified age; the criterion for inclusion in this study being that the mothers should have at least one dependent child under five years (Gavron 1966). From talking to the same fathers over the course of the first year of infancy, it would seem that the time-specificity of the study does matter. Taking the three basic caretaking tasks of feeding, nappy-changing, and bathing there were marked fluctuations between fathers' reports at three and twelve months after the birth. While some fathers had increased their involvement in one task, they had reduced their involvement in another, or some had increased overall involvement while others had lessened total involvement. This lack of consistency between individual tasks and between fathers' degrees of participation over time was explained in a number of ways, relating to either changes in the husband's or wife's employment status, to perceived changes in the infant, to changes in the nature of the infant care tasks themselves, or to other circumstantial or environmental demands. Five men changed jobs over the twelve-month period and this could either facilitate or restrict the opportunities for involvement. In one instance the father began working away from home and only returned at weekends, so his contact with the baby was severely curtailed. In another, the father returned to work after a period of studying and decided, because he would see less of the child on a daily basis, to participate more actively in her care. These case-study examples underscore the fine intermeshing and interdependence of men's home and work roles and reveal the impact that work can have on the form of family life (Moss and Fonda 1980). By twelve months two mothers were working and their husbands felt that this encouraged and necessitated a more equal division of childcare work. Surveys need to build into their design ways of evaluating the influence of both men's and women's employment statuses, ways of appreciating any changes in these, the effects of different kinds of occupations, and ways of assessing differential work patterns: shift-working, working nights, and part-time work. Perceived changes in the baby were felt to enable some men to participate more in primary care, whilst for others such changes were inhibiting. The baby was seen as becoming easier to manage, being less fragile; on the other hand, for others, she became less easy to handle, struggling and protesting more. It must be remembered too that a number of fathers expected their involvement to increase as the child got older (this had been commented on by several researchers), especially identifying the importance of the father's role when the child became 'sociable', walking and talking (Newson and Newson 1974). Increased involvement at twelve months may in part be a reflection of this ideology.

One of the most interesting observations is that fathers isolated changes in the nature and sequencing of the three primary tasks themselves. With a very small baby the tasks of feeding and changing were felt to be inextricably linked, and usually performed by a single caretaker, especially where babies were breast-fed. Bathing was, at this stage, the task least preferred by men, and was also closely tied to the nurturing tasks of feeding and changing. However, by twelve months, fathers felt these tasks to be much more divisible and segmented. This had a particular effect on bathing, and while at three months six fathers had never bathed the baby, by twelve months only one had never done so and six described themselves as regularly or always bathing the baby. Bathing had become a social task and was often characterized as an occasion for play. Babies had been transferred from baby baths to the 'big bath' and three fathers actually bathed *with* their babies as a routine occurrence. Interestingly, all these men had boy children. Bathing in these cases was a pre-bedtime activity and fathers also usually changed and prepared the baby for bed. This suggests that it may have been an important part of the father-child repertoire of contact.

Any shifts in feeding patterns from breast to bottle or to solids, the time of day when bathing routinely occurs, and the frequency of bathing also need to be noted when identifying father's participation. It may be that variations in family schedules affect this and are subject to change as the baby matures. The reasons why fathers' involvement in basic caretaking either increases or diminishes can be said then to be very complex, neither moving unilaterally nor equally between tasks. Studies that have attempted to capture shifts in performance rates over time usually attribute a decline in caretaking to a decline in interest, commitment, or motivation, or this assumption is implicit in their findings (Richards, Dunn, and Antonis 1977; Oakley 1979). However, such shifts are multifaceted and can be explained away in practical or external terms as well as in psychological or motivational ones.

A final empirical bias in the conventional survey findings on fathers' participation is the continued reliance on maternal reports of paternal behaviour. This is justifiable if investigators are mainly interested in mothers' perceptions of what fathers do. However, it cannot stand as an accurate report of fathers' activities, for this, it is necessary to turn to fathers themselves. This criticism is now being well heeded, and as the chapter by Simms and Smith in this book shows, social surveys are being designed with fathers in mind. However, it will not be enough for surveys to look at fathers 'as if' they were mothers, new questions may have to be devised and the 'old' questions may not translate very well when applied to men. This is especially important in deciding which variables to explore and trust, and as has already been suggested, men's physical or direct caretaking may be only a partial avenue of inquiry. What is compelling is that the direct incorporation of fathers' views will allow researchers to compare mothers' and fathers' accounts and to develop an appreciation of the *processes* by which mothers and fathers come to adopt and construct their current roles and how they feel about the existing division of labour. This will throw up insights about the nature of the power relations between husbands and wives and between parents and children. It will also help to show how couples build and sustain their family ideologies, how they set and achieve family goals and how they face and adapt to institutional and interpersonal change.

This is where the case-study approach is especially useful and draws its strengths. The couples in my study seemed from the beginning, as has already been said, to adhere to the conventional sex-gender division of man/breadwinner, woman/child-rearer during the period of infancy, but to negotiate what was felt to be a fair and equitable division of infant care within this context. What seemed to be important was not so much how labour was performed by which individual, but the *spirit* in which this was done and what each felt about that apportioning. The '*moral context*' of child care in terms of perceptions of fairness and justice seemed to be devised between couples and could be subject to change. The overall impression from this group of couples was one of an atmosphere of mutuality and satisfaction but the degree of satisfaction was always finely tuned and delicately balanced. One couple, Evan and Sheila Crowley, were in continual conflict about how the responsibilities of the home should be divided up and each envied the other's freedom and ease of life-style. For others, these issues flared from time to time or not at all. Having assumed the primary role of child-rearer, a number of mothers applied what can be called a 'maternal framework' in which to either directively encourage or discourage their husband's family involvement and by which to evaluate his efforts.

The application of this framework must be seen, however, in its wider context of the men's economic independence and often physical superiority — 'the power of the purse' and 'the power of the hand' — which meant that any bargaining powers that women had could be diminished or undermined (Bell and Newby 1976). This larger inequality and lack of symmetry between husbands and wives is especially noticeable in that many mothers were 'easy' on their husbands, praising their involvement even where it was minimal, accepting reasons for low involvement such as male inexperience, tiredness, disinterest, incompetence, physical unsuitability (clumsiness, large hands), and psychological unsuitability (rough, quick-tempered, impatient, squeamish) – reasons that would not stand up if applied to women. A few contrasting comments capture the complex processes of negotiation, chivvying, and bartering that result in a particular division of childcare across families. These insights have only been gained by talking to *both* parties and suggest that fathers' participation is closely linked to mothers' orientation and responses as well as fathers' own preferences:

> 'I don't think he's interested in the practical side (of infant care). He does now and again, he'll do things just to show willing more or less. He's not really interested in that side of it. He'll do it if he has to I think, but he doesn't really want to. So I do most of it . . . He's never fed her, no. He changes her occasionally and he'll dress her. He attempted once (to bath her) and he didn't get on very successfully and he offered to do it again but I said I'd do it (laughs). I think he's quite happy to keep away from that side of it, quite honestly (laughs). I don't want to force him to do it.'
> Angela Anderson, teacher, Infant School (five months after the birth)

> 'I wouldn't say I'm involved in that side (nappy-changing). Well, Angela takes, does it all really . . . There hasn't really been a decision, it's just worked out that way, you know. If it happened this afternoon that she started screaming and it was obvious that her nappy needed changing I'd go ahead and do it. (Bathing?) Angela always does that. I don't know. When she's a bit bigger, I'd feel a bit hopeless. I'd rather leave it. There again, in an emergency I suppose I could do it. I think I could manage it.'
> Keith Anderson, remedial teacher (three months after the birth)

'I think he needs to be involved for his own sake and for the baby's sake. I think he can comfort her very easily. I think she's very aware of the strength and steadiness of being held by him. The first time he bathed her I insisted that he did. I can do it very quickly having done it before but I'm very aware of her losing body heat and of course he isn't, he was messing about testing the water with his elbow and I found I really had to restrain myself not to say "come on, hurry up she's getting cold". He bathed her which took about half an hour and put her nappy on which fitted where it touched, it was awful, running down her legs and generally a mess.'

Beth Banks, midwife

Interpretive flaws in the survey approach

Three main interpretive flaws recur in surveys of father involvement in childcare. First, there is the very general problem of the relationship between what people say they do and believe and 'real' behaviour. All methods relying solely on verbal reports face this difficulty and some would argue that it can only be overcome by the inclusion of observational techniques. What surveys can and should do, however, but often fail to, is to make this issue explicit and treat it self-consciously. Secondly, and more critically, there is often the unspoken assumption in the presentation of survey findings that fathers' reported practices match or reflect fathers' ideologies. By focusing the attention on what fathers say they do there is a tendency to neglect how this connects with what they believe and to treat reports of overt behaviour as harmonizing with attitudes and values. Lastly, and relatedly, there is a frequent assumption that any observed change or lack of change in reported behaviour is necessarily accompanied by a change or lack of change in belief and value systems and that the two move in a progressive or continuous fashion. For example, any reported increase in fathers' participation in infant caretaking is interpreted as an indication of a loosening of sex-role definitions and stereotypes: high paternal participation is 'good', low participation is 'bad' (Parke 1979). However, it would seem that all these assumptions are naive, that the relationship between reported behaviour and values may not be obvious or consistent, and that behavioural and attitudinal changes may not occur at the same pace or with the same potency. It has been noted elsewhere that social change can occur even when there have not been massive changes in overt behaviour and that social change might be simply the time when new forms of behaviour appear 'plausible' (Gagnon and Simon 1970; Skolnick and Skolnick 1974). The simplistic marrying of overt measures of behaviour to conclusions about the quality of marriage, the nature of contemporary sex roles and social change can be detected in the extracts below. The Newsons' pioneering study on infant care is selected not because it is the most flawed or blameworthy but rather because it has been taken as a model and a basis for comparison by so many authors (Richards, Dunn, and Antonis, 1977; Gallagher 1978). Here the rationale for studying fathering activities is described (Newson and Newson 1965: 133, 134, 147):

> 'However, there is a great deal of evidence to suggest that the traditional pattern of family life is changing. Marriage today is ideally envisaged as a partnership in which husband and wife share each other's interests and worries, and face all major decisions jointly . . . Against such a background, it seemed natural for us to inquire into the extent to which fathers actually do participate in the care of one-year-olds. The procedure we adopted was to ask the mothers whether the fathers took an active part in doing things for the children . . . '

And in finding that 79 per cent of their sample of fathers (by mothers' report) 'take a part in the care of their small babies' they go on to conclude that:

> 'both mother and father are becoming home-centred, finding their interests, their occupation and their entertainment within the family circle. At a time when he has more money in his pocket, and more leisure on which to spend it, than ever before, the head of the household chooses to sit at his own fireside, a baby on his knee and a feeding bottle in his hand: the modern father's place is in the home.'

Turning to the case-study fathers, it is possible to document ways of uncovering men's parental values and beliefs that go beyond the mere enumeration of childcare tasks and that allow for a comparison between participation rates and paternal ideologies. Already it has been argued that the range of tasks traditionally counted is too limited, and some positive suggestions have been advanced to widen the existing range. Here the argument developed begs for an even more radical reappraisal of what fathers do and asks not just whether sufficient areas are being reviewed, but how this fits in with men's and women's beliefs about their roles, their marriages, and their definitions of masculinity and femininity. Again, it is not possible to do full justice to the data (McKee 1979); however, some of the crucial and interesting findings will be summarized. Asked 'do you think it is important to share baby care?' eleven fathers answered in the affirmative and subscribed to some general principle of 'democratic and participant parenthood'. However, there appeared to be much variation in both the structuring and meaning of sharing, and in the supporting explanations. Some fathers advanced 'the notion of sharing primarily because of a commitment to the child: child-rearing was felt to be part of a 'shared reality' (Backett 1980). Sharing was also seen as fostering the parent-child relationship. This view was backed up in statements such as 'it's all part of bringing her up', 'if you keep it even stevens they grow up to admire you both' and 'it gets you more involved with the baby'. Other fathers emphasized the importance of sharing mainly as a gesture aimed at alleviating the burden of care placed on their wives. These fathers alluded to the desire to establish some kind of symmetry or egalitarianism in their marital relationship. Two such fathers, Stephen Banks, accountant and Nigel Owens, electrician, expressed strong concern about their wives losing touch with the outside world, being overburdened and housebound.

This view of sharing, to release the wife from excessive domestic and familial demands, did not necessarily mean that fathers took on direct physical care of the infant; two elected to share domestic workloads instead, washing nappies, washing clothes, cooking, and doing general housework. (For a discussion of the relationship between men's involvement in housework and infant care see Oakley 1979.) Bound up with the view that mothers should be supported there was also a strong orientation to the child and a sense of commitment towards the child's upbringing and upkeep. This sense of responsibility toward the child has been mentioned earlier and men no longer felt footloose or 'able to vanish to Paris' (Simon Shaw). The fathers who contested that baby care should be shared did not reject the ideology of sharing but in one case felt that couples should be left to work out a routine that best suits them, overlaying the concept of sharing with the concept of individualism (Keith Anderson). While in the other case, the father found difficulty in reconciling the dictate of sharing with other demands of the male role which centred outside the home (see the earlier quote by Evan Crowley).

It should be stressed that for the majority of fathers this notion of sharing was not always perceived as a fifty/fifty division of infant care labour but instead was something shifting, arbitrary, personalized, and negotiated. It was as if fathers, along with mothers, established their own criterion of sharing, ranging in some instances from an occasional 'mucking in' to an ideal of equality in others. They had few standards by which to compare or judge their own degree of participation and what they did was largely invisible to public scrutiny. Men who did not contribute at all to childcare or who displayed a casual attitude toward parenthood were castigated: classified by one father as 'sky-larkers'. However, the meaning of sharing was elastic and private and, as already shown, carried out within a context where there was an assumed asymmetry in the division of roles from the outset. While fathers could opt into childcare and influence the sex-role division of childcare work, mothers did not feel that they had an equivalent facility for opting out of childcare or into full-time waged work.

A number of other questions serve to highlight men's parental values and reveal how these relate to their overall contributions to infant care. Answers to a series of questions about male attitudes to infertility, adoption, family planning, and the desire to have children suggest that most men saw having children as part of the 'normal' fabric of adulthood; marriage and having babies was ineluctably a natural part of the human life-cycle (see also the chapter by Owens). Husbands and wives were perceived as being equally implicated by the decision to have children, in that each would have to adjust their own life in some way both to accommodate and create a 'family'.

When asked about the existence of maternal and paternal instincts, the competence levels of mothers and fathers, the qualitative difference between being a mother and father, attitudes to working mothers, and men's general interest in babies, the replies from this group of men form a fascinating and complex patchwork. What is striking is that their dominant ideological positions fall into three categories: *'traditionalist'*[2] (Evan Crowley, British Rail guard); *'modified traditionalist'* (ten fathers are characterized here); and *'neo-feminist'* (Stephen Banks, accountant; Simon Shaw, postgraduate) (Komarovsky 1973). In the 'traditionalist' mode, childcare, especially the care of small babies, is felt to be women's work; women have special nurturing aptitudes — wives and mothers should not work and their 'proper place' is in the home; and men's chief fathering roles are to provide financial security and discipline and to teach children, especially boys, about gender-specific activities: 'boy's things'. In the 'modified traditionalist' stance, which is the majority position for the fathers in the present study, early infant care is held to be women's work but fathers have an important contribution to make and should share some of the practical care; men can nurture babies, but perhaps not so well as mothers – mothers having a 'special touch', being able to cuddle babies differently, acting out a more comforting role; wives and mothers should withdraw from work during the child's early years but return to work when the children are school age and at the same time keep up their interests in the outside world — while men's chief roles in infancy are to provide financial security for the family; to create a caring and supportive environment for wives and babies; to offer 'back-up' to the mother, to provide sex-role models for their children, to entertain children, and to instil a shared moral code in a spirit of fairness and collaboration with their wives. The 'neo-feminist' value constellation is one in which the fathers espoused an egalitarian belief about the interchangeability or symmetry of men's and women's roles. However, they were not truly 'feminist' in that they did not feel that they could modify their behaviour to facilitate this goal and wives' careers were still sacrificed or suspended.

These classifications should not be read as too fixed or exclusive and there were many inherent contradictions and ambivalences *within* men's value positions. More interesting was the frequent clash between their reported performance of and orientation to childcare duties. For most, these apparent inconsistencies and conflicts seemed tenable or manageable and were not remarked upon. For example, Evan Crowley espoused the belief that married women should not work yet later did not feel the need to comment on his wife taking up waged work almost immediately after the birth of their baby. Or alternatively, Tommy Hooper felt women to be more able in the care of small infants, yet his almost equal care of the baby during the early months was presented as unproblematic. The fathers who reported the most unease because of the disjunctions between what they believed about being a father and what they did as fathers were, interestingly, the 'neo-feminists'. This might suggest something about the lack of cultural supports for this value position and be a comment on the absence of real social opportunities for parents to swap or at least equalize their roles when their babies are young. As well as the confusion and tension within men's belief systems and between their ideals and practices there was some further hint that their feelings did not always complement those of their wives. Although this cannot be developed here it serves to further underscore the inherent complexity of men's experiences both in defining and in carrying out their fatherhood roles. Two brief comments reflect on this, one is chosen from the 'modified traditionalist' group while the second represents the 'neo-feminist' type:

'I do very little with being away during the week on the practical side. I give him a lot of his meals and I help prepare them while Janet's preparing our meal. And just generally playing with him, that's all really. It's difficult with just the weekends to spend as much time as I can with him . . . I think they (parents) have slightly different roles now but I think the roles join or should join as time goes on. And I think fairly soon they should become the same, the same role. Because the mother is able to satisfy the needs of the baby with her being at home most of the time, sort of most mothers who stay at home with the baby and the husband goes out to work, so I think the roles are different there — where the husband is the person who plays with the baby whereas the mother is the one who deals with its needs.'   Ralph Price, bank security clerk

'In the beginning I was very keen to try and work on a sort of equality, you know, try and work an equality out. We didn't want Sally to do all the traditional things simply because women do the traditional things. But we found for one reason or another that's the way it works out that the traditional demarcations did occur. And I got very sort of guilty about it, probably up to six months. And I used to say — "Look do you want me to do more? Do you want me to do less?" and Sally would say "Well you don't do it right" or "you take hours doing it" or "one could have done it in a few minutes" or "what's happening?" and slowly things do settle out.'

Simon Shaw, postgraduate

The present data, while it shows much about the lack of coherence and uniformity in the modern fathering role, cannot reflect on whether social change has occurred without recourse to historically comparable material. This takes us back to where I began the chapter and to the work of family historians and historical sociologists (see the chapter by Trevor Lummis). The case-study fathers perceive that things have changed and in comparing their fathering experiences with those of their own fathers, felt fatherhood practices in particular had changed in a direction of 'progressive egalitarianism'. It is possible to speculate, considering the views and experiences of the 'modified traditionalists' (who constitute the largest group of fathers in the present study), that what may have happened is that the modern father's role has expanded to include some involvement in childcare as part of its repertoire and there now exists some ideological compatibility between caring for babies and breadwinning. Whether this is advancing in a linear fashion towards a 'feminist' pattern is more difficult to ascertain, as is the question of whether it has shaken the overall hierarchical nature of men's and women's gender-relationships. Certainly, this possible 'shift' of fathers toward greater participation in infant care does not seem to have been matched by an equivalent expansion of women's roles in the early phase of motherhood, and as has already been pointed out, women did not feel that prime responsibility for infant care was a matter of choice or could be easily combined either with other occupations or other individuals. That the 'dominant' social role may have the luxury and power to change first has been emphasized by other researchers (McKee and Sherriffs 1959). As well as returning to historical evidence, studies like the present one need to be set in the context of much larger and more extensive work: families where the mothers of infants are working full-time; families where couples have shared equally or swapped roles (Russell 1979b); families where the male breadwinner is unemployed; families where men act as primary caregivers (see the chapters by O'Brien and Hipgrave) and families where childcare is shared amongst a number of adults. Only then can a comprehensive impression of men's family roles be gained and any social changes be properly detected and monitored.

Summary and conclusion

This chapter has shown, through the use of the case-study approach, that social surveys have suffered some repeated limitations in their approach to fathers' participation. The weaknesses identified relate to the small range of childcare tasks isolated for study; the tendency to aggregate tasks; the failure to take account of the period of infancy under review; the frequent reliance on maternal reports and concealment of the processes of parental negotiation; the tendency to neglect the problematic relationship between reported behaviour and values; and lastly, the imputation of social change as revealed through reported practices alone. Some ways of tackling and improving on these drawbacks have been thrown up by the case-study findings and these include: widening the range of tasks to take account of 'indirect' and non-physical caretaking especially with regard to decision-making; looking at fluctuations within the performance of given tasks; assessing the impact of the time-specificity of the study and the value of a longitudinal approach, and especially exploring the effects of occupational and employment status on the organization of infant care; uncovering how each partner feels about the division of labour and how these patterns were established and are maintained – taking consideration of marital power relationships; and finally, directly asking men about their beliefs about marriage, parenthood, and sex roles and relating this to their behaviour.

This is a large programme and begs the question of whether any single approach can encompass this task. The answer is clearly no, and a combination of social surveys, ethnographies, and observational work all have their part to play. What is needed is for each of these methods to enter into occasional discourse and selfcriticism and to learn from one another, especially when a new field of inquiry is being opened up. It is felt that this paper moves in some way towards this end. That this critical endeavour may prove fruitful is given full support in the comments of Peter Townsend, author of one of the most far-reaching social surveys of this century. He asserts: 'The defects of any research method have to be spelt out so that modifications can be introduced into research and its results properly evaluated' (Townsend 1979:114).

Notes

1 This study was carried out during 1976–77 and emerged from a larger social survey on mothers' experiences. It was kindly supported by the Health Education Council to whom thanks are due. Only first-time parents were interviewed: once during pregnancy, again when the baby was (on average) eleven weeks, and again at twelve months. Seven fathers held manual occupations, while five worked in white-collar or professional occupations. One was a student. Their ages ranged from nineteen to thirty-one. Names of the respondents are disguised in the text.

2 Where the word 'traditional' is used it refers to conditions existing within modern family structures. It does not refer back to pre-industrial family structures.

9 Young fathers: Attitudes to marriage and family life

MADELEINE SIMMS
AND CHRISTOPHER SMITH

In recent years much anxiety has been expressed in the medical and social work literature, both in Britain and in the United States, about the medical, social, and personal problems confronting teenage mothers.[1] An editorial in the *British Medical Journal* (1975) typically observed that teenage pregnancy was now a 'world-wide problem' and stressed the social problems and social dislocation of which teenage pregnancy was both a symptom and a cause: 'The same sorry tale of broken homes, breakdown of family life, and poor education, as well as failure of education about contraceptives to reach those most in need of it'. We therefore decided to investigate a national sample of teenage mothers and to ask them, among other things, how they managed with their babies, how much support they received from their partners, whether married to them or not, and how they viewed their situation in retrospect. We hoped that the answers to these questions might provide some guide to social policy in this area. We decided also to put similar questions to the partners of these teenage mothers in order to obtain their views about the pleasures and problems of fatherhood and of life with a teenage mother and baby. We thought this worth attempting because it is obviously preferable to ask people questions directly, rather than to rely on interpreting answers about their activities and reactions, given by others, as is so often done in the case of fathers. Further, much less direct attention has been given to young fathers in the past than to young mothers. This is partly due to the 'mother centred bias in our culture' which, as Parke, Power, and Fisher (1980) observe is 'particularly acute for adolescent parents', and partly for severely practical and financial reasons. Young fathers are less likely than young mothers to be at home during the day. They are more mobile, so that the costs of tracing and interviewing them tend to be higher. One per cent of our sample turned out to be in prison. Gaining contact with these men was by no means straightforward. There are potentially awkward problems about seeking to interview unmarried fathers who might wish to deny paternity, or keep it secret. Working-class men, as most of the men in our sample were, are not much given to discussing their attitudes and feelings, least of all with passing visitors. So, interviewing young working-class fathers is beset by all kinds of difficulties, which is why, given a choice, as the literature on young parents amply demonstrates, a captive audience of housebound young mothers looking after new babies, or small groups of articulate middle-class men, will always constitute an easier, cheaper, more accessible sample for time- and cost-conscious social scientists.

Despite these considerations, having decided that it was worth attempting to interview a national sample of fathers, we had to be clear in our minds what we could and could not hope to accomplish by the large-scale survey method. Surveys are much better at eliciting what fathers (and other people) do, rather than what they feel deep down, and they more accurately gauge current thoughts and attitudes than chart the passage of changing responses, though repeating surveys with the same sample as we intend to do can go some way towards achieving this.

We also take the view that in social research it is more worthwhile to describe reported behaviour than to speculate about underlying beliefs that do not express themselves in action. We recognized of course, as nearly all social survey scientists do, that the quantitative approach has severe limitations when dealing with the subleties and complexities of life. It can never aspire to be the 'single index' of experience but is an important one without which it is not possible to determine whether small-scale intensive interviews have any significance beyond the particular group of perhaps very atypical persons selected. Additionally, we believe that observed changes in domestic behaviour are usually, though not invariably, the consequences of changes in attitudes and values as well as in economic circumstances. People who disagree must be continuously astonished at the vagaries and arbitrariness of human behaviour.

This study then aims to take a snapshot of entry into family life from the father's angle of vision. This is an area where folklore abounds, often leading to expectations that young men in this situation will give little support to their partners and show little interest in their children, perhaps because they are scarcely more than children themselves. One young father in our sample summed up the latter view when he re-marked: 'Weren t long ago we were children ourselves really. Now we've got one of our own'. In this chapter we present some of our initial findings about the (mostly young) fathers' attitudes to marriage and family life at the time when the babies were aged up to seven months and when the experience of fatherhood was still something of a novelty for the majority of the men. In future publications we intend to present comparable material for the mothers.

Methods and characteristics of the sample

This study was based on a probability sample of 623 births to women aged under twenty, occurring in twenty-six areas of England and Wales during July 1979. Eighty-six per cent of the mothers of these babies were interviewed when the babies were one and a half to four months old. During these interviews the women were asked for permission to interview the father of their baby and 84 per cent of the women agreed and gave us the name and address of the father. We managed to interview 83 per cent of these men between October 1979 and January 1980. A structured questionnaire was used and the interviews lasted up to one and three-quarter hours. So, of the 623 men who were eligible for inclusion in the sample, 369 (59 per cent) were ultimately interviewed, a quite high proportion (73 per cent) of the married men and a low proportion (36 per cent) of the single men.[2]

Nearly all (88 per cent) of the men we interviewed were born in Britain. A fifth were teenagers and a further two-thirds were aged between twenty and twenty-five. Over half, 56 per cent, had had no further education or training since leaving school and 12 per cent were unemployed at the time of the interview. Most, 87 per cent, were classified as working-class.[3] Just over half had married after their partner became pregnant. Altogether, four-fifths were married. Two-thirds lived in households that consisted of the man, his partner, and his children. Eighteen per cent had children other than the survey baby; a quarter of these men reported that not all their children had the same mother.

To what extent though is this sample a representative one? Comparison with Office of Population Censuses and Surveys data about births to women aged under twenty (OPCS 1980) and with data collected from the birth certificates of the babies, and during interviews with the partners suggests that single men, men aged under nineteen or over twenty-three, men in unskilled jobs, and men born in the West Indies, are under-represented in our sample. There was also some indication that the men we failed to reach had less stable relationships with their partner, were less pleased about becoming a father, and were less involved in baby care than the men we managed to interview. It is likely, therefore, that the data we present in this chapter give a more favourable view of young fatherhood than is really justified.

Becoming a father: intentions and attitudes

One-fifth of the men were attempting to use birth control around the time their partner became pregnant. What were the other four-fifths up to? Were they simply ignorant, were they careless or irresponsible, or did they really intend to have a child at that time?

In fact, almost half these men who were not using birth control said this was because both they and their partner wanted a child, and in a few other instances at least one or other partner did so. Often the reason for wanting a baby at that time seemed to be connected with seeing pregnancy as a pathway to marriage.

'She wanted to get pregnant so we could get married.'

'She wanted a baby, and I wanted to settle down and get married.'

'We wanted to get married quickly. We knew her mum wouldn't let her, being just 16 . . .'

In about a quarter of cases a mixture of ignorance, indifference, apathy, and timidity seemed to be at work. The ignorance may not be surprising. Only half the men had ever had any sex education at school and only a third had ever heard birth control discussed in lessons at school.

'I thought I'd get away with it and not get her pregnant.'

'We thought it would never happen.'

'We were a bit timid to go and ask anyone for help.'

The indifference may be more difficult to account for:

'I just didn't care. If she got caught, that was it. I didn't mind getting married.'

'She left home and left her pills behind so we didn't think about it.'

'It didn't bother us if she did, put it that way.'

An eighth had problems with or dislike of birth control devices:

'It wouldn't be the same if I was wearing something.'

'We took precautions at first but got so fed up.'

'She should take the pill because I don't like using the other thing.'

Others gave a variety of reasons for failure to use birth control, among which 'it just happened' was a common response.

It seems that a large number of these men were prepared to contemplate having a baby at that time even if not always with great enthusiasm. They seemed prepared to accept fatherhood even when they did not positively desire it. This may account for the fact that whereas 80 per cent had not used contraception around the time their partner became pregnant, 80 per cent had adopted a method after the baby had arrived; 66 per cent of those using birth control were relying on the pill and 29 per cent on the sheath. This use of effective contraception had developed despite the fact that only 12 per cent of these men had asked or been asked by a professional since the baby's birth whether they would like any further information about the subject. But, having had one baby, most now seemed determined not to have another in a hurry. In fact, 12 per cent did not want any more children, and 62 per cent of those who did, wanted to wait two years or more for their next child.

Consistent with the picture drawn above, 75 per cent of men said they were pleased when they first realized their partner was pregnant and another 20 per cent confessed to mixed feelings. Only 5 per cent were definitely upset by the news. As might be expected, more of the married men, 90 per cent, than of the single men, 66 per cent, were pleased about the pregnancy.

Few, 5 per cent, of the men thought their partner ought to have an abortion and even fewer, 4 per cent, went as far as suggesting this to her, though this was sometimes because it did not occur to them in time. 'We didn't want the child and our parents didn't want it and we tried to forget it. . . . However, it was too late when we thought of it (abortion).' The failure to suggest abortion as a solution to their 'problems' is not explained by the men's views on abortion. Half thought that in principle any woman who wanted an abortion should be able to obtain one. Only 10 per cent disagreed with this. The remaining 40 per cent thought abortion ought to be available where there were acceptable grounds for this. What these were, varied from narrow medical indications to the widest social indications: 'If she is too young, or has no husband, or cannot support herself'. One man who gave a qualified reply nonetheless went on to explain: 'Only if the woman wants it. I don't think the man should have any say. It's the woman who's got to go through having the baby'. Certainly, the majority of men could be described as having very liberal views on this subject.

Life together

As previously mentioned, four-fifths of the men in our sample were married. Only four of these men said their marriage was unhappy and only eight more had mixed feelings about it. This is a remarkably high index of satisfaction with matrimony and it will be interesting to see whether this has changed at the follow-up stage a year later. 'We just seem to do everything together. It's great.' 'We're ideally suited.' Though there were a few clouds, even among those who claimed to be happy: 'Somehow we get depressed with each other and the baby . . . I get depressed with my job. It's so boring doing the same thing all the time'. One man who admitted to being unhappy observed: 'I think it's the kids that's not making it very happy . . . We're always having arguments about not having enough money, what debt we're in'. And another: 'I don't like married life. I'm tied down with it 'cos we have the kids'.

Half of the married men in our sample had married while their partner was pregnant with the survey baby. Nearly three-fifths of these men said the pregnancy was the main reason for getting married at that time. However, all but three also said they would have got married to their wife anyway at some time in the future.

Nearly all the men who remained single had talked about the question of marriage at some time with their partners. Reactions varied:

'I did when I found out she was pregnant, but she turned me down and said to wait until the baby was born. I respect her for that and as it's turned out she was right.'

'We'd rather wait first to see if we can live together and then maybe get married.'

Just over two-fifths had also discussed the question of marriage with their parents or others. Most thought they would get married to their partners before long. Only 14 per cent said definitely not, the reasons varying from not being in love, being happy as they were, having no money or jobs, to the girl having gone off with someone else. Just one man was against the idea of marriage on principle.

A high proportion of young fathers, single as well as married, claimed to have helped their partner with domestic tasks the previous week. Shopping, cleaning, washing up, cooking, and household repairs were frequently mentioned. Fewer men, though, reported assisting with washing or ironing. Only some 5 per cent of men who were in a position to do so, said they had not helped with anything.

Father and baby

Almost all of the fathers said they felt responsible for the baby's welfare, in many cases simply because it was their baby: 'He's my son and I'm his father'. In a few cases their feeling of personal responsibility was linked to particular experiences of their own, both positive and negative:

'My parents have been good to me and I hope that I can teach him properly and not shirk his responsibilities.'

'I didn't want to leave her without a dad because I know how it feels. I was brought up just by my mum. I know how the baby feels and I didn't want that to happen.'

Several fathers said they had changed their life-style in order to take account of the baby's arrival: 'I got out to work to support her. I've cut down my drinking and I don't smoke so much'. Nearly half the men specifically mentioned their role as breadwinners as an aspect of their feelings of responsibility for their child.

Virtually all the fathers claimed to have helped look after the baby at least occasionally. The most frequently reported task seemed to be feeding the baby and the least frequently, bathing the baby. The proportions undertaking these tasks were 96 per cent and 48 per cent respectively. Few, only 5 per cent, thought their baby was rather difficult to look after.

They were asked what they enjoyed most about fatherhood. Watching the child grow and develop was often mentioned: 'more interesting than telly' as one father observed, as was the sheer fact of having a child: 'You've got something that belongs to you'. Another factor was having something that was admired by others, even strangers on the street. A few men, however, were indifferent: 'Nothing really . . . I don't think about it all that much at the moment, honestly'.

Noise and changing nappies were often mentioned as most disliked aspects of fatherhood. Other dislikes included the problems of taking a pram everywhere, and the dependence of baby-sitters which made it difficult to have much social life. Several also missed their previous freedom and 'Not being able to go drinking with the boys'.

Half the single men did not have their children living with them. Most, though, had seen their children at least once, and often several times, during the week prior to the interview. Of the ten men who had not seen their children during this period, four reported that it was at least a month since they had seen their children and one that he had never set eyes on his child. These five men seemed, to varying degrees, upset by this lack of contact. For example: 'I don't like it at all. She's my kid. I'd like to see her'. In all, 70 per cent of the men who were not living with their children declared that they would like to see them more often.

Work, money, and social life

Had becoming a father so young affected their job prospects? Only 17 per cent thought so, but not all these regarded the effect as entirely negative: 'Given me some motivation, something to work for'. More of this group, however, felt that the effects were adverse in terms of mobility and learning skills:

'Now you're stuck . . . I can't look round now, I've got to keep working.'

'I'm not very free to do the things I wanted to do.'

'I had intended to continue what I was doing but left a "good" technician's job to earn more money . . . there's so much scope in technician's work, and you never stop learning — whereas the work I'm doing now, there's nothing more to learn . . . now possibly might have trouble getting back into being a technician.'

Despite this, only 7 per cent were unhappy with their current jobs while another 16 per cent had mixed feelings.

The men's earnings were relatively low. Almost half earned less than £60 per week after deductions and only one-fifth earned more than £80 per week. Not surprisingly, more than half of all men said money was a problem for them, in some cases acutely so: 'I'm always short of grub and that'; 'I owe money to people'. About one sixth of all men thought they were actually worse off than their contemporaries: 'We must be the worst dressed couple around'. This was often associated with the expenses of having a baby: 'A lot of people my age aren't married, haven't got a family, so just themselves to support'. On the other hand, just over a fifth of men thought they were better off than their contemporaries, many of whom were unemployed or living on very low wages.

Turning to financial assistance, three-fifths of the unmarried men claimed to give their partners money regularly, and a few more gave money intermittently. Of the men who gave regularly, half gave less than £10 per week. One man explained why he did not give regular financial assistance: 'I'm putting my money away for when we get married and I do buy clothes for the baby. She gets money from the Social so I don't need to give her any'.

Money problems obviously affected social life. Most fathers went out less often in the evenings than before the baby arrived. Fifteen per cent never went out at all, 20 per cent went out once a week or less. Three-quarters of those who now went out less often than before were content to accept the situation, finding their domestic preoccupations and hobbies an agreeable substitute for their previous social life, much of which took place in pubs:

'Doesn't bother me. Whereas before the wife would go out numerous times, now we've got an activity in the baby and an interest at night when we're all at home.'

'Not bothered. When we did go out, it was just sitting in the same pub with the same people. We don't miss it that much.'

'I prefer it 'cos I like home life. It's better than boozing all the time.'

'I don't mind 'cos I have a lot of home hobbies now and my time is taken up by them.'

It seems that in the past many young men often went out simply because they had little privacy at home in which to conduct their social life. This is not surprising since two-thirds had three or more siblings. So their previous social life was often not greatly regretted. But this was not universally true. One-sixth of men who went out less often did have complaints:

'It affects me 'cos if I want to go out I have to suffer and stay in, or have an argument with the wife when I get home.'

'I feel bad about it. If you are at work all day you want to get out in the evening.'

Some reflections

Looking back over their experience of fatherhood, nearly 60 per cent thought things had worked out better than they had expected when they found out their partner was pregnant. Only 8 per cent thought things had gone worse than expected. The reasons given for this deterioration were what they regarded as external factors: interfering social workers, tiresome in-laws, the appearance of another woman on the scene, or adverse economic factors. 'With me not being in work our marriage is breaking up. She says she's going to leave me soon if I don't get a job, and get her mother to look after the baby and go out to work herself.' Where things had gone well, it was because the man now earned more money than he had expected to, the couple had managed to obtain a house more quickly than anticipated, the relationship with parents and in-laws had improved, the couple had got on together much better than expected, and problems generally had proved less intractable than at first feared: 'I thought there'd be more things to it — having the baby would make things complicated — but it doesn't'.

Nearly three-fifths of the men thought they had changed since becoming a father, and in virtually all cases for the better. They felt they were now no longer simply youths out for a good time, but mature and responsible citizens:

'I didn't use to give a damn about anything – but now I have to.'

'It made me older.'

'Quietened down, less of a hooligan.'

'Don't drink as much. Take pride in myself . . . Have to keep hold of my money these days 'cos I need to look after my wife and kid.'

'I haven't got a police record or anything. I'm glad I got married early. It's made me settle down.'

Similarly, nearly two-thirds of the men thought their partner had changed since becoming a mother. Becoming more mature was again a common observation:

'She's become more of a woman. She's got responsibility which she didn't have before, like having a baby to look after. And she's got to watch where the money goes, work out the shopping, pay the bills, which she didn't have to do before. She's become more mature and responsible, having to do the housework, things like that.'

However, not all the changes were approved of. Some women were felt to be more tired, more preoccupied, more moody, more fraught, and less good tempered, another aspect perhaps of the impact of their new responsibilities:

'More possessive . . . she likes me stopping in with the baby. More niggly over small things. She makes an issue of things that don't really matter. Very moody. I think she feels tied down as well.'

'She used to be really easy going but now can lose her temper at the slightest things.'

All but 13 per cent of men thought life was going well for them, although half the men said they wished to change some parts of it. Another 7 per cent said they wished to change many parts of life. What this often meant was better housing, more pay, a more agreeable job, and more social life. Some regretted that they had not saved more money before the arrival of the baby and thus got off to a better and more comfortable start to their married life.

Discussion

Eight times more fathers in our sample were teenagers than might have been expected from a sample of births to mothers of all ages, and more than three times as many were in the next youngest age group, twenty to twenty-four years (OPCS 1980). In addition to being very young, as we have seen, the members of our sample were mostly working-class, with relatively low earnings and quite high levels of unemployment. The majority who were married had married women already pregnant, so one might suppose there had been some pressure on them to get married quickly. Despite all these potentially adverse factors, the men expressed a high degree of satisfaction with marriage. Only 1 per cent said they thought their marriage was not happy. There are of course dangers in accepting people's statements on this subject at their face value. Nobody who has married only recently likes to admit that things are not going well or that they may have made a mistake. There is a natural tendency to gloss over any problems, so one has to look around for corroborative evidence of marital harmony. Nearly all the men said they helped their wives with at least some domestic tasks. Few seemed to regret their previous, more active, social life. Pursuing hobbies at home, helping around the house, and helping with the baby seemed in most cases to compensate amply for their previous freedom to drink with their friends in local pubs. In so far as they thought their wives had changed since marriage, these changes were perceived as being mostly for the better. Achieving rapid maturity was highly regarded in a way it might not be in more middle-class circles, where preserving the freedom and anarchy of youth and adolescence for a longer period would be more highly valued.

In addition to being so pleased with marriage, they were also extremely pleased with fatherhood, which again, with a young and not very well-off group of men might be thought surprising. Only 5 per cent said they had been upset on originally learning of the pregnancy. Perhaps in the intervening year they had begun to forget how upset they really felt at the time, or perhaps they suppressed their feelings once the baby had actually arrived? Again, one looks for other evidence. Though most men approved of abortion in principle on very wide grounds, hardly any thought this was a relevant solution in their own case. Only a handful even suggested it to their partners as a possibility, and none had considered adoption. Four-fifths of the men stayed with their partners during some part of labour and many said they would have liked to stay longer had circumstances permitted. Nearly all claimed to help look after the baby at least occasionally, and nearly all said they felt personally responsible for the baby's welfare.

So, supposing that these young men are really as pleased with marriage and fatherhood as they claim to be, what might be the explanation for their perhaps unexpected degree of satisfaction?

One explanation might be family background. The men came from very large families. Two-thirds came from families of four or more children and one-fifth had six or more brothers and sisters. Nearly one-third of their own mothers had been teenage mothers themselves. Ten per cent of the grandmothers were still in their thirties at the time of the interview. This must surely have affected the men's expectations. Their parents had married young and had a lot of children. So in getting married young themselves and having a child right away, they were behaving quite conventionally in relation to their own background. The fact that they did not intend to repeat this large family pattern lay in the future. Most of the men intended to have only two or three children themselves. Meanwhile, the marriage enabled them to get away from their crowded homes. Much of their social life, as we have seen, took place in pubs before, less from choice than from lack of space and privacy at home. Now two-thirds had a place of their own. This must surely have contributed a good deal to the satisfaction they voiced with their present way of life.

In addition to getting away from home, another more positive factor might have been at work. Can it be that the men in our sample have chosen marriage, fatherhood, and domestic life because they genuinely felt ready for it? Those who strongly did not, may have opted out of this situation at an earlier stage by recourse to birth control and abortion — a tribute to the improvement in the family planning and abortion services during the past decade. Hence the satisfaction expressed. This then is not the traditional captive audience of young men frogmarched into matrimony as a result of accidental pregnancy. Indeed, rather the other way round. Some, as we have seen, achieved marriage through pregnancy. If this is a realistic interpretation of these findings, then it suggests that there may at last be light at the end of the tunnel, and that we are well on the way to achieving the Mecca of the family planners, expressed in their slogan 'Every Child a Wanted Child' though that might be putting it a little strongly. Perhaps 'Every Child an Accepted or Tolerated Child' might be a more accurate if somewhat less exhilarating slogan.

Forty per cent of the men said they wanted a baby. In answer to another similar question, 52 per cent said they intended their partner to become pregnant then. One may conclude therefore that around half the men had a positive attitude to having a child at that time. At one level this is very welcome news; but at the same time, their immaturity and their economic prospects both might suggest that it would have been wise to wait. This raises complex questions about the role of social policy in discouraging people from doing potentially damaging things they may feel impelled to do. In relation to smoking, drinking, and driving, many people would now accept that social policy does have a role to play, but with very young parenthood there is less consensus, and the issues seem less clear-cut to some people.

Twenty per cent of men, as we have seen, said they were using birth control around the time their partner became pregnant. Most relied on the pill, followed by the sheath. Many of them, however, admitted they did not use their chosen method consistently, nor always correctly, and some doubted whether the method itself was very reliable. In addition to the men who were using a method, albeit inefficiently, there was another group of just over 10 per cent of the sample who had used a method in the past but had had problems with it and had temporarily abandoned birth control, or were between methods when the pregnancy occurred.

These two groups most surely constitute the natural target for the next phase of family planning endeavour. Here are a group of young men whose motivation is established even though their current practice is weak. What is the most effective way of bringing birth-control services to young working-class men who are aware of their need for birth control without having any very clear idea of what to do about it? They are probably healthy enough at that age and do not see much of their general practitioners, most of whom anyway do not readily accept the role of distributors of male methods of contraception. Cossey (1979) notes that there is evidence from Holland, Sweden, and elsewhere, that brand advertising of male methods of contraception on television, commercial radio, in the cinema, and in the press may have an important role to play in contraceptive education. The Independent Broadcasting Authority's continued refusal to permit such advertising on television (while allowing advertising for beer despite mounting evidence of rising alcoholism in the community) is particularly damaging to the interests of this group and the health and welfare of their female partners.

The general picture that emerges from this survey is that these fathers indicate a high degree of satisfaction with their relationship with their partners, domestic life, and fatherhood. It may be that the delightful novelty of their situation was still uppermost in their minds at the time of interview. The follow-up survey one year later will begin to show whether this happy state of affairs has been maintained over a longer period in face of a more mobile and demanding child, possible further additions to the family, growing national unemployment, and the failure therefore of at least some of the fathers to improve their standard of living in accordance with earlier ambitions and expectations. One can, however, conclude that in the initial phase at least, the attitudes of most of the current generation of young married men to family life are very positive.

Notes

1   We are grateful to Ann Cartwright for encouragement and advice, to Dr Val Beral, members of the Advisory Committee, and our colleagues at the Institute for Social Studies in Medical Care, for their ideas and comments, to Irene Browne for much secretarial help, and to the young fathers who gave their time so generously. We thank the Office of Population Censuses and Surveys for undertaking the interviewing, and the Department of Health and Social Security for supporting the study on which this chapter is based.
2   Attention has only been drawn to differences which statistical tests suggest are unlikely to occur by chance more than five times in 100.
3   The index of social class was the father's occupation, classified according to the six social class groups distinguished in the Registrar General's Classification of Occupations, 1970.

10 The observation of father-infant relationships: An 'attachment' to outmoded concepts

CHARLIE LEWIS

It may seem ironical that observational studies of father-infant inter-actions now comprise one of the largest areas of research into father-hood.[1] For, despite much evidence to the contrary (for example Newson and Newson 1965; Schaffer and Emerson 1964), developmental psychologists have long accepted Freud's stress upon the paramount importance of the symbiotic relationship between a mother and her infant. Attachment theory, which expresses the views of both psycho-analysts (Bowlby 1969) and learning theorists (Maccoby and Masters 1970), provides the clearest statement for the belief that early experi-ence is vital in the development of the individual and that the 'primary attachment figure', or mother, stimulates this growth. Nevertheless it is under the auspices of attachment theory that research on father-infant interaction has developed within the last ten years.

In this chapter I will outline three areas of father-infant research in their historical perspective. The first two areas, the study of new-born babies and the 'strange situation' experiment, represent the first phase of father-infant studies and are the direct product of attachment theory, in that they were originally developed to measure the nature and strength of the mother-infant 'bond'. These are by no means as important in theoretical terms as the third area of work, that of fathers, mothers, and their infants interacting 'normally' at home, but I hope to show that all three share a common framework still very much linked to traditional assumptions about the implications of infant development and the need for this to be stimulated by caregivers in the medium of close dependent relationships.

So dramatically has the research focus altered that the editor of a recent collection of papers on father-infant interaction (Pedersen 1980a) likened its authors to a group of cyclists who make a 'break' in a cycle race. Pedersen claims that this group is leaving the main 'pack' of developmental psychologists and is setting a new theoretical pace for the field to follow.

Having outlined the three areas of research into fathers and their babies, I will consider just how different the orientation of these new studies really is, and will suggest that in many respects the 'break' they have made is not significant enough, by itself, to alter the course of developmental theory.

The father's contact with his newborn child — a sensitive period?

Bowlby (1969) claimed that in humans, as in animals, there exists a 'sensitive period' during the first days after delivery when the formation of the 'bond' between mother and baby is facilitated. This assertion is thought to be supported by research in hospitals which normally keep newborns in nurseries. Klaus and Kennell (1976a, 1976b) found in these hospitals that the simple procedure of allowing mothers and babies to become acquainted with one another after the birth and for a few hours in the following days, seems to make women become more involved when observed with their offspring. Moreover their follow-up studies were taken to suggest that this feeling of closeness persisted and that, two years after delivery, high-contact mothers stimulated their children more. In turn, these children had significantly higher IQs than those not allowed additional contact in the early days.

Work on 'sensitive periods' in the mother-child relationship gave rise to research on how fathers greet their newborns. These studies reveal that fathers, like mothers, explore their newborns in stereotypical ways, touching the infant's arms and legs for a few minutes before examining the trunk (Parke, O'Leary, and West 1972; Parke and O'Leary 1976; Rödholm and Larson 1979). A few differences between the 'exploratory behaviours' of men and women have been noted, but as Rödholm and Larson suggest, these seem best explained by the fact that fathers are sitting or standing when meeting their baby, while mothers are usually lying down with the infant on or next to them.

Again, like mothers, fathers seem very preoccupied or 'engrossed' with their new babies. Greenberg and Morris (1974) interviewed thirty men shortly after the birth of their first children and found that each one felt compelled to touch his baby and felt that his own was perfect and prettier than the others in the nursery. These responses led to the assumption that certain events trigger adaptive or unconscious caring mechanisms in fathers, as attachment theory had suggested. For example, Greenberg and Morris (1974:526) felt that a man's presence at the birth 'seems to be significant in releasing engrossment'; a suggestion also made by Peterson and her colleagues (1975). In addition, Margaret Mead (quoted in Klaus and Kennell 1976a:44) noted that societies in which men are not involved in child-rearing never allow fathers to touch their newborns, supposedly in case they get 'hooked' on their offspring.

The belief that both parents are predisposed to care for their young infant once contact is made is intuitively appealing, but the evidence from studies of both mothers and fathers is hardly conclusive. Theoretical speculation about the effects of 'behaviours' during 'sensitive periods' originated from ethological observations of young animals. Yet the irreversibility of such behaviours in other species has been questioned (Bateson 1979). Also, findings that increased early contact between mother and baby gives rise to dramatic changes in their early relationship need not be explained in simple cause-effect terms. In fact when greater controls are imposed to prevent 'high contact' mothers from realizing that the treatment they are receiving is special, the early differences in maternal 'sensitivity' between them and 'normal contact' groups are greatly reduced (De Chateau and Wiberg 1977; Svedja, Campos, and Emde 1980). It seems possible that the long term effects of Klaus and Kennell's experiments resulted simply from factors associated with the mother's awareness of the interest of the experimental team. Similarly the anthropological evidence suggests that taboos and rituals excluding fathers at the time of birth probably reflect more the political power struggle between husband and wife than they do the potential effect of a man's exposure to a newborn baby (Paige and Paige 1973).

Studies comparing mothers' and fathers' interactions with their new babies suggest further that the simple biological or mechanistic account of events, proposed by attachment theorists, does not suffice. Although people handle newborns in a similar fashion, Parke and O'Leary (1976) found that the way parents stimulated the baby was partly determined by the infant's birth order and sex. First children tended to be clutched in mothers' and fathers' arms, perhaps for fear of dropping them! Parents also touched their same sex babies more than ones of the opposite sex but only in certain social settings. So, mothers and fathers do not demonstrably become 'engrossed' or 'attached' in a uniform manner. Parke's and O'Leary's findings suggest that an explanation for the behaviour of parents in the early days of the child's life should take into account the complexity of social influences.

Clearly the arrival of a baby does not occur in a cultural vacuum and any attempt to infer from evidence about the way parents handle their newborn child must take into account their perceptions of events leading up to the delivery and also of how one is expected to act in these circumstances.

The 'strange situation' experiment

The second procedure developed to measure mother-infant attachments but which came also to be used for father-infant studies is Ainsworth's 'Strange Situation' (Ainsworth and Wittig 1969). Whereas observers of men with their newborns were interested in the effects of contact upon the father's behaviour and attitudes, this experimental paradigm was designed to measure the attachments of infants towards their parents. In a simple procedure the baby or toddler, having been settled in a strange room with a few toys, is exposed to a sequence of events in which his mother or father leaves him alone or with a stranger for a few minutes. During these interludes observers measure the reactions of the child to the stranger and to his parent's departures from and entrances into the room. Despite evidence which suggests that children may be attached to a variety of people at one time (Schaffer and Emmerson 1964; Ainsworth 1967), Bowlby (1969:366–68) maintained that infants distinguish between one primary attachment figure, who acts as a haven in times of stress, and 'secondary figures' who serve mainly as play-mates. As a result, 'strange situation' experiments involving both mothers and fathers have been carried out to find whether infants do make this distinction, particularly by Kotelchuck and his associates (Kotelchuck 1972; Spelke and colleagues 1973; Ross and colleagues 1975).

Kotelchuck's experiments with 'traditional' American families (with only the husband working outside the home) revealed that infants came to show separation anxiety at the end of the first year. This anxiety reached a peak at eighteeen months. However, infants did not exhibit attachment behaviour exclusively to one particular parent. Overall, 55 per cent of infants from one to two years showed definite preference for their mother, 20 per cent sought either parent and 25 per cent preferred only their father (Kotelchuck 1972). Similarly, so long as at least one parent was present together with the stranger the departure of the other parent did not elicit separation anxiety (Spelke and colleagues 1973). The findings suggest that infants will seek either parent in times of stress.

Perhaps the most striking significance in the results of these 'strange situation' experiments is the variation in infants' responses. An easy explanation for this diversity would be that infants' reactions are deter-mined by the relative amount of contact they habitually have with their mothers and fathers. Indeed in cultures where fathers' participation is very low, children protest at their mother's departure at an earlier age (for example Ainsworth 1967; Lester and colleagues 1974), and infants in regular day care are less likely to choose their mother as the only haven in times of stress (Barahal 1977). Yet other findings are more equivocal. A father's involvement in family life appears not to determine his child's preference in the strange situation (Kotelchuck 1972). His participation seems only to raise the age at which the child becomes sensitive to parental departures or the arrival of a stranger (Spelke and colleagues 1973).

A close look at the 'strange situation' reveals complications and inconsistencies that make it difficult to deduce much about father–infant relationships from the experimental findings. Some studies, for example, have replicated Kotelchuck's results and have concluded that infants are equally attached to both parents (for example Willemsen and colleagues 1974; Feldman and Ingham 1975). Others, on the other hand, have found that mothers were sought after much more than fathers (Cohen and Campos 1974; Lamb 1976c). Such fundamental differences in the research findings have been attributed to the fact that many variations on the original experiment have been used (Ainsworth and colleagues 1978; Lamb 1978b; Parke 1969). These reviewers make mention of basic differences in, for example, the number of different episodes the child is put through, which varies from four (Lamb 1976c) to thirteen (Kotelchuck 1972). They claim, however, that the crucial factor is the degree of stress to which the child is exposed. The greater the stress the more likely that children will choose their mothers, for example after the episode when they are left completely alone with the stranger. Although there is evidence for this claim (Lamb 1976c), Kotelchuck's original experiment compared infants' behaviour towards each parent after having been left, with and without the stranger present, and found no difference in their reaction (Kotelchuck 1972).

A great deal of effort has gone into standardizing the procedures of the strange situation (Ainsworth and colleagues 1978), but such moves towards standardization must lead only to limited generalizations about an infant's 'adaptive response' in one setting. As soon as that setting is altered the infant's behaviour becomes less predictable. It has been found, for example, that children spend more time exploring if the toys in the room are a brighter colour, and exhibit more attachment behaviours on their second visit to the laboratory than on the first (Willemsen and colleagues 1974). An active, friendly stranger elicits much less anxiety than a passive one (Ross and Goldman 1977), and children tested in the familiar setting are influenced much less by the comings and goings of fathers, mothers, and strangers (Ross and colleagues 1975).

These variations suggest that the 'strange situation' tells us very little about the similarities and differences betwen mothers' and fathers' relationships with their young children. Additionally, the whole procedure is bizarre. For the sake of the experiment parents are given strict instructions not to initiate contact with their child, to sit quietly aside and suddenly to leave at a given signal. In some cases they are not even permitted to turn to the child and say 'bye-bye'. The results of such procedures can hardly help except in explaining an infant's behaviour in very odd circumstances.

The two research areas discussed so far reveal that mother–infant and father–infant 'attachments' during the first days of contact and in the 'strange situation' are, by and large, similar. Yet the problems generated in trying to relate both approaches to an understanding of father–infant relationships have led to a new vogue in the study of mothers, fathers, and their babies in the natural setting.

Fathers and infants observed at home: the findings

Recent observational studies of fathers and infants have acquired a number of new characteristics, most of which reflect changes throughout developmental psychology. There has been a gradual recognition that infants have as much of an 'effect' upon their caregiver as vice versa (Bell 1968; Lewis and Rosenblum 1974). Second, criticism of the artificiality of experiments like the 'strange situation' has grown, and psychologists have been persuaded to study parents and children in their natural context, taking into account more than just the child's attachment behaviours. Researchers have also taken advantage of new recording devices like 'event' and video recorders.

The new father–infant studies take place in people's homes, and families are usually asked to carry on 'normally' so that a representative sample of their activities and interactions can be investigated. As this approach does not, in theory, interrupt the daily routines of these families, these researchers believe that their methods are superior to the traditional fare of interviews, questionnaires, and experiments (Pedersen 1980b). They observe the baby and record the frequency and nature of each parent's involvements with him. As a result they compare mothers' and fathers' 'parenting behaviours' in relation to their infant's responses. Moreover, many of these studies measure family interaction patterns over a specified period of the family life-cycle, often attempting to correlate parental handling with aspects of the infant's later development.

Frequent mention is made that, as yet, these research programmes are few in number, they study children of varying ages and use methods that are difficult to compare with one another. Despite this initial caution there is a pervasive mood that underlies theoretical discussion of each of their findings. This optimism is enough to generate the belief that a 'scientific revolution' is starting and that the 'break' from the rest of developmental psychology has been made.

Many who use similar observational techniques, like Schaffer (1977a), have concluded that the necessary ingredients for normal development are stimulation, a sensitivity to the child's needs, affectionate bonds between children and their caregivers, and a relative amount of consistency between these caregivers. In contrast the members of the 'break' think otherwise:

> 'Our point of departure from Schaffer is to assert that there are significant experiences associated with the other adult in the nuclear family, the father, and that mothers and fathers are generally not interchangeable objects in relation to the baby.'
>
> (Pedersen and colleagues 1979: 46)

The reason for this belief comes from small strands of evidence in many but by no means all of these projects. Indeed the vast majority of 'behaviours' measured show no difference between parents. However, even at a very early age (Parke and Sawin 1980) there are a few differences between the ways in which each parent is seen to handle their baby. Over the first three months Parke and Sawin noticed what they called a shift in parental 'roles' in different contexts. In some circumstances parental behaviours 'converged' over the time period and, in the case of playing with and smiling at the infant, their styles, initially different, became similar. Other 'roles', such as wiping the infant's face and routine 'grooming', were 'reversed', with the father, initially doing less, coming to do more than his wife. Parke and Sawin concluded that parental 'roles' are distinguishable even when the baby is very young and that these roles change perhaps as a result of 'mutual modelling'.

As the child gets older, it is felt that the process of adopting some of the other parent's strategies continues (Clarke-Stewart 1978), but at the same time differential styles are also in evidence. As early as ninety-six days after birth parents interact with their babies in different ways, at least when being filmed (Yogman 1977). Mothers are characterized by the rhythmic nature of their communications with their babies, made up of short cycles of verbal 'games' with longer pauses. The nature of a father's play, on the other hand, consists of longer, more abrupt episodes, which continually alternate between verbal and physical stimulation. Indeed in Yogman's small sample fathers played 'tapping games', like walking their fingers up the infant's arms, whereas mothers did not. Yogman suggests that both these types of play foster different aspects of the infant's development, and his finding is complemented by studies of older children.

While carrying out their study in the homes of five-month-olds,

Pedersen and his co-workers (1979) noted that mothers differed from fathers in that they smiled and verbalized more. In this and other studies, even when fathers are at home, traditional sex-role patterns are in evidence and wives attend to caretaking tasks more than their husbands (Pedersen and colleagues 1980; Clarke-Stewart 1980). Fathers, on the other hand, are thought to adopt the role of the child's playmate, perhaps developing the skills seen in Yogman's 'tapping' game (Lamb 1977b; Clarke-Stewart 1978; 1980). Lamb argues that this role differentiation is evident around the end of the first year, with fathers specializing in 'rough and tumble' or physical play. After twelve months infants tend to be held more by their mothers for caretaking and to respond more to their fathers' play initiatives (Lamb 1977b). By the end of the second year this affiliative preference is clear in Lamb's observations (Lamb 1977d). Clarke-Stewart's findings, however, suggest that the father does not take over as a playmate until the child is at least two. Whatever the age at which the father adopts this role, it is generally agreed that the distinction between mothers as caregivers and fathers as playmates is important.

It is not only what parents do that has come to be regarded as influential. These observers have also carefully documented the effects of the presence of others upon parent-child interaction. Although Parke and O'Leary (1976) found that fathers tended to hold firstborn sons more when their wives were present than when they were not, it has commonly been found that each parent's interaction with the infant in a three-person group (a triad) occurs less than when parent and child are alone (in a dyad). Lamb (1978b) points out that the size of a group does not influence the type of stimulation the baby gets, it just reduces the amount of attention given by each parent.

Great stress is placed upon the fact that both parents and children act differently in these contexts (for example Lamb 1977c, 1977d; Brazelton and colleagues 1979; Pedersen and colleagues 1979). The evidence that infants are exposed both to the differential styles of their parents and to the differences between dyadic and triadic group interaction patterns, has given rise to the suggestion that the third member of this triad, the father, is *more* than just another 'object' in the child's social network. It is felt that he plays an important role in his infant's development. Lamb (1977a:79), for example, writes: 'There is a compelling, albeit correlational, case that early differential mother–infant and father–infant relationships play a critical role in the formation of social skills and the development of personality'. Indeed, it has been widely speculated that each parental style has an important impact upon two crucial aspects of the infant's growth, namely sex-role and cognitive development.

First, mothers and fathers have been observed to treat their infants differently according to their sex. Just as they perceive their newborn in sex stereotypical ways (Rubin, Provenzano, and Luna 1974), Parke and Sawin (1980) found that, in front of an observer, parents will show affection to their same-sex three-month-olds more readily than to opposite-sexed children. Lamb (1977d) similarly found that in the second year of life fathers more readily invite sons to play (as opposed to daughters) and in return their sons tend to be more exploratory. As a result, Lamb (1977a) suggests that fathers facilitate the development of the male sex-role, by teaching boys to play rough boys' games.

Other evidence supports Lamb's claim, but makes the picture more complicated. Clarke-Stewart, for example, found that a boy's developmental quotient was related not only to the amount of physical and intellectual stimulation he received from his father whilst playing at home, but also to the amount of physical contact and 'socio-physical' play he received from his mother. Meanwhile a girl's intellectual development was correlated with the verbal and intellectual stimulation of her mother and the social and verbal responsiveness of her father at play (Clarke-Stewart 1980). Although some further studies reveal no differences in the way mothers treat their girls and boys (Belsky 1980; Pedersen and colleagues 1980), there is a general feeling that fathers' and mothers' interactional styles harness different aspects of the infant's intellectual growth. Parke, for example, refers to 'the unique role of the father in fostering the infant's cognitive development' (Parke 1979: 575). Like others he suggests that little attention has been paid to this area of study where the father must have an impact. His assertion is supported by some direct and indirect evidence. When children's cognitive development, as measured by a novel task or a standardized test, is compared with the observations made of them playing with their parents, it has been found that the ones more intellectually advanced tend to have fathers who stimulate them (Belsky 1980) or play with them in a family group (Clarke-Stewart 1980). Similarly, it has been found that although fathers simplify their speech to their two-year-old children, they use more complex linguistic structures than their wives including imperatives, 'stock expressions' (like 'right-on') and rare terms, like 'aggravating' or 'brontosaurus' (Gleason 1975); Engle 1978; Vendell 1977). In response, there is some evidence to suggest that two-year-olds modify their speech with each parent, being more polite (Ervin-Tripp 1977:83) or using longer utterances (Rondal 1980) with their fathers. These findings have given rise to the suggestion that the father acts as a 'bridge' to the outside world (Gleason 1975), testing and extending his children's abilities while his wife accommodates to their needs.

The findings discussed in this section have suggested to many that mothers and fathers serve different yet complementary roles in the child's development. It is suggested (for example by Pedersen and colleagues 1979) that the father assists early on by enabling the child to become aware of people outside the tight symbiotic mother–infant link. He is seen to act in very much the same way as Bowlby's (1969) secondary attachment figure, even though the majority of these studies reveal that, at home, children demonstrate their 'attachments' in much the same way to both parents (for example Hegland 1977; Lamb 1977d; Clarke-Stewart 1978). The importance of the father is seen to emerge after the child is at least one and possibly much later. For example, Clarke-Stewart (1978; 1980) having correlated parents' 'input' with the child's intellectual performance at fifteen and thirty months, argued that mothers 'effect' development during this period, while fathers react to improvements in the child's performance and become involved as a result.

There is surprisingly little discussion as to the origins of the difference between mothers' and fathers' interactions with their babies. In fact it is usually assumed that these differences are somehow inherent. A study by Field (1978) has shown that 'primary caretaker' fathers (those looking after their babies full-time) interact with their four-month-olds in ways more similar to mothers than 'secondary caretaker' fathers (who go out to work). Her findings have inspired new research programmes, but still the underlying assumption behind parent–infant interaction styles is that men and women are constrained, perhaps even biologically, to treat their children differently: 'there are two biologically based and culturally supported interactive styles – a masculine style involving physical play and a feminine style involving caregiving and conversation' (Clarke-Stewart 1980:141). In the next section I will attempt to analyse the validity of this and other conclusions gleaned from parent–infant studies.

Father–infant interaction studies in perspective

The recent wave of research into father–infant interaction has led to the suggestion that there are differences between mothers and fathers in their handling of babies and that in consequence each parent has a special contribution to the child's development. I will suggest that this conclusion is not a necessary deduction from 'hard' evidence. Rather, there is compelling evidence to show that there are at least three theoretical weaknesses implicit in the way these researchers infer from their findings. First, they assume that these observations of people interacting are objective measurements of typical 'behaviour'. Second, it is argued that it is possible to infer a good deal about the nature and causes of family interaction styles from these observations. Finally, it is suggested that these observed behaviours 'influence' changes in the infant in a very direct way. I will criticize each of these assumptions in turn.

THE OBJECTIVITY OF OBSERVATIONAL METHODS

As many father–infant studies have been carried out by counting 'observed behaviours', it may seem timely to make some generalizations about the ways in which mothers and fathers interact with their children when an observer is present in their home. The nature of any conclusion must, however, be dependent upon both the reliability and the validity of the findings on which they are based.

If we consider the amount of agreement between studies we find that the evidence is not clear. Nearly every 'finding' can be contradicted by counter-evidence. This fact is frequently acknowledged, but either discrepancies in results are attributed to differences in the methods used by each project, or else a theoretical explanation is invoked post hoc to fit the data. Having found, for example, no significant sex differences in the ways that five-month-old boys and girls were handled by their parents, Pedersen (1980c) suggested, because significant differences had been reported in studies with older and younger infants, that parents distinguish between boys and girls only at earlier and later ages. There is also much evidence to indicate that parents and infants do not fit the stereotypes they have been given. For instance, fathers in some studies do not play more with their infants (Parke and Sawin 1980; Belsky 1980) nor does their language always contain more imperatives (Rondal 1980).

More important than the fact that research findings have been contradictory is the problem of just how valid behavioural observations are. Some comparison has been made between home observations and other methods of studying families (Parke, 1978a; Pedersen 1980b), but there is insufficient discussion about what happens when an observer enters into a household and starts either to take notes or to press the keyboard of an 'event recorder'.

This omission is rather surprising given the wealth of literature on methodology in social psychology and the fact that developmentalists have long been aware of the problems involved in inferring from observations (Blurton Jones 1972b; Cooper and colleagues 1974). Unlike other psychologists using observational methods, father–infant interaction researchers assume that the effects of their presence are minimal simply because they carry out their work in the 'natural setting' and they claim not to interrupt daily routines. This assumption may not be valid. In some of these studies, parents were asked to intervene in ways determined by the experimenters.

However, even in studies where parents are allowed or encouraged to 'go about their normal routines' it is highly unlikely that their behaviour is still 'typical'. Indeed there is evidence to show that an observer's presence dramatically alters parental behaviour. In a near laboratory experiment for example (Randall 1974, in press), it was arranged that mothers and their ten-month-olds playing freely together would be observed when Randall was sitting in the corner taking notes and also after he had been called out to an 'urgent telephone call' by a stooge. A comparison of mothers' activities in each condition ('observed' and 'unobserved') revealed that ten of the twenty-seven behaviours he was measuring changed significantly. Among these many differences, for example, was the finding that while being watched mothers showed a preference for cuddling their sons, but when the observer was called out they tended to cuddle their daughters more. This finding is particularly relevant as it suggests that we should exercise caution when attempting to infer, from observational studies in a particular context, that parents universally treat their boys and girls differently. Although most of the father–infant studies observed family routines for longer periods than did Randall, and the families were in their own homes, it seems implausible that the observer's presence was unimportant in determining the outcome. Sue Golden (1975) reported that even living with families continuously for a whole week was not enough to reduce 'observer effects' completely.

Being watched may influence the behaviour of the 'observed' in a number of ways. For example, parents' perceptions of what the psychologist expects are likely to play an important part in the way they present themselves. Yet there is little discussion in this and other research literature about the rationale given to parents by the investigators before they move into a family's front room for a couple of hours every few weeks or months. In a very recent research project into the development of communication and play between mothers and their children, Gregory (in preparation) analysed the effect of the instructions she gave to mothers before an observational play session. She found, perhaps not surprisingly, that if told that the observer was interested in the way children learn to play, mothers, without being asked, attempted to engage their child in play. When told instead that the observer was interested in the development of language, she found that mothers began to elicit speech rather than play.

Clearly, the total social setting is a complicated one right from the outset. In order to gain any valid insight into the meaning of the 'behaviours' of participators in the circumstances generated by the intrusion of a stranger/observer into a household, we need to do more than note what goes on and make inferences simply from counting frequencies of selected activities. The effects of an observation may interact with many other circumstances. For example, Clarke-Stewart (1978) found that mothers were observed to interact less with their baby when the father was at home. The possible reasons for this finding are numerous. It might be that mothers 'bow out' to give father a chance to play with the baby when he comes home from work, in conformity with an assumed cultural expectation. Alternatively the result may have arisen from the fact that the mothers knew they were going to be watched playing with their children on another occasion when their husbands were not at home. Additionally, it may well have been communicated by implication that the psychologist was specifically interested in recording father–infant behaviours.

If it is important to assess how parents construe the nature of an observer's presence at any one time, it becomes even more necessary when we try to understand how interactions change over time. Parents' roles may indeed be altering, but it is also likely that their feelings about the observer's presence and their attitude towards the nature of the investigation will change with time.

The validity of this observational methodology is again called into question when the measurement techniques are critically reviewed. As Pedersen (1980b) admits, each study has few subjects but many 'variables'. So many measurements are taken and statistical tests applied, that the probability of obtaining chance 'findings' is always high; a point that has been made by Lamb (1978b) in considering Clarke-Stewart's (1978) findings.

GENERALIZING FROM OBSERVATIONS

Even if observers can integrate themselves into a household to obtain a representative sample of 'behaviours' at a given time, further problems arise. There is a tendency to suggest that parents' and infants' interactional patterns remain constant through time, that 'behaviours' have given or fixed meanings in every setting and that observations can illuminate the nature of parents' 'roles' (Parke and Sawin 1980). This leap from the specific to the general is dangerous at the outset because researchers observe families at specific times of day, and usually in the early evening. Toddlers' affiliative preferences for fathers at this time could well reflect the fact that they have not seen them all day (Hegland 1977). They may become just as excited playing with their mothers after a midday rest.

Generalization from these research findings is complicated by further issues. The small samples used in most studies, being white and middle-class and also fitting traditional family patterns, are not representative of all parents and children. Discussion, as I mentioned earlier, focuses upon the few differences between parents that prove to be statistically significant regardless of the real magnitude of the differences demonstrated and the overwhelming majority of similarities between parents. Little mention has been made until recently of the common finding (for example Rendina and Dickerscheid 1976), that irrespective of their sex, parents interact with their children in a variety of ways. The variations between possibly 'good' fathering styles are many and the suggestions that there are 'inherent' or 'biological' constraints on such behaviours seem highly dubious.

THE 'EFFECTS' OF PARENT–INFANT INTERACTIONAL STYLES

Home-based father–infant studies do more than make the dubious assumption that observed behaviours are representative of typical or fixed interaction patterns. In keeping with the traditional beliefs underlying the research into sensitive periods and attachments in the 'strange situation' discussed earlier, these studies have a tendency simply to accept that parents somehow induce development into their infants (for example Lamb 1978a:39). For instance many hold that correlations over time reflect causal and measurable influences which parents have upon their infant's development. Leaving aside the methodological problems overlooked in these studies, such cause–effect explanations appear simplistic on theoretical grounds. For a start they rely on the notion that infants are malleable and have to be 'socialized'. This view overlooks the large body of work that shows that from an early age babies are 'competent' (Stone and colleagues 1974); not only do they influence their caregivers, but their relationships with their parents are dynamic and reciprocal affairs (for example, Schaffer 1977b). Theoretical writings have come increasingly to suggest that early experience does not necessarily determine later development (for example Clarke and Clarke 1976, 1979). Such a conclusion has been reached partly because growing criticism has transformed the attachment concept from a specific biological theory, stressing the key role of the mother (Bowlby 1958), into a set of general metatheoretical propositions which are difficult, if not impossible, to test (Ainsworth and colleagues 1978:4). Without a concrete theoretical foundation, assertions about the effects of people interacting with others seem very problematic.

Conclusion

The observational studies reviewed in this chapter represent a 'break' from other areas of research in developmental psychology, if only because they do more than pay lip service to the father's role in family life. Like other researchers they have discovered the need to carry out their work in a setting that is as natural as possible. Yet, despite the large body of empirical literature that has accumulated, these particular studies seem to reveal surprisingly little about the nature of the relationship between a father and his young children, because they assume that theoretical conclusions about relationships can be inferred simply by comparing the frequencies of parents' and infants' 'behaviours' during short observation periods.

The little we can learn from these studies suggests that father–infant and mother–infant interaction patterns share more similarities than differences. Whether or not these differences signify anything about the relationships between members of a family cannot be inferred from observations alone, as many researchers in the field now realize: 'Unless the investigator attempts to see the world through the research participant's eyes, there is a great temptation to impose one's own constructions upon research findings' (Pedersen 1980c:161). In fact, although still methodologically committed to 'behavioural observations', many of these researchers have recently broadened their theoretical writings to incorporate the findings of social psychological and sociological studies of people's family roles and relationships (for example Lamb and Bronson 1978; Lewis and Feiring 1979; Parke 1979; Pedersen 1980b).

Each participant construes the significant events and daily routines that make up family life in a complexity of ways, as McKee (this volume) and many others show. Slight modification of behavioural methods, like the use of limited questionnaires to accompany observation data (Parke 1978b) and statistical methods measuring the sequences of behavioural interchanges (Parke and colleagues 1979), cannot by themselves explain the nature or development of people's perceptions and actions during the course of family interactions. As Pedersen (1980c) claims only a combination of approaches, whose findings ultimately are comprehensible to each participant, can begin to understand the reasons why families exist and change as they do. Cooper and his colleagues (1974:7) argue 'Direct observation may be a useful tool if it is appropriate to the area being explored (dare we say hypothesis being tested), but it is not an end in itself'.

Father–infant observation studies, particularly the recent wave of research based in people's homes, have warranted discussion in this chapter for two reasons. First, such a large and expanding body of re-search, whatever its pitfalls, deserves serious consideration because it represents a serious move toward understanding both fathers and their infants. Second, and more importantly, the shortcomings of the pro-cedure of simply observing people is leading these psychologists, like others before them, to a real 'break' away from behavioural methods towards an interdisciplinary approach for studying families.

Notes

1   I would like to acknowledge the help of John Newson, Joy Raynor, Beryl West, and Mary Dawson.

PART THREE

Fathers and some alternative family patterns

11 Lone fatherhood: A problematic status

TONY HIPGRAVE

This chapter will attempt to define the personal and cultural factors that commonly affect the position of lone fathers — men who, whether by accident or design, have become the sole care-takers of their children (though the term 'lone father' has been used by some authors to include men with a regular cohabitee (Ferri 1973, 1976) or even non-custodial fathers (Gatley and Koulack 1979)).

This will be done by outlining the statistics and research literature on the subject, and by amplifying identified potential problems for lone fathers. The primary focus will be on the father rather than his children, though it should not be forgotten that the influence of one on the other is mutual and inextricable. What this chapter seeks to demonstrate is that any stance that regards motherless families as inherently problematic and doomed to personal distress and psychological disturbance is too simplistic and that such problems as may exist in an individual family need to be analysed in terms of the particularistic interaction of personal and cultural elements.

Personal, interpersonal, and cultural factors

The effect on a particular family of losing a mother will reflect a mixture of *personal* and *cultural* dynamics. The *personal dynamic* includes such factors as, for example, a history of significant relationships, experience of parenting, and attributions of motivation or responsibility, and in essence applies equally to men and women. The *cultural dynamic* consists largely of an amalgam of attitudes and structures that push men towards the role of economic provider and women towards that of nurturer (see for example Fasteau 1974).

Each motherless family will present a particularistic interaction between these two basic dynamics. At the same time there are complex links between the cultural and personal aspects of lone fatherhood. Cognitive and experiential factors will determine the extent to which cultural expectations are incorporated on a personal plane by individual fathers, and cultural norms can only be maintained whilst certain personal styles and decisions remain prevalent. Furthermore, cultural expectations are manifested in structural forms, notably legal and welfare systems (and differentially by the individuals who work within these systems), as well as through other less formal social representations.

In addition, much research and a number of lay assumptions rest on the importance of particular dyads, notably the mother–child relationship. Families do not happen to work in conveniently dyadic ways. A language of dyads can often serve to distort the psychological and sociological realities of an environment within which each individual is influencing, and being influenced by, those around him. Families, of whatever type, are units in a constant state of negotiation, internally and externally, both as individuals and as a collective entity. The tendency to reduce this ecological complexity to linear models based on particular dyads needs to be readily recognized and treated with appropriate caution.

Lone fatherhood: research and statistical evidence

According to the Office of Population Censuses and Surveys there were an estimated 825,000 single-parent families caring for 1,250,000 children in Great Britain in 1978. Of these, 100,000 families with 180,000 children were headed by men (Hansard 1980a). Assuming a growth rate of 6 per cent per annum, as was the case between 1971 and 1976 (Leete 1978) at least 115,000 families and 200,000 children may, at the time of writing (1980) fall within the scope of this chapter.

In Great Britain in 1980 one family in eight with children is a single-parent family, and in some metropolitan areas the ratio is as great as one in four (*One Parent Times* 1980). In the USA, with its slightly higher divorce rate – 40 per cent of current young adult marriages (Hetherington 1979) – it has been estimated that 45 per cent of all children born in 1978 will spend some time as part of a single-parent family before they are eighteen, if present circumstances continue (Norton and Glick 1979). If one combines these statistics with American evidence (Lewis 1979) that on average lone fathers remarry within two years, it is clear that the present numbers of men and children in motherless families represent only a proportion of those who will

spend part of their parenthood and childhood respectively in motherless families.

Forty-eight per cent of lone fathers in Great Britain are caring for
one child, 32 per cent for two children, and 20 per cent for three or
more children; 80 per cent are over thirty years of age, and 90 per cent
of the children are of school age (that is, over five) (Leete 1978; *OPCS
Monitor* 1978).

Official statistics on single mothers are considerably more comprehensive than those on lone fathers, who are treated as an homogeneous
group (*OPCS Monitor* 1978). Thus, as yet, no official statistics are kept
on how many motherless families are created by divorce or separation
as opposed to death.

Of the research conducted so far into the phenomenon of single
parenthood and its effects, most has concerned the larger group of such
families, the fatherless (see for example Herzog and Sudia 1970).
Nevertheless, in the last decade studies of lone fatherhood have increased
dramatically and have attempted to extract common characteristics of
such families.[1] There have also been books and articles describing
personal experiences of lone parenthood, both fathers and mothers (for
example Barber 1975), offering practical advice to lone parents of
either sex (for example Brown 1980; Davenport 1979; Itzin 1980;
Bowskill 1980), and describing social work intervention with lone
fathers (Murch 1973; Brown and Stones 1979).

As we simply do not know what a representative sample of lone
fathers would look like, most of the studies above are open to methodological criticisms. One should thus be cautious about comparing data
between studies. In his review of the literature on motherless families,
however, Schlesinger (1978) identifies a number of common themes:
(1) financial problems; (2) childcare problems — mainly to do with
obtaining help or relief; (3) problems to do with the father's own
personal life; (4) homemaking and housework difficulties; (5) personal
stress; (6) problems to do with relating to the community at large.
More succinctly, George and Wilding (1972) assert that there are
problems of *time*, of *money*, and of *feelings*. We shall examine these
potential problems in more detail later in the chapter.

Becoming a single parent involves a double adjustment: it means
both becoming single and becoming the sole major parent (see Hetherington, Cox, and Cox 1976), a combination which for men does not
admit of any readily available social role or status. The circumstances
by which a man becomes a single parent will vary enormously. These
encompass death of a spouse, separation, divorce, and, rarely, being
left with a child though unmarried. Separation may occur in an atmosphere of grief, hostility, or mutuality, and the father may have fought

to keep his children or simply have been left with them. Further compounding factors include the age, sex, and number of children, the father's employment, the nature of any continuing relationship with a spouse or ex-spouse, and the ready availability of support. With so many intervening variables, to speak of lone fatherhood as if it were a unitary phenomenon is thus misleading. One American study has identified (allowing for remarriages) at least nine different types of single-parent status (Greenberg 1979).

It is not easy to assess how similar or different the situations of widowers and separated or divorced husbands might be. It may perhaps be thought that the position of the widower is generally an easier one, but in their study of 588 motherless families, George and Wilding (1972) found that feelings of loneliness and depression lasted considerably longer for widowers than for divorced or separated fathers. To borrow a distinction used in another context by Townsend (1957) it may be that cultural factors combine to increase their *desolation* (a term referring to the absence of a particular individual) by maximizing their *isolation* (referring to a position in the community); in cases of marital breakdown the tendency may be towards relatively greater isolation and relatively less desolation. Whatever the similarities or differences between the different types of lone fatherhood, there is little doubt that the course of marital breakdown can be negotiated or distorted in a much more active manner by the marriage partners (see the following chapter), and that the uncertainty inherent in processes involved in negotiating marital separation creates a complex series of personal peaks and troughs that vary considerably according to the aggressive or conciliatory stances adopted by the separating parties (Chiriboga and Cutler 1977).

Potential difficulties: time, money, and feelings

We can now return to look in more depth at the kinds of difficulties that lone fathers may face, and we shall examine in turn each of the three broad groups suggested by George and Wilding. It is worth recalling that these are only *potential* difficulties; the extent to which individual lone fathers experience any of what follows below is determined by the particularistic interaction of cultural factors (structural and attitudinal) and personal factors (historical, practical, and psychological). Thus, a separated lone father who is in aggressive dispute with his wife, who has previously undertaken little in the way of care-taking activity with his children, and who has had to give up his job, is in a vastly different position from, say, a widower, whose wife has died after a long illness, who has a well paid job with flexible hours, and a number of helpful relations and friends. Further, lone fathers are not bound to have problems and may, indeed, derive considerable satisfaction from their new-found lifestyles.

Where appropriate, I have attempted to illuminate particular points from an in-depth study that I conducted of sixteen lone fathers (one unmarried, two widowed, nine divorced, four separated) caring for thirty-three children. Each father had at least one child of under school age, and all had been caring for their children for more than twelve months (average period three and three-quarter years; range one and a quarter to nine years). Interviews were based on a structured questionnaire and lasted on average three and a half hours. The study was designed to complement the British survey studies with a series of subjective perceptions and all the interviews were recorded and transcribed (Hipgrave 1978).

PROBLEMS OF TIME

When lone fathers talk of time problems, they usually mean one of two things: either they have too much time on their hands or too much to do and too little time. Which, if either, of the two extremes is experienced will largely be determined by whether a father is able to keep working or not.

In a random street survey, George and Wilding (1972) found that 86 per cent of those questioned considered that single-parent mothers should stay at home to care for their children, but a staggering 78 per cent felt that fathers in the same position should go out to work rather than become househusbands. Full-time fathers consistently report being regularly confronted with this attitude, including by professionals operating in welfare and social security agencies.

In practice roughly five out of six lone fathers in Great Britain do manage to continue working (Hansard 1980b). For working lone parents, the 'time' problem can consist of having too little time for the pleasanter aspects of parenting or for personal pursuits, and of a constant attempt to allocate time and resources in the best interests of the children. The problem of combining employment with homemaking and parenting is a common one for all lone parents and free social time as a family is often scarce. School holidays are particularly bad times due to limited day-care provision (George and Wilding 1972; Hipgrave 1978). A major series of structural recommendations by the Finer Committee on One Parent Families (Finer 1974) — like the majority of its recommendations, still awaiting implementation — concerned the need for more flexible working arrangements and vastly improved day-care facilities for single parents.

Although the majority of lone fathers do continue working, some 35 per cent of George's and Wilding's (1972) sample had been forced to give up work at some point to care for their children full-time. Most had returned to work, but there is a significant minority of lone parents who become full-time parents to their children. (American studies, incidentally, do not seem ever to include a group of such fathers.)

For many men, work is a vital social outlet from the sometimes claustrophobic pursuits of single parenthood: 'My advice to any lone father would be to keep his job on. I couldn't sit inside these four walls — it'd drive me insane. Funny though it sounds, my work is my social life — you know, just that bit of ordinary adult company'. Those fathers who choose to give up work renounce consciously this often unappreciated aspect of work life, perhaps without realizing that their social life outside work is also likely to alter drastically. A reduction in income reduces leisure options for the family, at least those which cost money. One full-time lone father put his problem thus: 'You've got time on your hands, but it's not usable time, you can't do anything with it. You've got time on your hands but you haven't'. Thus a con-sciously-taken decision to leave work can sometimes have devastating and unforeseen consequences for the full-time father, at least in the short-term. Most full-time fathers go through periods of lethargy or extreme aggressive frustration — nearly always displayed privately — at the feeling of being trapped at home, especially in the first few months after giving up work. A number of incidents illustrating this were described to me by full-time fathers, including screaming long and loud at the walls, throwing cutlery and head-banging. One full-time father recalled his first few months alone in a slightly less dramatic vein:

'I can remember times when I had to consciously, physically, drag on every last reserve of tolerance to stop myself from doing something drastic. That happened at least two or three times. I took the kids upstairs, put one in the bedroom, locked the door, put the other in the other bedroom and just went downstairs, sat down and cooled down. It really surprised me that I never blew.'

FINANCIAL PROBLEMS

Financial problems may involve either the size of family income or how it is managed, and represent a common headache for lone parents of both sexes. George and Wilding (1972) found that in 44 per cent of their motherless families, the family income had decreased as a result of the family's new status. Only 12 per cent of these cases could be ac-counted for by loss of a wife's earnings; thus, if their study is of general application, George's and Wilding's findings indicate that around one-third of motherless families suffer reduction in income that is attributable to the father actually bringing home less money.

At one extreme, full-time fathers can find themselves having to live on social security. In Great Britain, for householders with a mortgage this may result in having to sell the family house and move into rented accommodation, as social security payments do not generally cover mortgage repayments adequately. Three of the fathers in my own study had been put in this position. As one, about to sell his house after four years as a lone father, put it:

> 'I'm just fed up of having no money. It's been nine years since I married and I feel I've had nothing out of life yet, and I feel if I get a bit of money, I'll get something nice. I resent moving, though. I resent it because to me it was security to the kids. If owt happened to me, they'd got the house which could, you know, be sold.'

For fathers still in employment, overtime may be limited for the sake of the family, or a new and more convenient job found (O'Brien 1980b). Whatever the reason for a drop in income, its effect will be not only to reduce a family's material standards but also to limit the number and nature of activities open to them. A young separated lone father with two young children, living on social security and having had to sell his house, expressed his difficulties as follows:

> 'I've never enough in my pocket to feel like I'm the average everybody. If I go to the shop, I've got to look at the prices and think "I can't afford that today", whereas if I had the money in my pocket, I'd have that extra choice. You're always saying to the kids "I'm sorry, no treats". I mean, I can accept a lower standard of living myself, but why should I have to force it on these [children]?'

Some fathers have difficulties — at least initially — in managing the household budget. This will depend on what experience individuals have had of managing the weekly household finances, and for most fathers any such problems represent merely a new, short-term learning task. For men who have never had to shop wisely, or to place priorities on purchases, however, money management can be another significant stress at a time when other practical or emotional strains are also at their peak.

In Great Britain the Finer Committee (Finer 1974) has recommended a change in the financial arrangements regarding single-parent families, incorporating a guaranteed allowance for all children and a means-tested allowance for parents. Although single parents do now receive an extra allowance — at the time of writing this is £3 per week, though this sum is deducted where fathers receive supplementary benefits — there is no evidence that this gesture has eased in any significant measure the relative poverty that single-parent status brings with it for many families (Ferri 1976).

EMOTIONAL DIFFICULTIES

There are probably as many combinations of problems broadly to do with emotions as there are individual lone fathers. The general context of these emotional factors is a series of fundamental conflicts, notably between the demands of the past and the future, and between the needs of the father and those of his children. Thus, broadly speaking, stresses involving time and money factors already mentioned can be linked with any of the following:

Feelings related to attitudes expressed by the community

Men are not in general socialized into admitting personal difficulties or asking for help or reassurance. Although there is some evidence that lone fathers are more likely than their female counterparts to receive practical help in childcare activities (Ferri 1976), and interview studies suggest no shortage of sympathy from the community, most lone fathers feel that they get neither the reassurance nor the practical advice and assistance that they need. Furthermore an American author (Mendes 1976a) has suggested that those fathers most likely to mobilize helping resources are those who need it least.

The issue of sympathy is an interesting one. Sympathy can sometimes unwittingly stem from a belief that by breaking one of society's developmental codes — namely that an intact family unit is the ideal mode of rearing children — lone fathers are doomed to personal difficulties and their children to developmental harm. This is illustrated in the following quote:

'A lot of people are sympathetic, but I'm not too struck on them being too sympathetic. A bit of sympathy's all right, it boosts your ego a bit, but if they come out and say "You're coping very well, but it is a pity", it sort of clashes, doesn't it? You're saying the opposite to what you mean.'

Another put it this way:

'In a way, you get too much sympathy. I think you need a bit of saying "the kids are being brought up all right". I mean it's all right your mum saying it, but I'd like someone who knew about kids to say "Well your kids seem to be all right". Then I'd feel more at ease, like.'

Feelings of isolation or loneliness

This cluster of feelings can involve any of at least three components. First, it is linked to the availability of support systems, formal or informal. Second, many lone fathers have met very few, if any, men in a similar position to themselves. Some may do so via single parents' groups, notably, in Great Britain, Gingerbread, but such groups by no means attract the majority of lone parents in a particular area. Exceptionally, attempts have been made to bring together motherless families on a social or therapeutic basis (Brown and Stones 1979). Third, there is the issue of personal intimacy with other adults: 'You know your kids love you, but it's a different sort of love, you know. I suppose I feel as though I want to be wanted'.

In an American study, Greenberg (1979) sought to highlight differences in this area of adjustment between lone fathers and lone mothers. Whilst both sexes considered that personal autonomy was the major benefit of single parenthood, both groups felt problems of sexual adjustment, enjoying neither the freedom of a single 'swinger' nor the comforts of marital sex. Men seemed to be allowed more behavioural latitude in terms of sexual relationships, but discomfort from *loneliness* was almost exclusively limited to lone fathers. The less liberal sexual scripts afforded to women were effectively counterbalanced by a strong same-sex friendship network, which made for greater 'leisure-role satisfactions' and thus appeared to allow single mothers greater appreciation of the benefits of independence gained by being single again. Intimacy, in the sense of intimate relationships, may be an important factor militating against the onset of depressive reactions (Brown and Harris 1978).

With male friends, lone fathers often find that their personal priorities have shifted in a way which makes these same-sex relationships less reciprocal. Informal, non-sexual, relationships with females outside the father's own family can be problematic. As one father put it: 'With being a bloke and talking with someone's wife the neighbours automatically think "Ey up, he's trying to knock her off" or something — chatting her up, you know'.

When lone fathers do establish an intimate relationship with a member of the opposite sex, in addition to the problem of how the woman friend and children interact, the role, or potential role, of the new female in the household causes fathers some concern, as they will have taken over many of their former partner's practical, as well as parental, functions:

> 'When you've got the opportunity of having a relationship with another bird, you can't really say "Here you are, you do that job" — a job that the wife was doing — and then you revert to your old job, because you're so conditioned to doing things yourself. You become that critical that you often ruin your relationship with the bird.'

Feelings connected with sexual identity

Many of the issues discussed in the previous subsection are also relevant to the issue of the father's perceptions of his own manhood, particularly with reference to the changed nature of the same and opposite-sex friendships. So-called 'masculine' rewards are generally inconsistent with the personal and generally intangible rewards of child-care.

A particular element in this complex group of feelings concerns public tasks that are usually the preserve of a mother. Evidence from the Newsons' (Newson and Newson 1965; 1968) and other studies (for example McLaughlin (in press)) of child-rearing patterns in intact families seems to indicate that the more public nurturing tasks become, the less likely fathers are to participate in them. Having to shop with adolescent daughters for clothes is an example of a difficult public exercise for fathers. A similar one, this time related to young daughters, is quoted below:

> 'You feel a bit — er — you get one or two queer looks. You notice it especially when you're looking through kiddies' pants and things like that. There you are, looking through kiddies' pants and they're thinking "Ey up, we've got a right one here". You can see it, you can feel them looking at you.'

Feelings connnected with parental competence

There is no reason to suppose that lone fathers themselves should be — in varying degrees — immune from the prevailing assumptions that the mother is the more important parent, particularly of younger children, and that a two-parent family is the 'proper' environment for the healthy development of children. Mendes (1979) has called this 'the tyranny of the two-parent model'.

Three common elements in popular assumptions of parenthood can affect the sensitivity of a number of lone fathers particularly strongly.

First, there is what one might call the 'Volcano Effect', which states that being brought up in a one-parent family inevitably involves psychological stresses, which simmer slowly under the surface and are bound to erupt at some later point in the child's development:

> 'People are always complimenting you on how well she's behaved and all the rest of it. I don't think much about that, because you're always sort of waiting for the next kick in the face. I don't know whether it will all sort of pop out when she's fourteen or fifteen or whether she is genuinely growing up adjusted.'

Second, feelings of parental inadequacy are usually less concerned with the *tasks* involved in childcare — most men will already be experienced in childcare activities (see, for example Newson and Newson 1963; 1968) — than with potential emotional deficits, in particular children's needs for what in common parlance is termed 'mother love': 'I wish I could be more emotionally involved with them rather than being a man and staying a man, like. I wish I could give them more feminine love, if you understand'.

Third, there is the issue of whether men can provide suitable parenting for daughters. Surprisingly, although a number of studies have described greater adjustment problems for boys in fatherless families (see for example Biller 1974; Wallerstein and Kelly 1980; Hetherington, Cox, and Cox 1976), there is little hard evidence in favour of the popular assumption that rearing daughters is problematic for men, although a recent piece of American research (Santrock and Warshak 1979) suggests that same-sex pairings of lone parents and children make for better social adjustment in children. Most of the arguments invoked against fathers rearing daughters — the need for same-sex models, the mysterious 'feminine touch', critical periods such as adolescence and so on — apply equally to mothers and sons, which seem to be a less contentious pairing. Many lone fathers — and mothers — are aware of the dangers inherent in opposite-sex pairings and plan appropriate strategies to counteract them (Orthner and Lewis 1979; Hipgrave 1978).

Feelings to do with household tasks

This group of feelings tends to be of relatively short-lived intensity and can be expressed in either terms of anxiety over tasks that one is unable to perform well, or in a continuing belief that, like 'mother love', there is a phenomenon, customarily called a 'woman's touch', which is always missing in the motherless family, however competent and tasteful the father might be in the home.

Feelings directly related to the former spouse

As has already been noted, most lone fathers find the process of structuring a new parenting and homemaking role less arduous than that of negotiating an appropriate separation from a former spouse (Todres 1975; O'Brien 1980a). This applies whether the new family unit is created by death or marital breakdown. For widowers the nature of these feelings and patterns of adjustment have been documented in the literature on bereavement and widowhood (Marris 1958, 1974; Parkes 1972; Marsden 1969). In cases of marital breakdown the adjustment of fathers and mothers is linked to the spirit underpinning the 'strange kind of intimacy' (Gatley and Koulack 1979) that characterizes their new relationship (see following chapter).

A particular difficulty for lone fathers is that the intensity of each of the various pressures outlined above tends to reach a peak during the first year of lone parenthood, when a number of different stresses tend to interact to produce a period of speeding confusion and personal crisis for many lone fathers:

'Your mind's like a gambling machine — you know, clicking and spinning — you find yourself looking at all the aspects of everything at the same time.'

'That first year takes the worst part out of you, because your're learning all the time and often you're running into a brick wall. You think you're almost there, you're coping, then — bang! — you've hit a bullet again and you really feel down, and you think "is it blinking worth it?" '

Conclusions

A general theme running through this chapter is the need to move from a language of *pathology* to one of *process*, acknowledging that the process of transition and adjustment may involve both strengthening and weakening factors for any individual or family (Weiss 1979).

It would be misleading to offer a 'typical' model representing lone fathers' reactions to their new status. Any such 'model' would simply not be able to incorporate the complexities of the interplay between personal and cultural factors in any individual case. Nevertheless, a number of common variables have been identified, both institutional and interpersonal, that can seriously affect both fathers and children in adjusting to the loss of a wife or mother. On the institutional level such variables may be structural or attitudinal. Structural factors include particularly the material disadvantage and downward mobility associated with single parenthood, and the manner in which welfare, employment, and legal systems deal with lone parents and their children.

Attitudinal factors are less easy to delineate with any precision. The attitude of the community at large can often serve to isolate one-parent families – and fathers in particular. Ferri's finding that:

> 'Far from being conducive to the re-integration of one parent families into the social fabric, the ambivalent and often negative attitudes which society adopts toward such families seems only to isolate them and add to the multiple difficulties they face.'

(Ferri 1976:149)

applies with particular force to motherless families for and to whom there are no readily available behavioural conventions. The belief that children need mothers — as opposed to the more reasoned position that children have developmental needs which can be met by a number of familial models, as well as remain unmet in the traditional family unit — remains hard to shake in present-day society.

In conclusion, then, it can be said that the individual personal and interpersonal difficulties that lone fathers (and mothers) face in reconstituting a social and parental role for themselves are compounded by cultural variables that make this potentially difficult process of transition even more stressful. There is, in short, no evidence that lone fathers cannot plan and organize a healthy developmental environment for themselves and their children. There is a good deal of evidence that we, the community, make it extremely hard for them to do so.

Notes

1 Examples of these studies include: George and Wilding (1972); Bain (1973); Todres (1975); Ferri (1976); Ferri and Robinson (1976); Gasser and Taylor (1976); Keshet and Rosenthal (1978a, 1978b); Levine (1976); Orthner, Brown, and Ferguson (1976); Mendes (1976b, 1979); Katz (1979); Hipgrave (1978); O'Brien (1978, 1980a).

12 Becoming a lone father: Differential patterns and experiences

MARGARET O'BRIEN

> 'I'm going to refer to myself as being a mother, because there is no male, no name for men doing the job that I'm doing.' (A lone father)

In contrast to the voluminous literature on lone motherhood, until the last decade, social scientists have given little consideration to the phenomenon of lone fatherhood. One consequence of this omission is that the experience of being a lone father has in some ways been hidden from public attention. The relative invisibility of this group may be connected to the fact that dominant in their lives are activities and concerns that are not usually associated with the conventional 'manly' role. It could be argued that men becoming lone fathers cross the traditional boundaries of female and male terrains: on an interpersonal level by being involved with the process of *'mothering'* (the intimate one-to-one caring and giving relationship) and on a structural level by entering into the institution of *'motherhood'* (with its home-centred, unwaged, and ambiguous status). However, this proposition needs to be carefully contextualized, since transitions to lone fatherhood in contemporary society are taking place at a time when there is great conflict over what actually constitutes the female and the male terrain. Thus, while some individuals are active in blurring sexual and gender divisions others are active in accentuating them. As far as men are concerned, on the one hand there are groups who are *contesting* the aggressive and tough image of man and the notion of the father as sole economic provider, while concurrently there exist groups who are busy *reasserting* the importance of these very same images (see Harrison 1978 for overview; Seidler 1978). Within the area of single parenthood itself there are also conflicting sets of attitudes and practices. For example, Britain has recently seen the formation of two complementary pressure groups that both criticize the conventional practice whereby mothers automatically become the custodial parent after divorce. Families Need Fathers (FNF) believe that the courts and social services should give more consideration to the man's relationship with his child, while Mothers Apart From Their Children (MATCH) argue that some women, at some periods in their life, need to give up full-time mothering in order to develop their own identity. Men becoming lone fathers are surrounded by these sets of beliefs. In addition they have to work their way through the 'contradictory complex of masculinity' (Willis 1978: 152); no longer will their personal identity and status be totally connected to their occupation outside the home. For some men it may be the first time that feelings associated with 'self as father' gain precedence over those associated with 'self as worker'.

In order to explore men's entry into lone fatherhood and its interrelationship with their perceptions of gender identity I decided to study one particular sub-group of lone fathers in depth: men who become lone fathers after marital separation.[1] Because of the importance that motherhood has assumed it could be suggested that men who eschew lone parenthood in this situation have a lower risk of public censure and private self-condemnation than women in comparable positions. I was interested therefore to discover why these men took up single fatherhood. Could it be that they were very committed to and involved with parenting before separation and wanted to continue this type of arrangement afterwards, or were other factors more important, such as the nature of the marital separation or their relationship with their ex-wife?

The study

The study consisted of semi-structured in-depth interviews with fifty-nine London-based lone fathers. The main criteria for selecting the sample were: (a) that the men were maritally separated or divorced, and (b) that they had taken on a major day-to-day care of their dependent children after marital separation. In other words, the respondents were not selected on the basis of precipitating causes (for example, the study was not restricted to men whose marriages had ended by the process of mutual agreement or to men who had become lone fathers because they felt no other option was available) but rather on the basis of the outcomes themselves, marital separation and lone fatherhood. As the study was primarily concerned with men's parental experiences with young children, only men who had one of their children in the five to eleven-year age group were considered eligible. The group of lone fathers was collected from as wide a variety of sources as possible, since, of course, there is no sampling frame available from which separated and divorced lone fathers can be randomly drawn.

Table 12 (1)   *Source of sample[2]* *(Total = 59)*

Ginger-bread	National Council for one Parent Families	Families Need Fathers	Adverts	Primary Schools	Divorce Welfare Office/ Social Worker	Personal Contacts
29	5	10	6	2	2	5

Overall, the extent of the sample's representativeness of the general population of separated/divorced lone fathers is not known, for there is only limited demographic information available on this group of men (see Hipgrave, Chapter 11). However, an effort was made to attain a sample reflecting a wide variety of social backgrounds. Table 12 (2) gives a summary of the general characteristics of the sample.

Differential trajectories into lone fatherhood

In previous studies of single parents investigators have rarely asked their respondents to reflect *separately* on the transition from couplehood to singlehood and the transition from joint parenthood to lone parenthood, with the consequence that any distinctive patterns are either confounded or obscured. Therefore, in this study during each interview the events and feelings surrounding marital separation and the decisions about childcare arrangements were established independently of each other. I will very briefly describe the major patterns, taking first the transition from couplehood to singlehood.

A common theme emerged from the men's accounts of their marriage breakdown, in that most felt their wives had initiated the separation. Forty-eight (81 per cent) of the men felt they had been 'acted against' rather than 'active in' the end of the marriage. This pattern of transition to singlehood is in line with other studies on separated/divorced lone fathers (George and Wilding 1972; Hipgrave 1978). There was no established common pattern however, that characterized the transition from joint to lone parenthood.

Other studies of lone fatherhood have suggested that the issue of choice, whether or not a man chooses to become a lone father, is an important distinguishing factor in determining the texture of the transition to lone fatherhood (Mendes 1975). However, for men in this study, choice proved to be just one of an array of important dimensions. Other elements emerged: for example, whether there was any discussion; the extent of hostility involved; the degree of abruptness in the transition; and whether the needs of the child were put before or after the

Table 12(2) General characteristics of sample (N = 59)

Occupation		Age		Family size (no. of dependent children)	
'Middle-class' (N = 26)		25–29	9	1	21
Professional	11	30–34	21	2	24
Intermediate	15	35–39	32	3	8
'Working-class' (N = 33)		40–44	22	4	6
Skilled non-manual	12	45+	12		
Skilled manual	16				
Partly skilled	2				
Unskilled	3				

needs of self. From a consideration of these dimensions it became apparent that the different routes into lone fatherhood could be broadly separated into three major (although not necessarily totally exclusive) types:

(a) *The conciliatory negotiators*

These were a group of men (N = 20) who described the process of becoming a lone father as one which involved relatively amicable discussions with their wives, sometimes over a long period of time. The eventual outcome of these negotiations was that both parents considered the child would benefit most from living with and being mainly cared for by the father.

(b) *The hostile seekers*

A second group (N = 20) can be characterized as men who wanted to become lone fathers very much irrespective of the wishes of the children's mother and actively forced their wives to accept the situation.

(c) *The passive acceptors*

A final group (N = 19) could be described as men who passively acceded to their wives' active 'desertion' of the children and who therefore literally had little or no initial choice over the childcare arrangements. This schema, it will be noticed, emphasizes the character of the transition. So that although (formally) the wife 'left' the husband in about 80 per cent of the cases, it was possible to differentiate between couples who mutually negotiated childcare after separation and couples who found this type of communication either unacceptable or impossible to carry out. In many cases, then, the transition from couplehood to singlehood and the transition from joint parenthood to lone parenthood did not simply run in parallel. In the rest of the chapter I will describe more fully the three trajectories and I will attempt to explore any unifying and distinctive characteristics within and across these three routes in relation to men's parent, gender, and husband identities.

The conciliatory negotiators

It appears that when conciliatory negotiators' marriages were coming to an end there developed a realization that *joint* decisions would have to be made about the children's general welfare. These men described how sometimes intense personal antagonisms were suspended to allow space to decide what was the most suitable solution for the children and in some cases for each individual of the couple. A lecturer, who had been separated for over three years, related the following account:

> 'We negotiated how we were going to do this and . . . we worked out the best way we could do anything was to raise a mortgage on a second flat nearby which she now has. She didn't like this house very much and I stayed . . . We decided between us that the children would basically live with me but also have very close contact with her.
>
> *Why did you decide that?*
> Well, I like children, I like my children, I enjoy them, I like fatherhood and my wife wanted to go back to full-time work. So all round it was the best thing for all of us.'

Conciliatory negotiators tended not to perceive their ex-wives as opponents but rather as partners involved in very unfortunate proceedings: 'it was an awful decision to make, but we just had to sit down and work it out'. This particular route into lone fatherhood was only reported by a third of the men I interviewed and proved to be connected with an array of other factors only some of which will be developed here (for further discussion see O'Brien (forthcoming)).

Materially, the conciliatory negotiators were more advantaged than the other groups. Seventy-five per cent (N = $\frac{15}{20}$) were in professional and managerial occupations, all were in full-time employment or studying, and few had housing or money problems.[3] At the time of the separation their ex-wives also possessed substantial material resources: half were in professional and managerial occupations and only a minority were full-time housewives. It could be argued that this material base created a situation in which more options were open to the separating couple and particularly to the woman. Many of these women were sufficiently well-off to set themselves up independently of their husbands and this economic power may have been useful in the bargaining process over childcare arrangements. Further discussion of the marriage and parental roles before separation threw more light on the men's motivations for lone fatherhood. Generally the marriages were construed as being fairly egalitarian unions where decision making was normally shared and marital communication thought to be very important. Most of the men reported sharing quite extensively in the physical and emotional arenas of childcare and in some cases felt they had in fact had the *main* responsibility for the children. Thus, one respondent who had been married for ten years had taken a year off work to look after the three children while his wife retrained. During this period his wife met another man and felt she wanted to separate. He described how he felt at the time:

> 'I was shocked, amazed — it wasn't as if we had a long period of marital trench warfare, we never had that at all . . . our marriage was never static, there was a sort of dynamism about it, we talked a lot to each other, but it's funny . . . one of the things she said was that she found marriage too claustrophobic that we were too dependent on each other. But I said that was because of the kids . . . she would never have become a social worker without my support. I in a sense carried it, but carried it because I thought we were doing it together.'

Amidst all the hurt feelings this couple were still able to reach a common understanding about the children. Both felt very strongly that their children should not suffer prolonged anxieties and so continued their previous arrangement whereby the father had major responsibility for the children and the mother moved out of the marital home. Along with most of the conciliatory negotiators, this respondent could not bear the idea of being a 'Sunday father' and felt that lone fatherhood 'was the first major thing that I'd ever done, it's completely changed my life'. At the time of the interview (two years after separation) flexible and frequent access arrangements had been established, the lone father had become a student and the non-custodial mother was financially contributing quite substantially to the family unit.

In general, conciliatory negotiators actually saw lone fatherhood as the preferred outcome following marital breakdown because they felt quite committed to and involved with parenthood. They enjoyed looking after children and, in comparison to the other two groups, were less likely to believe that children were really a mother's concern. As one father commented: 'You can come out with all these clichés about the softness of women but we can be equally soft and sensitive. The stereotype of a man being aggressive and not being able to relate to things that are gentle is just untrue'. They themselves felt little conflict between their gender identity and their position as primary caregiver, but it was reactions from others that often caused disquiet (see also Hipgrave 1981: Chapter 11).

> 'No I don't feel at all uneasy about my position, I've spent so much time in her life looking after her on a daily basis . . . but sometimes other people make you question it . . . you get the feeling that they think you are odd . . . that there is something rather peculiar about a man who can cook and look after a house and kids and so on.'

Within the conciliatory negotiators' group most of the marriages had ended at the wives' initiation, but there were substantially more mutually agreed separations than in the other two groups. (None among hostile seekers, two among passive acceptors, but seven among the conciliatory negotiators.) Perhaps partly as a result of this, the conciliatory negotiators had significantly more contact with their ex-wives at the time of interview,[4] felt more friendly towards them, and were more positive about mother–child contact. Although some of the separations did involve a 'third party' this group of men appeared to have more cultural armour for accepting the existence of marital infidelity and did not feel it necessary to 'punish' their ex-wives in the ways expressed by our second group – the hostile seekers.

The hostile seekers

For some separating couples decisions about their children's welfare are intricately connected to the internecine marital conflicts. Intentionally, or sometimes by default, children of hostile seekers' marriages became pawns in a highly emotional 'game'. Most of the hostile seeker marriages involved the wife leaving, at least initially, for another person. In fact nine of the twelve divorced men in this group (the other eight were still separated at the time of the interview) had based their petitions on the wife's adultery. Many were *morally outraged* by this adulterous behaviour and wanted to take revenge on their wife. Keeping main care and control of the children became a symbolic way of *punishing* her.

The following account was from a respondent, whose wife left him for another man, but who had come back 'on and off' to the marital home because of the children.

'She wanted to have joint custody of the children and I wouldn't give her that. I said you've got to be here and look after the children and look after them properly. So I went to court and told them all about her and the court ordered me custody of the children, with her having access.'

In this particular case the mother attempted suicide, for, as her husband put it, 'she was twisted up between the love of the man and the love of the children'. For some, intertwined with the punishment motive was the hope that by keeping the children they might eventually entice their wife back; a subtle form of emotional blackmail appeared to be in operation. Connected with this was the feeling that they had 'lost' their wife, but they were certainly not going to lose their children. Furthermore she had someone else to go to, while they were alone, they 'had nothing'. In other words a few appeared to want their children mainly for emotional security and this was reflected in the comment, 'them being dependent on you, makes you feel wanted'. Many of these men became intensely insecure after separation and interestingly a few adopted very 'macho' styles, as if they were compensating for what they perceived as demasculinization. One respondent started going to body-building and karate classes four or five times a week: 'Her boyfriend he was dead scared of me because he thought I was a right what's it. So he started doing karate and so he started trying to be a little hard, coming on a bit strong . . . he found out I was going to the club so he stopped you see'. This man was extremely hurt and dejected by his wife's departure and his response was utter bewilderment on the one hand, mixed with intense loss of pride on the other. At the time of the interview hostile seekers reported the most extreme negative feelings towards their ex-wives and their past marriages: 'She made out I was a little boy . . . two years before it happened she made me have a vasectomy. What a dirty trick! You know children are the only mark I'm going to leave when I die'.

Few admitted any part in the relationship breaking down, feeling their wife was the 'guilty' partner: 'I feel very bitter towards her because I gave her everything. She had no reason to go', commented one man. Prolonged court battles and tugs-of-war, at times across continents, were more characteristic of this group. Some men who took the drastic step of kidnapping their children undoubtedly did this to 'punish' their wives, but other sincerely felt they were the better parent and rationalized their behaviour by pointing to the unequal treatment they would receive in court (see Lowe, Chapter 2). One respondent involved in a cycle of international kidnapping felt:

'Judges, in spite of masses of contradictory evidence, think men are incapable of running a home and looking after a child . . . in my case I've always had a particularly close relationship with my son, because of my job I always spent more time looking after him . . . nowadays a father's rights have been virtually reduced to nothing, he's at the complete mercy of his wife.'

In general, however, when compared to the other groups, hostile seekers recalled relatively lower levels of pre-separation child involvement, perhaps suggesting that all were not necessarily becoming lone fathers because of continuing commitment to parenting. 'When my wife was with me I did feel very distant. I rarely saw them, she used to leave them at my mother's a lot.' Hostile seekers were married for the shortest time and separated for the shortest time so that their family situation was more 'in flux' than the other two groups. Some were still involved in custody disputes at the time of the interview. They tended to be worried about their children's future and experienced more conflicts between their gender and parental identities as compared to the conciliatory negotiators. But in general they had reasonable material resources, having come from a wide variety of social backgrounds and they had actively 'fought' for lone fatherhood, unlike our next group — the passive acceptors.

The passive acceptors

Although it is far more common for men than women to desert their families, recent legal evidence points to an increase in number of husbands using wives' desertion as grounds for divorce (see Maidment 1980: 1169, who asks, 'Is this a consequence of greater equality all round?'). All of the passive acceptors became involuntary lone fathers after their wives desertion and some likened themselves to widowers in that they had no say in the matter at all. As one manual worker put it:

> 'Carol was abandoned! I came home on a morning of a night shift, about eight o'clock in the morning, and she'd been dumped at a neighbour's . . . the wife disappears and abandons the child, you just don't know what's happening, where she's gone, what she's doing . . . we got a letter from her after a while.'

This group in fact emerged as the most socially deprived; they were more likely to mention housing or money problems; more were in semi-skilled and unskilled occupations; they had larger families and a greater proportion had health problems. For example, one man lived with his six-year-old son in appalling temporary accommodation for the homeless where he had to share all amenities. His wife had left them two years previously, and since then they had lived a fairly itinerant lifestyle, roaming from town to town. He felt he was 'a no-hoper' but that his son 'kept him going'.

Many passive acceptors were absolutely devastated by their wives' desertion and from their accounts it appeared that many either denied that something was going wrong in their marriage, or were completely unaware of their wives' dissatisfaction with it. A man in this group described how his wife left him and their five children just a few weeks after he had prematurely retired because of ill-health. His job entailed long hours away from home during the day 'and all the while she was carrying on behind my back. As far as I was concerned I was happily married. I just couldn't believe it'. In this particular case the woman was nine years younger than her husband and she had married him at the early age of seventeen. Overall a large proportion of the respondents' brides were young at marriage (40 per cent of the total sample were nineteen years or under), but this was particularly so in the passive acceptor group. In fact, ten out of nineteen passive acceptor brides were in this category. A recent British study on the characteristics of 'Who Divorces' (Thornes and Collard 1979) concluded that a teenage bride and a premarital pregnancy were two 'high risk' factors in predicting later divorce. The present study has, perhaps, provided some confirmatory evidence of this trend. Passive acceptors often commented that their wives were too young at marriage, and that subsequently the women had often grumbled that they had 'missed out on something'. As one respondent who had married a nineteen-year-old woman related:

> 'She wanted children straight away but then after she had the children she was bored at home, and I let her go out with her friends because I could see it was a drag being at home . . . then she falls in love with this other bloke . . . when I look back I think she only married me to get away from her parents.'

In the sample as a whole not all the women left their families for other men: some were said by their husbands to have rejected the wife/ mother role and did not want another marriage-type relationship. However, women in the passive acceptor group who wanted this 'independence' were not as financially well off as the wives of conciliatory negotiators. Proportionately more wives of passive acceptors were either in poorly paid unskilled work or were full-time home-makers at the time of separation. Consequently some had to return to their family of origin as the first port of call. One respondent explained: 'She was the typically bored suburban housewife and she couldn't stand kids . . . She left to go and live with her family to start with but she's got a flat somewhere now.' Very few passive acceptors had frequent contact with their wives and there were some who reported, 'I haven't seen her since the day she left'.

Although a majority had substantial amounts of childcare responsibility before their wives' departure (determined mainly by the woman's continual absence or non-participation) passive acceptors were the most likely to express feelings of conflict attached to the lone father role. Perhaps because they had little choice in determining their situation, passive acceptors tended to over-emphasize the importance of the mother as the major nurturant parent ('the woman's touch') and to deny their own caring capacities.

> 'A father cannot provide all the child's needs, there is no way you can. A child must have a good loving mother.'

> 'I've got to be strict and stern or I've got to be loving and warm. I haven't got the right shape to give them cuddles they like.'

Of all the lone fathers interviewed, passive acceptors most clearly conformed to Mendes's (1975: 143, 144) hypothesis:

> 'Fathers whose wives forced them or otherwise aggressively propelled them into single parenthood will have a greater amount of negative sentiments . . . about their parental roles than will any other type of single father.'

Conclusion

Single-parent families constitute an increasing proportion of family arrangements in Britain today. It is sometimes forgotten, however, that within this grouping are located many lone-father families. In this chapter I have attempted to trace the variety of routes into lone fatherhood for men whose marriages have come to an end. After separation, some fought to retain custody of the children, often against the wishes of the wives; others had lone fatherhood thrust upon them by their wives' desertion; still others mutually negotiated the transition to lone fatherhood with their partners. These different routes into male single-parenthood clearly highlight the fluidity and complexity of parental experiences for many men today.

Notes

1 I would like to thank Dr A. N. Oppenheim for his supervision of this project, the Social Science Research Council for their financial support, and Evelyn Tovey for her secretarial assistance.
2 I would like to thank Gingerbread, One Parent Families, Families Need Fathers, William Patten Junior School, Sir Thomas Abney School, Edith Neville Primary School, and the North East London Court Welfare Service for their invaluable assistance in the location of the sample.
3 Most of the tendencies quoted are statistically significant at or beyond $p < .05$ (using Chi-square or Kendall's Tau tests).
4 The mean length of *de facto* marital separation was 3.2 years for the conciliatory negotiators, 2.4 years for the hostile seekers and 3.6 years for the passive acceptors.

13 From father to step-father

JACQUELINE BURGOYNE
AND DAVID CLARK

Even a cursory glance at the annals of family history will indicate that step-relationships, and what sociologists like to call 'family reconstitution', are by no means new phenomena. With the development of a deeper understanding of family life in former times has come both a greater appreciation of the diversity of kinship and social networks and a questioning of previously idealized assumptions about the supportive function of the 'extended' family (Laslett 1977:177). Evidence concerning the prevalence of marriage and step-parenthood has also been uncovered, and as Laslett puts it when describing seventeenth-century England, 'something like one quarter of all marriages were not first marriages at all' (1971:103). A more recent estimate suggests that the numbers remarrying did in fact decrease during the modern period, from 33 per cent of all who married once in the sixteenth century, to 12 per cent of that population in the nineteenth century — a trend that may have been linked to the declining death rate (Trumbach 1978:51). It was, of course, the death of a spouse that most frequently occasioned the remarriage of a bereaved adult, especially a parent, for whom remarriage might be seen to have both immediate and long-term advantages in the context not only of childcare and domestic help, but also of inheritance and financial settlement. In spite of, or perhaps because of, these expectations, step-parents have an unfortunate place in family history, where one of the most enduring consequences of second marriage has been the creation of a figure so powerful in negative associations and malevolent imagery that her kinship apellation has entered into the language as a synonym for all that is callous, cruel, and uncaring. We speak, of course, of the 'wicked' step-mother, whose unfeeling and vindictive behaviour towards her charges has so pervaded folk tales, children's stories, and popular wisdom. In general, it has been she, rather than her male counterpart, who has borne the brunt of history's disfavour, though at least one writer suggests that step-fathers were numerically in the majority (Laslett 1977:166). Such negative images of step-parenthood and step-relationships seem to persist in popular consciousness and continue to be present both in everyday language and in the assumptions that might surround family life after remarriage.

In recent years, step-parents have once again attracted a certain amount of public scrutiny as high rates of divorce and remarriage have assigned large numbers of men, in particular, to step-parental roles. In England and Wales in 1977 there were 356,954 marriages, approximately one-fifth of which involved the remarriage of a divorced woman (the proportion containing a divorced person of either sex was nearly one-third of all marriages). It is not possible to say from registration statistics how many of these remarrying women were mothers (and thereby 'created' stepfathers in remarrying) though we do know that the majority of children stay with the mother when their parents separate and that even in contested custody cases, the courts tend to favour the continuance of existing arrangements (Eekelaar *et al.* 1977: 8, 31). Another perspective is gained from consideration of the number of couples with children under sixteen years who divorce in a given year. In 1977 there were 77,501 such couples. Remarriage rates indicate that over half of these would go on to contract second marriages (Leete and Anthony 1979). If we combine these with unpublished data from the OPCS Family Formation Survey, which shows that in 1976, 7 per cent of all children under the age of sixteen were living with a step-parent (Dunnell, private communication), we are able to form some impression of the significant and growing extent of step-father families.

To study step-fathers is to confront two kinds of intellectual difficulty. On the one hand, and most obviously, it is to be concerned with the characteristics of a form of parental experience which, when set against a background of changing patterns of marriage and family life, is becoming increasingly prevalent and which may present peculiar problems for adults and children alike. Such an approach is predicated on the assumption that 'fathering' is in itself an understood and, typically, non-problematic activity. Any intellectual appraisal of step-fathers would therefore be concerned with examining the extent to which step-fatherhood differs from some consensual set of norms relating to fatherhood in general and the consequences which this might have for family life. On the other hand, when considering step-parenting as a whole, such an approach remains unwarranted so long as we continue to lack a full and adequate understanding of the constituent elements, practices, and meanings relating to 'normal' family life. Informed by these difficulties, and aided by other papers in this volume, we are therefore seeking to develop not only our knowledge of the singular, deviant, and problematic aspects of step-fatherhood (if indeed these can be said to exist at all as discrete entities) but also to throw further light on our understanding of what fathers 'are' and 'do' and the meanings that they attach to their behaviour.

Types of step-father

It is important to recognize first of all that subsumed under the general term 'step-father' are four distinct types of relationship. As we have seen, step-fathers are most usually 'created' by the remarriage of divorced, custodian mothers.[1] The fundamental characteristic of the step-father is thus the assumption of certain forms of parental obligation in relation to his partner's child(ren) by a previous union. He may or may not be previously married; he may or may not already be a parent – he may or may not have custody of his child(ren). This can be illustrated diagramatically (Figure 13 (1)).

Figure 13 (1)

Divorced woman with	+	Bachelor
custody of children	+	Divorced, non-parent
by a previous	+	Divorced, non-custodial father
marriage	+	Divorced, custodial father

There are therefore four distinct divorce-related 'pathways' whereby a man might become a step-father, each of which will combine experience and expectations to different effect. Orientations towards step-fatherhood are likely to vary with these pathways, as are subsequent outcomes. The bachelor marrying for the first time will therefore face and be prepared for step-fatherhood in a very different way, for example, to his divorced counterpart, especially the one who has had children in a previous marriage. Bachelors, for example, may only have the haziest of notions about the texture of daily domestic life with small children and the ways in which this may affect their relationship with their new partner. By contrast, the orientations of a non-custodial father towards a new partner's child(ren) may be distinct from a father who has retained custody of his children and must now encourage them to establish day-to-day life alongside their newly acquired step-siblings.

We have suggested elsewhere that the process of becoming a step-mother is essentially more problematic than that of becoming a step-father (Burgoyne and Clark 1980b). Despite recent trends towards increased involvement of fathers in childcare and home management, it is still usually the case that a greater proportion of the domestic burden of child-rearing falls to mothers, rather than fathers. Moreover, it is often argued that it is the mother who is more likely to feel a sense of public accountability for the kind of people that 'her' children become and the way that they 'turn out' in general. Step-mothers are therefore likely to be pitched immediately into the mêlée of everyday family life, with its routines of meal-times, bed-times, work, play, and so on, whereas the step-father, like the 'natural' father, is left hovering on the sidelines, uncertain as to his role, function, or warrant. There are of course, certain dangers in this assumption, which may reflect more upon conventional wisdoms relating to gender than upon the social reality of the differences themselves. Yet these can both be examined through a consideration of step-fatherhood as an activity, together with the beliefs about fathering that underpin it.

In a sample of forty remarried couples and their children that we studied in Sheffield between 1977 and 1979,[2] there were thirty-five step-father families of various types and five step-mother families. Three of the step-fathers were ex-bachelors, eight had childless first marriages, eleven were non-custodian fathers, and thirteen were custodian fathers[3]. When compared with the remarried population as a whole, the couples in our study exhibit a number of important differences. The various combinations of previous marital status in the sample are listed in *Table 13 (1)*, along with the proportions of each category in the total re-marrying population for 1977.[4]

Table 13 (1) *Combined marital statuses, Sheffield study*

	No. in sample (N = 40)	Percentage of those remarrying in 1977
Divorced man–single woman	3	26*
Divorced man–widow	2	4
Widower–spinster	2	3
Both widowed	1	7
Widower–divorcee	1	less than one
Bachelor–divorcee	3	24
Both divorced	28	40
Total	40	100

*Source: Marriage and Divorce Statistics 1977, Population Series FM 2 No 4. Derived from Table 2.1.

There was therefore too great a proportion of two-divorcée couples in our sample as well as, and more importantly for the present purpose, an over-representation of custodian fathers. We have already referred to findings presented by Eekelaar and Clive (1977), which indicate that only between 10 and 15 per cent of fathers can be expected to retain or gain custody of their children after divorce, whereas over half of the divorced fathers in our sample had custody of children from a previous marriage. It seems likely that for many of these it was personal recognition of an unusual and perhaps slightly pioneering status that encouraged them to take part in the research project as a means of 'stating their case' to a wider public.

Each of the men and women taking part in the study was interviewed separately on at least three occasions. In the first interview we concentrated on the collection of detailed life histories, focusing particularly on the subjective experiences of marital break-up, second courtship, the decision to cohabit/remarry, and the process of family reconstitution. In the second interview we asked more structured questions about custody, access, and maintenance arrangements, as well as contacts with professionals such as lawyers, social workers, and doctors during the period of divorce and remarriage. We also looked at the effects of marital dissolution on family and social networks. The third interview was concerned specifically with childcare and parenthood in second marriages. Throughout all the interviews we were anxious to avoid leading questions about the potential problems of step-parenting and we therefore tried to encourage our respondents to designate and discuss the issues which they themselves saw as important. In many respects our interests were the same as those of the Newsons:

> 'Many issues which define characteristic styles of child-rearing only assume importance because of the cultural values which parents have learned to attach to them . . . At the individual level, the degree to which parents perceive themselves to be behaving like everyone else, giving their statements an 'of course' quality, or whether they feel themselves to be out on a limb in relation to other parents, must necessarily colour the whole pattern of their child-rearing.'
>
> (Newson and Newson 1973:13, 14)

Stepfathers and 'conscious parenthood'

From their work in Nottingham, the Newsons have isolated some general characteristics of contemporary beliefs about and patterns of childcare. These include the expectation that the activities and attitudes involved in caring for children are usually carried out spontaneously and relatively unselfconsciously. In contrast to professional care-givers, who are expected to maintain a relatively formalized and consciously considered attitude which is consistent with their relationship with their clients, 'parents can afford to show a degree of flexibility and indeed inconsistency which more formal educative relationships cannot' (Newson and Newson 1976:441). Accordingly, parent-child relations take on an almost instinctive quality, so that being a parent becomes synonymous with the achievement of full adult status. By contrast, the step-fathers in our study frequently appeared highly reflective and self-conscious about relationships with their step-children. Their 'conscious parenthood' was demonstrated in a number of ways. For example, when we asked questions about relationships and routines within the new family, they frequently referred to discussions and joint decisions about both detailed and mundane aspects of day-to-day care as well as more obvious major child-rearing events. Indeed, being able to share the responsibilities and activities of childcare more fully in a second marriage were frequent themes in interviews when our respondents compared past and present partners. There was also a good deal of indirect evidence from comparison of husbands' and wives' accounts of how they had arrived at some sort of shared understanding of the step-father's role in the new family. This was often reached during second courtship and the early phases of family reconstitution when considerable energy might be invested in the establishment of a joint identity. A step-father's assessment of his role and responsibilities within the new family group, and his responses to specific issues and crises, are therefore likely to be shaped by both partner's definitions of the obligations of step-fatherhood. Custodian fathers, however, tended to be more likely to expect their second wives to cope with step-motherhood 'by instinct'.

Such conscious parenthood can only be understood in terms of the emotional and material legacy of former marriage. Remarried parents typically feel responsible in some measure for the management of a series of transitions in their children's lives that are frequently regarded as upsetting and harmful. In particular, beliefs about the personal and emotional consequences of parental divorce are part of a web of widely-held folk beliefs concerning the effects of childhood experience on subsequent personality development. Bad behaviour, poor progress at school, adolescent delinquencies, difficulties in making relationships, as well as a variety of adult eccentricities may all be explained as the consequences of a 'broken home'. Such beliefs are legitimated in the occupational ideologies of teaching and the therapeutic professions, as well as through the media. Consequently, many of the parents in our study demonstrated persistent feelings of guilt and uncertainty about the potential effects on their children of their divorce and remarriage, even when they were at the same time at pains to point out the benefits which the recreation of 'ordinary family life' through remarriage had for the children.

The accounts of both husbands and wives clearly point to partners' investments in the creation of a secure home life for themselves and their children. This 'home-centredness' may prove especially significant for step-fathers. As the 'affluent worker' studies of the early 1960s showed, a relatively privatized involvement in home life on the part of skilled manual workers has become increasingly prevalent (Goldthorpe and others 1969). Others have seen the phenomenon as part of a more general trend towards the 'symmetrical family' (Young and Wilmott 1973). It was evident however that for many of the stepfathers in our own study, the change from a traditional and 'typically male' pattern of minimal involvement in childcare and domestic life towards an increasingly home-centred life style, was associated for them with the events and changes of divorce and remarriage. This was explained, in part, as an attempt to avoid the 'mistakes' of the past, but also symbolized the relief which many felt at being able to 'settle down' into ordinary life once more, often after a period of conflict and disturbance. As one man put it:

'I used to go gallivanting around and everything but I always used to envy a chap who were happily married. Y'know, "I'm on holiday with the wife and kids", I always used to envy them and I've always known, deep down, I'm a family man.'

Another man described how he had stopped drinking heavily once he had settled down, because:

'Days are too full . . . By [the] time you've got through your day and got two, and now three, kids ready for bed and got them to bed, it's just, er, I don't feel I need alcohol, you know I'm happy to stay in the house, with [wife], I don't feel I need to go off drinking.'

For those custodian fathers who had looked after children on their own for a time, the acquisition of additional responsibility for their step-children was matched by a concomitant relief at being able to share the duties and burdens of childcare with a new partner. One mother described how her husband, who had also brought with him children from a previous marriage, had 'tried to be a mother *and* a father to his two [children]'. Although they had both felt capable of taking on such a task, it was apparent that remarriage had eased the pressure on each of them and allowed them now to take great pride in the family life that they jointly offered their children. An understanding of how the step-fathers in the study saw their role should be grounded therefore in the context of a shared, negotiated commitment to a way of life that was frequently much more home- and family-centred than they had experienced in first marriage.

Father and step-father

It also became clear as we analysed our data, that evaluations of step-fatherhood were made in terms of more generalized beliefs about male parental obligations and an appropriate sexual division of labour. Whether step-fathers were describing for themselves their part in family life, or whether this was being outlined appreciatively by their wives, most couples drew attention to the *supportive* aspects of a step-father's contribution to the family unit. Women who had supported children on their own prior to remarriage might therefore point to the greater financial security that they now enjoyed. Step-fathers, in their turn, were often able to recount detailed incidents illustrating their wives' former financial difficulties and frequently showed great pride in the fact that the children were now 'well turned out' or 'wanted for nothing'.

Financial security was not, of course, an inevitable consequence of remarriage and the question of maintenance payments received from non-custodial fathers illustrates how divorce and family reconstitution can produce unsettling and long-standing consequences. Attitudes towards receipt of these payments varied among the families in our study and the issue of 'maintenance' was often a sensitive one for step-fathers. Among some of the large families on low incomes, the payments were clearly a vital component of the weekly budget, sorely missed if they failed to arrive. In general, however, step-fathers seemed anxious to shoulder financial responsibility for their step-children, almost as a demonstration of commitment, and were therefore prepared to lose such payments, especially if, as was frequently the case, the cessation of maintenance produced an attendant diminution in contact between child(ren) and non-custodial father. Where this applied, and the step-father was able to see himself, and be seen, as the new family's principal source of economic support, then the sense of being 'just like an ordinary family' could be more easily achieved. Consequently, where a step-father still had to make maintenance payments to an ex-wife and/or non-custodian children and where these posed a heavy additional burden on the new family's budget, there was frequently a sense of resentment towards a situation which appeared to undermine his ability to support his new family.

There were also other ways in which step-fathers might support their wives in the day-to-day organization of family life; for example, through accompanying them on visits to schools and hospitals, as well as sharing the burden of visits from social workers and other officials. Again, the mothers frequently made comparisons between their first and second husbands in these respects: '[He] will go down to the school with me on open days and things like that, which my ex-husband didn't do, I always ended up going on me own'.

One specific area in which step-father support clearly emerges is in the everyday management and control of children. Thus mothers who had spent a period as single parents tended to link their perceived lack of control over their children with more general feelings about difficulties in coping with the varying demands that growing children made upon them. The arrival of a step-father, heralded by a greater degree of economic security and some help with everyday tasks, might therefore enable mothers to cope more effectively, even when their new partners were, perhaps deliberately, playing no direct part in disciplining the children. For example, step-fathers often brought new interests into the family and in this respect were especially welcomed by mothers of boys. Many of the step-fathers were clearly pleased to be able to describe passing interests on to and sharing enthusiasms with newly acquired step-children. Interestingly, parents were most likely to point to the advantages for the child of having a step-parent of the same sex so that there were fewer obvious examples of shared hobbies and so on between step-father and step-daughter. As one man remarked, 'It's difficult to pass interests on to girls, isn't it?'.

Whereas descriptions of step-fathers' gradual and indirect involvement in the lives of their new partners and step-children were generally couched in positive terms, some couples commented on particular problems which they had encountered when first coming together as a family. For example, a step-father might find difficulties in the early stages when attempting to reprimand or discipline a child who was clearly aware that he was not the child's 'real' father. Where such difficulties had been overcome however, mothers frequently expressed relief at being able to leave certain aspects of discipline to a husband who was able to manage them better.

'They take more notice of him than they do of me, they seem to be playing me up more.'

'I think he could quell them with a word.'

'[My husband] only has to say something to him and Jeremy [the step-son] looks at him in amazement . . . and instantly stops what he is doing.'

It is clear from these descriptions, that for the couples in our study, 'being a step-father' was frequently bound up with a contribution to parent-child relationships and family life in general which was grounded in the economic, emotional, and domestic support which he might provide. Being a *step*-father is therefore seen in the more general context of expectations about fatherhood and in particular, beliefs in the naturalness of a sexual division of labour within marriage. For whilst there were considerable variations in how the couples defined this division and allocated male and female tasks, its existence and effects were always apparent.

In other respects there were clear differences between 'natural' and 'step' fatherhood. Step-fathers often expressed regret that they had only known and been able to influence the lives of their step-children for a relatively short time. Some also felt that being a father to someone else's child(ren) was frequently complicated by the continuing, if at times intermittent, presence of the non-custodial natural father. Even a symbolic presence, found perhaps in the sending of a gift or birthday card, was unsettling to some step-fathers, who were clearly sensitive to the fact that, as one of them put it, 'blood is thicker than water'. Thus even where the social dimensions of fatherhood were incumbent entirely upon the step-father, a continuing concern about being 'only a step-parent' might serve to inhibit family reconstitution and undermine his efforts to become a 'complete' or 'real' father to his step-children. Contradictions and ambiguities of this sort are also sharpened by aspects of welfare and legal policy that affect step-fathers. For example, step-fathers may become liable to pay maintenance for step-children if they divorce the child(ren)'s mother (Snow V. Snow 1972; see Cretney 1979:469f.) but would not take precedence over the non-custodial father if the mother were to die (Cretney 1979:Section 4). There are also many occasions when the ambiguous status of the step-father is powerfully reinforced by public bureaucracies. As one step-father explained:

> 'The word I don't like is step-father . . . I think it's a terrible word that, even if you have to cover up . . . you don't *have* to, but I think it's better to, like at work and things like that . . . 'cos, you know, it's all these forms, when you have to fill them in, like tax and that . . . you put "Father, yes" and then they send it back and say, "Are you guardian or step-parent"? "Then, you're not, their real father." I hate that word so.'

Conclusions

The process of becoming a step-father is perceived by both the men and their partners as an essentially private experience, confined within the sphere of home and family. Bringing with them a variety of expectations, norms, and ideals based upon the extent and quality of earlier parental experience, step-fathers and their spouses face the task of reconstituting family life, often out of the turbulent *sequelae* of marital break-up and divorce. In many cases they seek, above all, to become an 'ordinary family' once again. The objective is frequently quite self-consciously perceived. Couples in our study described in their accounts of 'getting to know one another' how, for example, even before any decision about cohabitation or remarriage had been made, they had been eager to discuss shared experiences of childcare and parental duty. As we noted in a paper on the decision to remarry, second courtships among divorced parents are likely to be domestically and family-oriented, with the children playing a central role in the development of the adult partner's relationship (Burgoyne and Clark 1980a). Such circumstances must undoubtedly serve to underline the incumbencies that the intending step-father might face and we found that in almost all cases the men we interviewed had seriously considered the implications of a situation where, as one of them put it, 'You're not just marrying her, you're marrying the kids as well'.

The degree of preparedness for their new life which step-fathers show may be shaped in various ways. On the one hand, the experience of inheriting a ready-made family might prove more problematic for the single man with no past experience of parenting or child-management than for the non-custodial father who in remarrying is eager to reinvest parental energies and skills in his new step-children. Alternatively, custodian fathers who consider themselves to have successfully negotiated the experiences of single parenthood may find life in a step-sibling family a considerable strain, especially in that oft-cited, though probably apocryphal situation where 'Your child and our child are picking on my child'. As we have tried to indicate, there are a variety of aspects of life in a step-family that can differ from that in an 'ordinary', 'unbroken', 'nuclear' family. Step-fathers' feelings about these and the responses which they believe to be appropriate will be influenced largely by their more general perceptions of the father's role. Accordingly, it is common for men to identify the obvious areas in which the absence of a father has affected their step-children, and to choose these as the focus of their attention. This manifests itself, typically, in an increased level of 'home-centredness' based on the provision of financial support, help in public encounters with officials, leisure-time pursuits shared with children, and so forth.

In all of these activities and responses however, the step-father may be liable to feel a sense of unease and insecurity. Unfavourable images of his role which persist in popular thought, along with occasionally lurid mass media coverage of child-abusing 'wicked step-fathers',[5] are likely to draw attention to the potential problems that he faces. Indeed, 'problems' relating to parenting and childcare, that might conceivably be a feature of any family at a similar point in the life-cycle, may come to be regarded as direct results of step-family life. Such negative stereotypes and feelings can have a powerful effect, and in the absence of any broadly based set of assumptions about what constitutes a 'good' step-father it is apparent that more normalized, though equally diffuse, images of the good *father* will serve as a model for action and belief. This can bring with it certain difficulties, since some attempts to 'be an ordinary father' will inevitable be frustrated by the structural constraints imposed on the family by post-divorce financial and legal settlements. At these points, the step-father, like other men and women who pass through the experience of divorce and remarriage, finds his private life heavily scripted by ideologies and forces largely outside his control.

Notes

1 A man might also, of course, become a step-father through marriage to either a widowed mother or the mother of an illegitimate child. We shall be concerned here mainly with families containing step-fathers which result from the divorce of one or other partner.
2 The project was funded initially by the Sheffield City Polytechnic and latterly by the Social Science Research Council. The support of both organizations is gratefully acknowledged.
3 Four of the custodian fathers were widowers.
4 Thirty-five of the forty couples in the sample were remarried in 1977–78.
5 See, for example, the banner headline 'Six Years for the Cruel Stepfather', which appeared on the front page of the *Scottish Daily Express* (23 February, 1980) in connection with the imprisonment of a man who had killed his step-daughter.

References

Ackermann, N. W. (1958) *The Psychodynamics of Family Life*. New York: Basic Books.

Ainsworth, M. D. S. (1967) *Infancy in Uganda: Infant Care and the Growth of Love*. Baltimore: Johns Hopkins Press.

—— (1969) Object Relations, Dependency and Attachment: A Theoretical Review of the Infant–Mother Relationship. *Child Development* **40**: 969–1025.

Ainsworth, M. D. S., Bell, S. M. and Stayton, D. J. (1974) Infant–Mother Attachment and Social Development: 'Socialisation' as a Product of Reciprocal Responsiveness to Signals. In M. P. M. Richards (ed.) *The Integration of a Child into a Social World*. London: Cambridge University Press.

Ainsworth, M. D. S., Blehar, M. C., Waters, E. and Wall,,S. (1978) *Patterns of Attachment: A Psychological Study of the Strange Situation*. Hillsdale, New Jersey: Laurence Erlbaum.

Ainsworth, M. D. S. and Wittig, B. A. (1969) Attachment and Exploratory Behaviour in One-Year-Olds. In B. M. Foss (ed.) *Determinants of Infant Behaviour*. London: Methuen.

Anderson, M. (1971) *Family Structure in Nineteenth Century Lancashire*. London: Cambridge University Press.

—— (1979) The Relevance of Family History. In C. C. Harris and others (eds) *The Sociology of the Family: New Directions for Britain*. Sociological Review Monograph No. 28. London: Bemrose Press.

Ariès, P. (1962) *Centuries of Childhood*. London: Jonathan Cape.

Arnold, F., Bulato, C., Buripalldi, B. J., Chung, J., Fawcett, T., Iritani, S. J., Lee, S. J. and Wu, T. (1975) *The Value of Children: A Cross National Study*. Honolulu: East-West Population Centre.

Askham, J. (1975) *Fertility and Deprivation: A Study of Differential*

Fertility amongst Working Class Families in Aberdeen. London: Cambridge University Press.

Backett, K. C. (1980) Images of Parenthood. In M. Anderson (ed.) *Sociology of the Family (2nd Edition).* London: Penguin Books.

Bain, C. (1973) Lone Fathers: An Unnoticed Group. *Australian Social Welfare* 3: 14–17.

Barahal, R. M. (1977) *A Comparison of Parent-Infant Attachments and Interaction Patterns in Day Care and Non Day Care Family Groups.* PhD thesis, Cornell University. University Microfilms 78-6326.

Barber, D. (ed.) (1975) *One Parent Families.* London: Davis-Poynter Books.

Barrett, M. (1980) *Women's Oppression Today. Problems in Marxist Feminist Analysis.* London: Verso.

Bateson, P. P. G. (1979) How do Sensitive Periods Arise and What are they for? *Animal Behaviour* 27: 470–86.

Becker, G. S. (1960) An Economic Analysis of Fertility. In Universities National Bureau Committee for Economic Research, *Demographic and Economic Change in Developed Countries.* Princeton: Princeton University Press.

Bell, C. and Newby, H. (1976) Husbands and Wives: The Dynamics of the Deferential Dialectic. In S. Allen and D. Barker (eds) *Dependence and Exploitation in Work and Marriage.* London: Longmans.

Bell, R. Q. (1968) A Reinterpretation of the Direction of Effects in Studies of Socialization. *Psychological Review* 75: 81–95.

Bell, R. Q., Weller, G. M. and Waldrop, M. F. (1971) Newborn and Preschooler: Organization of Behavior and Relations between Periods. *Monograph of the Society for Research in Child Development* 36 (142).

Belsky, J. (1980) A Family Analysis of Parental Influence on Infant Exploratory Competence. In F. A. Pedersen (ed.) *The Father-Infant Relationship: Observational Studies in the Family Setting.* New York: Praeger.

Benson, L. (1968) *Fatherhood: A Sociological Perspective.* New York: Random House.

Berardo, F. M. (1980) Decade Preview: Some Trends and Directions for Family Research and Theory in the 1980s. *Journal of Marriage and the Family.* November: 723–28.

Berelson, B. (1973) The Value of Children: A Taxonomical Essay. In *Population Council Annual Report 1972.* New York: Population Council.

Berkner, L. K. (1973) Recent Research on the History of the Family in Western Europe. *Journal of Marriage and the Family.* August: 395–405.

Bierkens, P. B. (1975) Childlessness from the Psychological Point of View. *Bulletin of the Menninger Clinic* 30(2): 177–182.

Biller, H. B. (1971) *Father, Child and Sex Role*. Lexington, Massachussetts: D. C. Heath.

—— (1974) *Paternal Deprivation*. Lexington, Massachussetts: D.C. Heath.

Biller, H. B. and Meredith, D. (1975) *Father Power*. New York: David McKay Co.

Blurton Jones, N. (ed.) (1972a) *Ethological Studies of Child Behaviour*. London: Cambridge University Press.

—— (1972b) Characteristics of Ethological Studies of Human Behaviour in N. Blurton Jones (ed.) *Ethological Studies of Human Behaviour* London: Cambridge University Press.

Bowlby, J. (1958) The Nature of the Child's Tie to his Mother. *International Journal of Psycho-Analysis* 39: 350–73.

—— (1969) *Attachment and Loss: Volume 1 Attachment*. Harmondsworth: Penguin.

—— (1969–1980) *Attachment and Loss*. Vols. 1–3. London: The Hogarth Press.

Bowskill, D. (1980) *Single Parents*. London: Futura.

Brazelton, T. B., Yogman, M. W., Als, H. and Tronick, E. (1979) The Infant As a Focus for Family Reciprocity. In M. Lewis and L. Rosenblum (eds) *The Child and his Family*. New York: Pitman.

British Medical Journal (1975) Editorial: 'Pregnancy in Adolescence.' 3: 665–66.

Brown, A. (1977) *Fatherhood in the Behavioural Sciences and other Professional Literature: A Selective Review*. Chapter in unpublished PhD thesis, University of Aberdeen.

Brown, A. and Stones, C. (1979) A Group for Lone Fathers. *Social Work Today* 10(47): 10–13.

Brown, G. W. and Harris, T. (1978) *Social Origins of Depression*. London: Tavistock.

Brown, R. (1980) *Breaking Up: A Practical Guide to Separation, Divorce and Coping on your own*. London: Arrow Books.

Bucove, A. (1964) Postpartum Psychosis in the Male. *Bulletin of New York Medicine* 40(12): 961–971.

Burgoyne, J. and Clark, D. (1980a) Why Get Married Again? *New Society* 52(913), 3 April.

—— (1980b) *Parenting in Stepfamilies*. Paper presented to Eugenics Society Symposium on Changing Patterns of Childbearing and Childrearing, 25–26 September.

Burnage, A. (1977) Effects of Infertility. *Adoption and Fostering* 88 (2): 47–48.

Busfield, J. (1972) Age at Marriage and Family Size: Social Causation and Social Selection Hypotheses. *Journal of Biological Science* 4 (1): 117–134.

—— (1974) Ideologies and Reproduction. In M. P. M. Richards (ed.) *The Integration of a Child into a Social World*. London: Cambridge University Press.

Busfield, J. and Paddon, M. (1977) *Thinking About Children*. London: Cambridge University Press.

Cartwright, A. (1976) *How Many Children?* London: Routledge and Kegan Paul.

Chard, T. and Richards, M. P. M. (eds) (1977) *Benefits and Hazards of the New Obstetrics*. Clinics in Developmental Medicine No. 64. London: Heinemann Medical Books.

Chaytor, M. (1980) Household and Kinship: Ryton in the Late 16th and Early 17th Centuries. *History Workshop* 10: 26-60.

Chester, R. (1972) Is there a Relationship between Childlessness and Marital Breakdown? *Journal of Biosocial Science* 4(4): 443–54.

Chiriboga, D. A. and Cutler, L. (1977) Stress Responses among Divorcing Men and Women. *Journal of Divorce* 1(2): 95–105.

Chodorow, N. (1978) *The Reproduction of Mothering: Psychoanalysis and the Sociology of Gender*. Berkeley: University of California Press.

Clarke, A. M. and Clarke, A. D. P. (1976) *Early Experience: Myth and Evidence*. London: Open Books.

—— (1979) Early Experience: Its limited effect on later development. In D. Schaffer and J. Dunn (eds) *The First Years of Life*. Chichester: Wiley.

Clarke-Stewart, K. A. (1978) And Daddy Makes Three: The father's impact on mother and young child. *Child Development* 49(2): 466–78.

—— (1980) The Father's Contribution to Children's Cognitive and Social Development in Early Childhood. In F. A. Pedersen (ed.) *The Father-Infant Relationship: Observational Studies in the Family Setting*. New York: Praeger.

Cohen, L. and Campos, J. (1974) Father, Mother and Stranger as Elicitors of Attachment Behaviours in Infancy. *Developmental Psychology* 10: 146–54.

Cooper, E. S., Costello, A. J., Douglas, J. W. B., Ingleby, J. D. and Turner, R. K. (1974) Direct Observation? *Bulletin of the British Psychological Society* 27: 3–7.

Cossey, D. (1979) *Teenage Birth Control. The Case for the Condom*. London: Brook Advisory Centres.

Coussins, J. and Coote, A. (1981) *Family in the Firing Line*. London: NCCL and CPAG.

Cretney, S. M. (1979) *Principles of Family Law*. Third Edition. London: Sweet and Maxwell.

Daley, E. A. (1977) *Father Feelings*. New York: Pocket Books.

Davenport, D. (1979) *One Parent Families: A Practical Guide to Coping*. London: Pan Books.

De Chateau, P. and Wiberg, B. (1977) Long-term Effect on Mother–Infant Behaviours of Extra Contact During the First Hour Post Partum. *Acta Paediatrica Scandinavia* **66**: 137–43.

Dennis, N., Henriques, F., and Slaughter, C. (1956) *Coal is Our Life*. London: Eyre and Spottiswoode.

Deutsch, H. (1947) *The Psychology of Women, Vol. II. Motherhood*. New York: Grune and Stratton.

Dinnerstein, D. (1978) *The Rocking of the Cradle: and the Ruling of the World*. London: Souvenir Press.

Dodson, F. (1974) *How to Father*. New York: Signet.

Douglas, M. (1975) Couvade and Menstruation. In *Implicit Meanings*. London: Routledge and Kegan Paul.

Dubbert, J. L. (1979) *A Man's Place: Masculinity in Transition*. Englewood Cliffs, New Jersey: Prentice-Hall.

Dunn, J. F. (1977) Patterns of Early Interaction: Continuities and Consequences. In H. R. Schaffer (ed.) *Studies in Parent–Infant Interaction*. London: Academic Press.

Dunnell, K. (1979) *Family Formation 1976*. London: HMSO.

Easterlin, M. A. (1969) Toward a Socio-economic Theory of Fertility: A Survey of Recent Research on Economic Factors in American Fertility. In S. J. Behrman and others (eds) *Fertility and Family Planning: A World View*. Ann Arbor: University of Michigan Press.

Edgell, S. (1980) *Middle Class Couples. A Study of Segregation, Domination and Inequality in Marriage*. London: George Allen & Unwin.

Eekelaar, J. (1973) What Are Parental Rights? *Law Quarterly Review* **89**: 210.

—— (1978) *Family Law and Social Policy*. London: Weidenfeld and Nicholson.

Eekelaar, J., Clive, E., Clarke, K. and Raikes, S. (1977) *Custody After Divorce*. Oxford: Centre for Socio-Legal Studies.

Emerson, J. (1970) Behaviour in Private Places: Sustaining Definitions of Reality in Gynaecological Examinations. In H. P. Dreitzel (ed.) *Recent Sociology No. 2*. New York: Macmillan.

Engle, M. E. (1978) *Do Fathers Speak Motherese?: An Analysis of the language of young children*. PhD United States International University, San Diego, California.

Ervin-Tripp, S. (1977) Wait for Me, Roller Skate. In S. Ervin-Tripp and C. Mitchell-Kernan (eds) *Child Discourse*. New York: Academic Press.

Espenshade, T. J. (1972) The Price of Children and Socio-economic Theories of Fertility. *Population Studies* 26(2): 207-21.

Etzkowitz, H. (1971) The Male Sister: Sexual Separation of Labour in Society. *Journal of Marriage and the Family* August: 431-34.

Farrell, W. (1974) *The Liberated Man*. New York: Random House.

Fasteau, M. F. (1974) *The Male Machine*. New York: McGraw Hill.

Fawcett, J. T. (ed.) (1972) *The Satisfactions and Costs of Children: Theories, Concepts, Methods*. Honolulu: East-West Population Centre.

Fein, R. A. (1974) Men and Young Children. In J. H. Pleck and J. Sawyer (eds) *Men and Masculinity*. Englewood Cliffs, N.J.: Prentice Hall.

— (1976) Men's Entrance to Parenthood. *Family Co-ordinator* 25(4): 341-48.

— (1978) Research on Fathering: Social Policy and an Emergent Perspective. *Journal of Social Issues* 34 (1): 122-35.

Feldman, S. and Ingham, M. (1975) Attachment Behaviour: A Validation Study in Two Age Groups. *Child Development* 46: 309-30.

Ferri, E. (1973) Characteristics of Motherless Families. *British Journal of Social Work* 3: 91-100.

— (1976) *Growing up in a One Parent Family*. Slough: NFER Publishing Company.

Ferri, E. and Robinson, H. (1976) *Coping Alone*. Slough: NFER Publishing Company.

Field, T. (1978) Interaction Behaviours of Primary versus Caretaker Fathers. *Developmental Psychology* 14: 183-84.

Finer, M. (1974) *Report of the Committee on One Parent Families (Cmnd 5629)*. London: HSMO.

Firestone, S. (1972) *The Dialectic of Sex*. London: Paladin.

Flandrin, H. L. (1979) *Families in Former Times*. London: Cambridge University Press.

Gagnon, J. and Simon, W. (1970) *The Sexual Scene*. Chicago: Aldine Press.

Gallagher, E. B. (1978) *Infants, Mothers and Doctors*. Lexington: D. C. Heath.

Gasser, R. D. and Taylor, C. M. (1976) Role Adjustment of Single Parent Fathers with Dependent Children. *The Family Coordinator* 25: 397-401.

Gatley, R. H. and Koulack, D. (1979) *The Single Father's Handbook*. New York: Anchor Press/Doubleday.

Gavron, H. (1966) *The Captive Wife*. London: Routledge and Kegan Paul.

George, V. and Wilding, P. (1972) *Motherless Families*. London: Routledge and Kegan Paul.

Gersick, K. E. (1979) Fathers by Choice: Divorced Men who Receive Custody of their Children. In G. Levinger and O. C. Moles (eds) *Divorce and Separation: Context, Causes and Consequences.* New York: Basic Books.

Gibson, C. (1980) Childlessness and Marital Instability: A re-examination of the Evidence. *Journal of Biosocial Science* 12(2): 121–32.

Gleason, J. B. (1975) Fathers and other Strangers: Men's Speech to Young Children. In D. P. Dato (ed.) *Developmental Psycholinguistics: Theory and Applications.* Washington D. C.: Georgetown University Press.

Golden, S. G. (1975) Preschool Families and Work. PhD thesis, University of Michigan, Ann Arbor.

Goldstein, J., Freud, A., and Solnit, A. J. (1973) *Beyond the Best Interests of the Child.* New York: Free Press.

Goldthorp, W. O. and Richman, J. (1974) Maternal Attitudes to Unanticipated Home Confinement. *The Practitioner* 212: 845–53.

—— (1977) A Reevaluation of Domiciliary Confinement. A Follow up Study of the Effects of the Hospital Strike of 1973. *The Practitioner* 219: 863–66.

Goldthorpe, J. H., Lockwood, D., Bechofer, F. and Platt, J. (1969) *The Affluent Worker in the Class Structure.* London: Cambridge University Press.

Graham, H. (1977a) Women's Attitudes to Conception and Pregnancy. In R. Chester and J. Peel (eds) *Equalities and Inequalities in Family Life.* New York: Academic Press.

—— (1977b) Images of Pregnancy in Ante-Natal Literature. In R. Dingwall, C. Heath, M. Reid, and M. Stacey (eds) *Health Care and Health Knowledge.* London: Croom Helm.

—— (1978) *Problems in Ante-Natal Care.* York: University of York.

Graham, H. and McKee, L. (1978) Family and Peer Group; Volume 5 of *The First Months of Motherhood: Report.* University of York.

—— (1980) *The First Months of Motherhood: Summary Report of Women's Experiences of Pregnancy, Childbirth and the First Six Months After Birth.* London: The Health Education Council Monograph Series, Number 3.

Graham, H. and Oakley, A. (1981) Competing Ideologies of Reproduction: Medical and Maternal Perspectives on Pregnancy. In H. Roberts (ed.) *Women, Health and Reproduction.* London: Routledge and Kegan Paul.

Greenberg, J. B. (1979) Single-Parenting and Intimacy: A Comparison of Fathers and Mothers. *Alternative Lifestyles* 2(3): 308–29.

Greenberg, M. and Morris, N. (1974) Engrossment: The Newborn's Impact Upon the Father. *American Journal of Orthopsychiatry* 44: 520–31.

Gregory, S. (in preparation) How mothers construe the experimental situation: the effect on interaction.

Hacker, H. M. (1957) The New Burdens of Masculinity. *Marriage and Family Living* 19 (August): 227–33.

Hall, J. (1972) The Waning of Parental Rights. *Cambridge Law Journal* B: 248.

Hansard, (1980a) Written Answers to Parliamentary Questions. *Hansard* 984(176): Col. 551.

—— (1980b) Written Answers to Parliamentary Questions. *Hansard* 988(208): Col. 63–4.

Hareven, T. K. (1977) The Family and Gender Roles in Historical Perspective. In L. A. Cater and others (eds) *Women and Men: Changing, Roles, Relationships and Perceptions.* New York: Praeger.

Harrison, J. B. (1978) Men's Roles and Men's Lives. *Signs: Journal of Women in Culture and Society* 4(2): 324–36.

Hartman, A. A. and Nicolay, R. (1966) Sexually Deviant Behaviour in Expectant Fathers. *Journal of Abnormal Psychology* 71(3): 232–34.

Hawthorn, G. (1970) *The Sociology of Fertility.* London: Collier Macmillan.

Hegland, S. M. (1977) Social Interaction and Responsiveness in Parent-Infant Interaction. PhD Ohio State University. University Microfilm No. 785854.

Herzog, E. and Sudia, C. E. (1970) *Boys in Fatherless Families.* Washington D.C.: U.S. Department of Health, Education, and Welfare.

Hetherington, E. M. (1979) Divorce: A Child's Perspective. *American Psychologist* 34(10): 851–58.

Hetherington, E. M., Cox, M., and Cox, R. (1976) Divorced Fathers. *The Family Coordinator* 25: 417–28.

Hipgrave, T. (1978) When the Mother is Gone: Profile Studies of 16 Lone Fathers with Pre-School Children. Unpublished MA thesis, University of Nottingham Child Development Research Unit.

—— (1981) Child-Rearing by Lone Fathers. In R. Chester, P. Diggory, and M. B. Sutherland (eds) *Changing Patterns of Child Bearing and Child Rearing.* London: Academic Press.

Hoffman, L. W. and Hoffman, M. L. (1973) The Value of Children to Parents. In J. T. Fawcett (ed.) *Psychological Perspective on Population.* New York: Basic Books.

Humphrey, M. (1969) *The Hostage Seekers.* London: Longmans.

Itzin, C. (1980) *Splitting Up.* London: Virago.

Katz, A. J. (1972) Lone Fathers: Perspectives and Implications for Family Policy. *The Family Coordinator* 28(4): 521–29.

Kerr, M. (1958) *The People of Ship Street.* London: Routledge and Kegan Paul.

Kerr, M. and McKee, L. (1981) The Father's Role in Child Health Care. *Health Visitor* 54(2): 47–51.

Keshet, H. F. and Rosenthal, K. M. (1978a) Fathering After Marital Separation. *Social Work* 23(1): 11–18.

—— (1978b) Single-Parent Fathers: A New Study. *Children Today* 7 (3): 13–20.

King, M. (1974) Maternal Love – Fact or Myth? *Family Law* 4: 61.

Klaus, M. H. and Kennell, J. H. (1976a) *Maternal-Infant Bonding*. St Louis: C. V. Mosby.

—— (1976b) Parent to Infant Attachment. In D. Hull (ed.) *Recent Advances in Paediatrics*. Edinburgh: Churchill Livingstone.

Komarovsky, M. (1973) Cultural Contradictions and Sex Roles: The Masculine Case. *American Journal of Sociology* 78(4): 874–84.

Korner, A. F. (1971) Individual Differences at Birth: Implications for Early Experience and Later Development. *American Journal of Orthopsychiatry* 45(4): 608–19.

Kotelchuck, M. (1972) The Nature of the Child's Tie to his Father. PhD Harvard University.

Kuhn, T. S. (1970) Falsification and the Methodology of Scientific Research Programmes. In I. Lakatos and A. Musgrave (eds) *Criticism and the Growth of Knowledge*. Cambridge, Massachusetts: Cambridge University Press.

Lamb, M. E. (1975) Fathers: Forgotten Contributors to Child Development. *Human Development* 18: 245–66.

—— (1976a) The Role of the Father: An Overview. In M. E. Lamb (ed.) *The Role of the Father in Child Development*. London and New York: John Wiley and Sons.

—— (ed.) (1976b) *The Role of the Father in Child Development*. London and New York: John Wiley and Sons.

—— (1976c) Effects of Stress and Cohort on Mother- and Father–Infant Interaction. *Developmental Psychology* 12: 435–43.

—— (1977a) A Re-Examination of the Infant Social World. *Human Development* 20: 65–85.

—— (1977b) Father–Infant and Mother–Infant Interaction in the First Year of Life. *Child Development* 48: 167–81.

—— (1977c) Infant Social Cognition and 'Second-order' Effects *Infant Behaviour and Development* 1(1): 1–10.

—— (1977d) The Development of Mother–Infant and Father–Infant attachments in the second year of life. *Developmental Psychology* 13: 637–48.

—— (1978a) Social Interaction in Infancy and the Development of Personality. In M. Lamb (ed.) *Sociopersonality Development*. New York: Holt, Rinehart and Winston.

—— (1978b) The Father's Role in the Infants' Social World. In J. H. Stevens and M. Matthews (eds) *Mother/Child, Father/Child Relationships*. Washington D. C.: National Association for the Education of Young Children.

Lamb, M. E. and Bronson, S. K. (1978) *The Role of the Father in Child Development: Past Presumptions, Present Realitites and the Future Potential*. Paper presented to a conference on Fatherhood and the Male Single Parent, Omaha, Nebraska, November.

Lamb, M. E. and Lamb, J. F. (1976) The Nature and Importance of the Father–Infant Relationship. *The Family Coordinator* 25(4):379–85.

Laslett, P. (1971) *The World We Have Lost (2nd edition)*. London: Methuen.

—— (1976) The Wrong Way Through the Telescope: A Note on Literary Evidence in Sociology and in Historical Sociology. *British Journal of Sociology* 27(3): 319–41.

—— (1977) *Family Life and Illicit Love in Earlier Generations*. London: Cambridge University Press.

Laslett, P. and Wall, R. (eds) (1972) *Household and Family in Past Time*. London: Cambridge University Press.

Leete, R. (1978) One Parent Families: Numbers and Characteristics. *Population Trends* 13. London: HMSO.

Leete, R. and Anthony, S. (1979) Divorce and Remarriage: A Record Linkage Study. *Population Trends* 16. London: HMSO.

Leiderman, P. M., Tulkin, S. R., and Rosenfeld, A. (eds) (1977) *Culture and Infancy*. New York: Academic Press.

Lester, B., Kotelchuck, M., Spelker, E., Sellers, M. and Klein, R. E. (1974) Separation Protest in Guatemalan Infants: Cross Cultural and Cognitive Findings. *Developmental Psychology* 10: 79–85.

Levine, J. A. (1976) *Who Will Raise the Children?* Philadelphia: Lippincott.

Lewis, K. (1978) Single Father Families: Who They Are and How They Fare. *Child Welfare* 57: 642–51.

Lewis, M. and Feiring, C. (1979) The Child's Social Network: Social Object, Social Functions and Their Relationship. In M. Lewis and L. Rosenblum (eds) *The Child and its Family*. New York: Plenum.

Lewis, M. and Rosenblum, L. A. (1974) *The Effect of the Infant on its Caregiver*. New York: Wiley.

Liebenberg, B. (1969) Expectant Fathers. *Child and Family* 8: 265–77.

Lindberg, I. and Fredriksson, U. (1973) Maternity Benefits to Become Parenthood Benefits. *Current Sweden* 9 (September). Stockholm: Swedish Institute.

Loane, M. (1910) *Neighbours and Friends*. London: Edward Arnold.

Lock, A. (ed.) (1978) *Action, Gesture and Symbol*. London: Academic Press.

Lomas, P. (1966) Ritualistic Elements in the Management of Childbirth. *British Journal of Medical Psychology* **39**: 207–13.

Long, S. (1979) *Attitudes of Young Working Class Men to Children and Family Formation*. Mimeograph, Cardiff: David Owens Centre for Population Growth Studies.

Lummis, T. and Thompson, P. (1977) *The Family and Community Life of East Anglian Fishermen*. London: Social Science Research Council, Final Report.

Lynn, D. (1974) *The Father: His Role in Child Development*. Belmont, California: Wadsworth.

Maccoby, E. E. (ed.) (1966) *The Development of Sex Differences*. Stanford: Stanford University Press.

Maccoby, E. E. and Masters, J. C. (1970) Attachment and Dependency. In P. H. Mussen (ed.) *Carmichael's Manual of Child Psychology (3rd edition)*. New York: J. Wiley.

Macfarlane, A. (1970) *The Family Life of Ralph Josselin, a Seventeenth Century Clergyman: An Essay in Historical Anthropology*. London: Cambridge University Press.

—— (1977) *The Psychology of Childbirth*. London: Open Books Publishing Co.

Macintyre, S. (1976a) To Have or Have Not: Promotion and Prevention in Gynaecological Work. In M. Stacey (ed.) *The Sociology of the N.H.S.* Sociological Review Monograph 22. Keele: University of Keele.

—— (1976b) Who Wants Babies? The Social Construction of Instincts. In D. L. Barker and S. Allen (eds) *Sexual Divisions and Society: Process and Change*. London: Tavistock.

—— (1977) *Single and Pregnant*. London: Croom Helm.

Maidment, S. (1976) A Study in Child Custody. *Family Law* **6**: 200.

—— (1980) Matrimonial Statistics 1979. *New Law Journal* December 11: 1168–1170.

Marris, P. (1958) *Widows and Their Families*. London: Routledge and Kegan Paul.

—— (1974) *Loss and Change*. London: Routledge and Kegan Paul.

Marsden, D. (1969) *Mothers Alone: Poverty and the Fatherless Family*. London: Allen Lane.

Marsh, P., Rosser, E. and Harré, R. (1978) *The Rules of Disorder*. London: Routledge and Kegan Paul.

Masters, W. and Johnson, V. (1966) *Human Sexual Response*. Boston: Little Brown.

McKee, J. P. and Sherriffs, A. C. (1959) Men's and Women's Beliefs, Ideals and Self-Concepts. *American Journal of Sociology* **64**(4): 356–63.

McKee, L. (1979) Fathers' Participation in Infant Care. Unpublished paper, University of Warwick, British Socioiogical Association.

—— (1980) Fathers and Childbirth: Just Hold My Hand. *Health Visitor* 53(9): 368–72.

McLaughlin, A. (1981) In R. Chester, P. Diggory and M. B. Sutherland (eds) *Changing Patterns of Child Bearing and Child Rearing*. London: Academic Press.

Meacham, S. (1977) *A Life Apart: The English Working Class 1890–1914*. London: Thames and Hudson.

Mead, M. (1949) *Male and Female: A Study of the Sexes in a Changing World*. New York: Morrow and Company.

Medick, H. (1976) The Protoindustrial Family Economy: The Structural Function of Household and Family During the Transition from Peasant Society to Industrial Capitalism. *Social History* 3: 291–315.

Mendes, H. A. (1975) Parental Experiences of Single Fathers. Unpublished PhD thesis, University of California, L.A.

—— (1976a) Single Fatherhood. *Social Work* 21(4): 308–13.

—— (1976b) Single Fathers. *The Family Coordinator* 25: 439–44.

—— (1979) Single-Parent Families – A Typology of Lifestyles. *Social Work* 24(3): 193–200.

Millett, K. (1972) *Sexual Politics*. London: Abacus.

Millgårdh, M. and Rollén, B. (1975) Parents' Insurance. *Current Sweden* 76. Stockholm: Swedish Institute.

Mitchell, J. (1974) *Psychoanalysis and Feminism*. London: Allen Lane.

Morgan, D. H. J. (1975) *The Social Theory of the Family*. London: Routledge and Kegan Paul.

—— (1981) Men, Masculinity and the Process of Sociological Enquiry. In H. Roberts (ed.) *Doing Feminist Research*. London: Routledge and Kegan Paul.

Morton-Williams, J. (1976) *The Role of Male Attitudes in Contraception*. London: Social and Community Planning Research.

Moss, P. (1980) Parents at Work. In P. Moss and N. Fonda (eds) *Work and the Family*. London: Temple Smith.

Moss, P. and Fonda, N. (1980) *Work and the Family*. London: Temple Smith.

Murch, M. (1973) The Motherless Families Project. *British Journal of Social Work* 3: 365–76.

—— (1980) *Justice and Welfare in Divorce*. London: Sweet and Maxwell.

Nash, J. (1975) The Father in Contemporary Culture and Current Psychological Literature. *Child Development* 36(1): 261–99.

Newson, J. (1979) Intentional Behaviour in the Young Infant. In

D. Shaffer and J. Dunn (eds) *The First Year of Life*. Chichester: Wiley.

Newson, J. and Newson, E. (1965) *Patterns of Infant Care in an Urban Community*. London: Pelican.

—— (1968) *Four Years Old in an Urban Community*. London: George Allen and Unwin.

—— (1974) Cultural Aspects of Child-Rearing in the English Speaking World. In M. P. M. Richards (ed.) *The Integration of a Child into a Social World*. London: Cambridge University Press.

—— (1976) *Seven Years Old in the Home Environment*. Harmondsworth: Pelican.

Nichols, T. and Beynon, H. (1977) *Living with Capitalism*. London: Routledge and Kegan Paul.

Niphuis-Neill, M. (1976) *Satisfactions and Costs of Children and Fertility Attitudes*. Netherlands Inter-University Demographic Institute, Working Paper No. 4.

Norton, A. and Click, P. (1979) What's Happening to Households? *American Demographics* **1**: 19–23.

Oakley, A. (1974) *The Sociology of Housework*. London: Penguin Books.

—— (1979) *Becoming a Mother*. Oxford: Martin Robertson.

—— (1980) *Women Confined*. Oxford: Martin Robertson.

O'Brien, M. (1978) Father Role and Male Sex Role after Marital Separation: Men Coping with Single Parenthood. Paper presented at the British Psychological Society, Social Psychology Section, September at UWIST, Cardiff.

—— (1980a) Lone Fathers: Transition from Married to Separated State. *Journal of Comparative Family Studies* **XI**(1):115–27.

—— (1980b) *Fathers' Perceptions of Work-Home Conflicts*. Paper presented at the London conference of the British Psychological Society, 18–19 December.

—— (in preparation) Fathers Without Wives: A Comparative Study of Married and Separated Fathers. PhD thesis, University of London.

Office of Population Census and Surveys Monitor (1978) reference FM2 78/2, Published by OPCS, St Catherine's House, 10 Kingsway, London.

Office of Population Census and Surveys (1980) *Birth Statistics 1977*. London: HMSO.

O'Leary, S. E. (1972) Mother–Father–Infant Interaction in the First Two Days of Life. Unpublished PhD thesis, University of Wisconsin.

One Parent Times (1980) 4 (Spring): 3. Published by the National Council for One Parent Families, London.

Orthner, D. K., Brown, T., and Ferguson, D. (1976) Single Parent

Fatherhood: An Emergent Family Lifestyle. *The Family Coordinator* **25**: 429–37.

Orthner, D. K. and Lewis, K. (1979) Evidence of Single Father Competence. *Family Law Quarterly* **13**(1): 27–47.

Owens, D. J. (1979) *Recourse to the Doctor: The Definition of Involuntary Childlessness as a Medical Problem*. Paper presented to the British Sociological Association, Medical Sociology Group Annual Conference, in September at York University.

Paige, K. and Paige, J. (1973) The Politics of Birth Practices: A Strategic Analysis. *American Sociological Review* **38**: 633–77.

Palme, O. (1975) The Sex-Role Problem. *Hertha* **2**(62): 9. Utgiven av Frederika Bremer-Förbundet.

Parke, R. D. (1978a) International Design. In R. Cairns (ed.) *Social Interaction: Methods, Analysis and Illustration*. New York: Laurence Erlbaum.

—— (1978b) Parent–Infant Interaction: Progress, Paradigms and Problems. In G. P. Sacket and H. Haywood (eds) *Application of Observational–Ethnological Methods in the Study of Mental Retardation*. Baltimore: University Park.

—— (1979) Perspectives on Father–Infant Interaction. In J. Osofsky (ed.) *Handbook of Infant Development*. New York: Wiley.

—— (1981) *Fathering*. London: Fontana.

Parke, R. D. and O'Leary, S. (1976) Family Interaction in the Newborn Period: Some Findings, Some Observations and Some Unsolved Issues. In K. Riegal and J. Meacham (eds) *The Developing Individual in a Changing World*. The Hague: Mouton.

Parke, R. D., O'Leary, S. E., and West, S. (1972) Mother–Father–Newborn Interaction: Effects of Maternal Medication, Labor and Sex of Infant. *Proceedings, 80th Annual Conference of the American Psychological Association* **7**: 85–6.

Parke, R. D., Power, T. G. and Gottman, J. (1979) Conceptualizing and Quantifying Influence Patterns in the Family Triad. In M. E. Lamb, S. J. Suomi and G. R. Stevenson (eds) *Social Interactional Analysis: Methodological Issues*. Madison: University of Wisconsin Press.

Parke, R. D., Power, T. G. and Fisher, J. (1980) The Adolescent Father's Impact on the Mother and Child. *Journal of Social Issues* **36**: 88–106.

Parke, R. D. and Sawin, D. B. (1976) The Father's Role in Infancy: A Re-evaluation. *The Family Coordinator* **25**(4): 365–72.

—— (1980) The Family in Early Infancy: Social Interaction and Attitudinal Analysis. In F. A. Pedersen (ed.) *The Father–Infant Relationship: Observational Studies in the Family Setting*. New York: Praeger.

Parkes, C. M. (1972) *Bereavement: Studies of Grief in Adult Life*. London: Tavistock.

Pedersen, F. A. (ed.) (1980a) *The Father–Infant Relationship: Observational Studies in the Family Setting*. New York: Praeger.

—— (1980b) Issues Related to Fathers and Infants. In F. A. Pedersen (ed.) *The Father–Infant Relationship: Observational Studies in the Family Setting*. New York: Praeger.

—— (1980c) Overview: Answers and Reformulated Questions. In F. A. Pedersen (ed.) *The Father–Infant Relationship: Observational Studies in the Family Setting*. New York: Praeger.

Pedersen, F. A., Yarrow, L., Anderson, B. and Cain, R. L. (1979) Conceptualization of Father Influences in the Infancy Period. In M. Lewis and L. Rosenblum (eds.) *The Social Network of the Developing Infant*. New York: Plenum.

Peel, J. (1972) The Hull Family Survey: Family Planning in the First Five Years of Marriage. *Journal of Biosocial Science* 4(3):333–46.

Peel, J. and Carr, G. (1975) *Contraception and Family Design: A Study of Birth Planning in Contemporary Society*. Edinburgh: Churchill Livingstone.

Pember Reeves, M. (1913) *Round About a Pound a Week*. London: G. Bell & Sons. Reprinted 1979, London: Virago.

Peterson, G. H., Mehl, L. F., and Leiderman, P. H. (1975) The Role of Some Father-related Variables in Father Attachment. *American Journal of Orthopsychiatry* 49(2): 330–38.

Pleck, J. (1979) Men's Family Work: Three Perspectives and Some New Data. *The Family Coordinator* 28(4): 481–89.

Pleck, J. and Sawyer, J. (eds.) (1974) *Men and Masculinity*. Englewood Cliffs, New Jersey: Prentice-Hall.

Poster, M. (1978) *Critical Theory of the Family*. London: Pluto Press.

Rainwater, L. (1960) *And the Poor Get Children*. Chicago: Quadrangle.

Randall, T. M. (1974) An Analysis of Observer Influence on Sex and Social Class Differences in Mother–Infant Interaction. PhD thesis, State University of New York, Buffalo, New York. University Microfilms No. 75-7788.

—— (in press) Effect of an Observer's Presence on the Behaviour of Middle Class and Working Class Mothers. *Journal of Social Psychology*.

Rapoport, R. and Rapoport, R. N. (1980) The Impact of Work on the Family. In P. Moss and N. Fonda (eds.) *Work and the Family*. London: Temple Smith.

Rapoport, R. N., Rapoport, R. and Strelitz, Z. with Kew, S. (1977) *Fathers, Mothers and Others*. London: Routledge and Kegan Paul.

Rebelsky, F. and Hanks, C. (1971) Fathers' Verbal Interaction with

Infants in the First Three Months of Life. *Child Development* **42**: 63–8.

Reik, T. (1914) Couvade and the Fear of Retaliation in Ritual. In T. Reik *Four Psychoanalytic Studies*. New York: Grove Press.

Rendina, I. and Dickenschied, J. (1976) Father Involvement with First Born Infants. *The Family Coordinator* **25**: 373–77.

Reynolds, D. (1910) *Alongshore*. London: Macmillan.

Rich, A. (1976) *Of Woman Born*. London: Virago.

Richards, M. P. M. (ed.) (1974a) *The Integration of a Child into a Social World*. London: Cambridge University Press.

—— (1974b) First Steps in Becoming Social. In M. P. M. Richards (ed.) *The Integration of a Child into a Social World*. London: Cambridge University Press.

—— (1981) Review of Attachment and Loss Volume 3. Loss: Sadness and Depression. *Journal of the Biosocial Sciences* (in press).

Richards, M. P. M., Dunn, J. F. and Antonis, B. (1977) Caretaking in the First Year of Life. *Child Care, Health and Development* **3**:23–36.

Richman, J. and Goldthorp, W. O. (1978) Fatherhood: The Social Construction of Pregnancy and Birth. In S. Kitzinger and J. Davis (eds.) *The Place of Birth*. Oxford: Oxford University Press.

Richman, J., Goldthorp, W. O. and Simmons, C. (1975) Fathers in Labour. *New Society* 16 October.

Roberts, D. (1978) The Paterfamilias of the Victorian Ruling Classes. In A. S. Wohl (ed.) *The Victorian Family*. London: Croom Helm.

Roberts, E. (1977) Working Class Women in the North West. *Oral History* **5**(2): 5–30.

Roberts, H. (ed.) (1981) *Women, Health and Reproduction*. London: Routledge and Kegan Paul.

Rock, P. (1976) Some Problems of Interpretative Historiography. *British Journal of Sociology* **27**(3): 353–69.

Rödholm, M. (1981) Effects of Father–Infant Postpartum Contact on their Interaction 3 Months after Birth. *Early Human Development* **5**: 79–85.

Rödholm, M. and Larsson, H. (1979) Father–Infant Interaction at the First Contact after Delivery. *Early Human Development* **3**: 21–7.

Rondal, J. A. (1980) Fathers' and Mothers' Speech in Early Language Development. *Journal of Child Language* **7**: 353–69.

Rosenberg, B. G. and Sutton-Smith, B. (1972) *Sex and Identity*. New York: Holt, Rinehart and Winston.

Rosengren, W. R. (1962) Social Sources of Pregnancy as Illness or Normality. *Social Forces* **9**: 260–67.

Ross, G., Kagan, J., Zelazo, P. and Kotelchuk, M. (1975) Separation

Protest in Infants in Home and Laboratory. *Developmental Psychology* II: 256–57.

Ross, H. S. and Goldman, B. D. (1977) Infants' Sociability Towards Strangers. *Child Development* 48: 638–42.

Rowbotham, S. (1973) *Hidden from History*. London: Pluto Press.

—— (1979) The Trouble with 'Patriarchy'. *The New Statesman* 21 December: 970–71.

Rubin, J. L., Provenzano, F. J., and Luna, Z. (1974) The Eye of the Beholder: Parents' Views on the Sex of Newborns. *American Journal of Orthopsychiatry* 44: 512–19.

Rushton, P. (1979) Marxism, Domestic Labour and the Capitalist Economy: A Note on Recent Discussion. In C. C. Harris and others (eds.) *The Sociology of the Family: New Directions for Britain*. Sociological Review Monograph No. 28. London: Bemrose Press.

Russell, G. (1979a) Fathers: Incompetent or Reluctant Parents? *The Australian and New Zealand Journal Of Sociology* 15(1): 57–67.

—— (1979b) *Fathers as Caregivers: A Study of Shared-Role Families*. Macquarie University, Australia (mimeo).

Rutter, M. (1972) *Maternal Deprivation Reassessed*. Harmondsworth: Penguin.

Santrock, J. W. and Warshak, R. A. (1979) Father Custody and Social Development in Boys and Girls. *Journal of Social Issues* 35(4): 112–25.

Scanzoni, J. and Litton Fox, G. (1980) Sex Roles, Family and Society: The Seventies and Beyond. *Journal of Marriage and the Family* November: 743–55.

Schaefer, G. (1965) The Expectant Father, His Care and Management. *Postgraduate Medicine* 38: 658–63.

Schaffer, H. R. (1977a) *Mothering*. London: Fontana.

—— (1977b) *Studies in Mother–Infant Interaction*. London: Academic Press.

Schaffer, H. R. and Emerson, P. (1964) *The Development of Social Attachments in Infancy*. Monograph No. 29, Society for Research in Child Development.

Schlesinger, B. (1978) Single Parent Fathers: A Review. *Children Today* 7(3): 12–18.

Scott, J. W. and Tilly, L. A. (1975) Women's Work and the Family in Nineteenth Century Europe. In C. E. Rosenberg (ed.) *The Family in History*. Pennsylvania: University of Pennsylvania Press.

Seidler, V. (1978) Masculinity and Fascism. *Achilles' Heel: A Magazine of Men's Politics* 1: 14–21.

Shills, E. and Rheinstein, M. (eds) (1967) *On Law in Economy and Society*. New York: Simon and Schuster.

Skolnick, A. and Skolnick, J. H. (1974) *Intimacy, Family and Society*. Boston: Little, Brown.

Smith, C. (1978) The Crisis of Childlessness. *Adoption and Fostering* **91**(1): 49–53.

Snodgrass, J. (ed.) (1977) *A Book of Readings for Men Against Sexism*. Albion: Times Change Press.

Spelke, E., Zelazo, P., Kagan, J., and Kotelchuck, M. (1973) Father Interaction and Separation Protest. *Developmental Psychology* **9**: 83–90.

Stangel, J. J. (1979) *Fertility and Conception: An Essential Guide for Childless Couples*. London: Paddington Press Limited.

Stedman–Jones, G. (1976) From Historical Sociology to Theoretical History. *British Journal Of Sociology* **27**(3): 295–305.

Stone, L. (1975) The Rise of the Nuclear Family in Early Modern England: The Patriarchical Stage. In C. E. Rosenberg (ed.) *The Family in History*. Pennsylvania: University of Pennsylvania Press.

Stone, L. H., Smith, H. T., and Murphy, L. B. (1974) *The Competent Infant*. London: Tavistock.

Sudnow, D. (1967) *Passing On, the Social Organization of Dying*. Englewood Cliffs, New Jersey: Prentice-Hall.

Svedja, M. J., Campos, J. L., and Emde, R. N. (1980) Mother–Infant 'Bonding'. Failure to Generalize. *Child Development* **51**: 775–79.

Taconis, L. (1969) The Role of the Contemporary Father in Rearing Young Children. *Educational Research* **2**(2): 83–94.

Tanzer, D. (1976) *Why Natural Childbirth? A Psychologist's Report on the Benefits to Mothers, Fathers and Babies*. New York: Schocken Books.

Thompson, E. P. (1976) On History, Sociology and Historical Relevance. *British Journal of Sociology* **27**(3):387–402.

—— (1977) Happy Families. *New Society* **41** (September 8): 499–501.

Thompson, P. (1977) *The Edwardians*. Hertford: Paladin.

Thornes, B. and Collard, J. (1979) *Who Divorces?* London: Routledge and Kegan Paul.

Todres, R. (1975) Motherless Families. *Canadian Welfare* **51**(4): 11–15.

Tolor, A. and di Grazia, P. V. (1976) Sexual Attitudes and Behaviour During and Following Pregnancy. *Archives of Sexual Behaviour* **5**: 539–51.

Tolson, A. (1977) *The Limits of Masculinity*. London: Tavistock.

Townsend, P. (1957) *The Family Life of Old People*. London: Routledge and Kegan Paul.

—— (1979) *Poverty in the United Kingdom: A survey of Household Resources and Standards of Living*. London: Allen Lane.

Trivers, R. L. (1972) Parental Investment and Sexual Selection. In

B. Campbell (ed.) *Sexual Selection and the Descent of Man 1871–1971*. Chicago: Aldine Press.

Trumbach, R. (1978) *The Rise of the Egalitarian Family*. London: Academic Press.

Tunstall, J. (1962) *The Fishermen*. London: MacGibbon and Kee.

Van Keep, P. A. and Schmidt-Elmendorf, H. (1975) Involuntary Childlessness. *Journal of Biosocial Science* 7(1): 37–48.

Vendell, D. L. (1977) *Boy Toddlers' Social Interactions with Mothers, Fathers and Peers*. PhD thesis, Boston University Graduate School, Massachusetts. University Microfilm No. 77-11: 428.

Wallerstein, J. A. and Kelly, J. (1980) *Surviving the Breakup*. New York: Basic Books.

Walters, J. and Walters, L. H. (1980) Parent–Child Relationships: A Review, 1970–1979. *Journal of Marriage and the Family* November: 807–21.

Webb, B. (1971) *My Apprenticeship*. London: Penguin.

Weiss, R. S. (1979) Growing Up a Little Faster: The Experience of Growing Up in a Single Parent Household. *Journal of Social Issues* 35(4): 97–111.

Welbourne, E. (1923) *The Miners' Union of Northumberland and Durham*. London: Cambridge University Press.

Wente, A. S. and Crockenburg, S. B. (1976) Transition to Fatherhood: Lamaze Preparation, Adjustment Difficulty and the Husband–Wife Relationship. *The Family Coordinator* 25(4): 351–57.

West, M. M. and Konner, M. J. (1976) The Role of the Father: An Anthropological Perspective. In M. Lamb (ed.) *The Role of the Father in Child Development*. New York: Wiley.

Whiting, B. B. and Whiting, J. W. M. (1975) *Children of Six Cultures*. Cambridge: Harvard University Press.

Willemsen, E., Flaherty, D., Heaton, C., and Ritchey, G. (1974) Attachment Behaviour of One-year-olds as a Function of Mother Versus Father, Sex of Child, Session and Toys. *Genetic Psychology Monographs* No. 90: 305–24.

Williamson, N. E. (1976) *Sons or Daughters: A Cross Cultural Survey of Parental Preferences*. Sage Library of Social Sciences Volume 31. London: Sage.

Willis, P. (1977) *Learning to Labour*. London: Saxon House.

Winnicott, D. W. (1958) *Collected Papers*. London: Tavistock.

Woolf, M. (1971) *Family Intentions*. London: HMSO.

Woolf, M. and Pegden, S. (1976) *Families Five Years On*. London: HMSO.

Wortis, R. P. (1972) Child-rearing and Women's Liberation. In M. Wandor (ed.) *The Body Politic*. London: Stage 1.

Yogman, M. (1977) *The Goals and Structure of Face to Face Interaction Between Infants and Fathers*. A paper presented to the Society for Research in Child Development, New Orleans, March.

Young, M. and Willmott, P. (1962) *Family and Kinship in East London*. London: Penguin Books.

—— (1973) *The Symmetrical Family*. London: Routledge and Kegan Paul.

Zweig, F. (1962) *The Worker in an Affluent Society*. London: Heinemann.

Name index

Subject index